W9-BPS-755

A DEFINING MOMENT

Lawrence W. Tyree Library
Santa Fe Community College
3000 NW 83rd Street
Gainesville, Florida 32606

A DEFINING MOMENT

THE PRESIDENTIAL ELECTION OF 2004

WILLIAM CROTTY, EDITOR

M.E.Sharpe
Armonk, New York
London, England

Copyright © 2005 by M.E. Sharpe, Inc.

All rights reserved. No part of this book may be reproduced in any form
without written permission from the publisher, M.E. Sharpe, Inc.,
80 Business Park Drive, Armonk, New York 10504.

Library of Congress Cataloging-in-Publication Data

A defining moment : the presidential election of 2004 / edited by William Crotty.
p. cm.
Includes bibliographical references.
ISBN 0-7656-1561-4 (hardcover : alk. paper); ISBN 0-7656-1562-2 (pbk. : alk. paper)
1. Presidents—United States—Election, 2004. I. Crotty, William J, 1946–

JK5262004 .D44 2005
324.973'0931—dc22 2005003760

Printed in the United States of America

The paper used in this publication meets the minimum requirements of
American National Standard for Information Sciences
Permanence of Paper for Printed Library Materials,
ANSI Z 39.48-1984.

∞

BM (c) 10 9 8 7 6 5 4 3 2 1
BM (p) 10 9 8 7 6 5 4 3 2 1

Contents

Part III: Conclusions

List of Tables and Figures

Tables

Figures

Preface

This is the story of the election of 2004, the most contentious and important in the contemporary history of the United States. Two candidates and two political parties with different views as to the future of the United States contested for the people's vote. The candidates faced each other, each with their strengths and their weaknesses, and each proposing contrasting solutions to the nation's problems. Terrorism, the war in Iraq, and national security were the principal concerns of the Bush presidency and would be the main areas of debate in the election. In addition, they established President George W. Bush's strength in the electorate.

Senator John Kerry (D-MA) and the Democrats were strongest on domestic social and economic issues. Kerry began his full-out campaign effort late, allowing the Republicans to go a long way in establishing his public image. It was not until the presidential debates that Kerry would revitalize his campaign and pull even with the president in what would become one of the closest and most acrimonious campaigns in modern political history.

The result was a highly competitive, if confusing, election with two candidates and two parties presenting opposing views as to what America needed from its government. The "values divide" could not have been greater. The candidates and the contrasting parties had little if anything in common beyond an appreciation, shared by the electorate, that this was an extremely important race offering clear policy choices and contrasting visions as to how the United States should act in both international and domestic affairs. It was, as virtually all acknowledged, a defining election in establishing the country's future course.

I wish to thank Niels Aaboe, Executive Editor for Political Science at M.E. Sharpe, Inc., and Angela Piliouras, Managing Editor, for their contributions to the development of this book. I would also like to thank research associate Ben Lampe in particular, Whitney Ritter, and the others at the Center for the Study of Democracy at Northeastern University for their help in completing this study. Janet-Louise Joseph, administrative officer of Northeastern University's Department of Political Science, has been a constant source of assistance. Most of all, I would like to express my gratitude to my wife, Mary Hauch Crotty, for her interest and support.

As editor, I would like to dedicate this book to Michael S. Dukakis, who for me embodies what public service is all about.

Part I

The Context

1

The Bush Presidency

Establishing the Agenda for the Campaign

William Crotty

Presidential Elections and Their Consequences

Every presidential election is important. Some elections, however, are more important in terms of their consequences for the nation than others; so it was to be with the election of 2004. Two opposing visions of the United States and its future were presented to the American public; one would prevail and set the country's course domestically and in relation to the international community for years, if not decades and generations, to come. They had little in common.

One emphasized unilateral military actions and a "go it alone" approach to international relations, resulting in a war in Iraq that had not gone well. It rejected international cooperative efforts to avoid or resolve crises, a redirection of a bipartisan approach that reached back to the post–World War II period (if not Woodrow Wilson's efforts to establish an effective League of Nations in the aftermath of World War I).

Domestically this vision focused on tax cuts, a revised tax code and a continuing distribution of wealth upward, severe budgetary deficits, and a curtailment of individual rights in meeting the threat of international terrorism. Security and the fight against terrorism dominated its thinking. It terms of internal politics, its agenda reflected the Republican initiatives of the Reagan presidency. This was the Republican vision.

The Democrats' vision, while less contextually cohesive, rejected virtually every one of these points. It placed its emphasis on international cooperative efforts in conducting the war in Iraq and promised to focus more on Al Qaeda and its leader Osama bin Laden and the broader "war on terrorism," which Democrats charged had been neglected in the move to invade Iraq. It also promised a more effective conduct of the Iraqi war[1]; a more restrained use of the "first strike" capability to declare war and invade a nation, a power given to the president by the Congress to engage in "preemptive" actions to protect American security and punish the country's enemies; the protection of civil liberties, not a strength of the Bush administration and its then attorney general, John Ashcroft; budget deficit reduction; medical care for the middle class and those less well off as well as a reduction in pharmaceutical costs; a living minimum wage; greater resources directed to health, education, and the protection of the environment; restructured and more equitable tax policies; and the safeguarding of Social Security benefits. In effect, it provided a virtual mirror image of the Republican agenda and actions of the previous four years. (Although not entirely; Kerry, it turned out, and in opposition to his perception in the primaries, supported the war in Iraq, but argued he would conduct it more effectively and in concert with the support from other nations.) The choices were clear.

The future direction of America was at stake, a point both presidential candidates acknowledged and one emphasized repeatedly. It was not to be just the normal campaign rhetoric. Two sets of choices, two futures, with little in common: the 2004 presidential race was truly a defining election.

An Unelected President

The United States had an unelected president for four years from 2000 to the election of 2004 (for a review of election results, see the Appendix). The 2000 election, the closest in history, had come down to the vote count. The U.S. Supreme Court overrode a Florida Supreme Court decision, suspended the state's vote count, and in a 5–4 decision declared George W. Bush the winner over Democratic candidate and former Vice President Al Gore.

The Bush campaign's petition to the nation's highest court asked for a "lawful resolution" of the election and went on to say that "absent a decision by this Court, the election results from Florida could lack finality and legitimacy. The consequence may be the ascension of a President of questionable legitimacy, or a constitutional crisis."[2] In its brief ruling, the U.S. Supreme Court employed the doctrine of "equal protection of the law." It was not a happy conclusion, and one that many on both sides of the partisan debate feared. The Court indicated that constitutional guarantees would be violated by continuing the recount because standards varied from county to county. As the *Wall Street Journal* noted:

"By that logic, the entire nation arguably engaged in an unconstitutional free-for-all on Election Day, as standards varied among many states."[3] It would surface as an issue again in the 2004 election.

Little had been achieved in modernizing the nation's often-antiquated and conflicting voting and registration procedures, ballot integrity, and in creating national electoral standards. Both campaigns were ready for a series of legal battles, with the Democrats vowing to meet the challenge and this time with an expenditure of resources and legal talent equal to the Republicans (not the case in 2000).[4]

Built on the acrimonious results from Florida in 2000, the 2004 election had become "the most litigious, lawyer fraught election in history."[5] The parties took legal and political positions completely opposed to each other: "Republicans, long suspicious of urban political machines and worried about record levels of new registrations in many swing states, say Democrats have abetted fraud. Democrats, who cite a bitter history of efforts to deny minority and low-income voters the ballot, contend that Republicans are trying to suppress the vote."[6] The charges were not new, and in fact had historical grounding. The intensity of the fights and the willingness to quickly and systematically appeal to the courts to the extent indicated represented a campaign tactic new to politics and now accepted as a legitimate, and even potentially decisive, extension of the normal campaign.[7]

Whatever the merits of the Supreme Court's intervention in determining the 2000 election's outcome, George W. Bush was declared the winner and was sworn in as president. His new vice president, Dick Cheney, was a former secretary of defense (under Bush's father), chief of staff under President Gerald Ford, a former congressman from Wyoming, and, most controversially when chosen, head of the Houston-based Halliburton corporation,[8] later to receive billions of dollars in reconstruction funds for Iraq and Afghanistan.

Cheney was considered the driving force in the Bush presidency and as close to an acting president in the immediate post-9/11 hours as one could ever be. Bush and Cheney ruled as if they had won by a significant voting mandate, never acknowledging the closeness of the 2000 race or the legitimacy of its debatable ending. Given this agenda, it could be said the administration was extremely successful in getting the Congress (Republicans controlled both houses) and the American people to support its policies. Domestically, the administration was Hard Right/conservative (despite the campaign slogan used in the 2000 election and resurrected periodically in 2004 promoting Bush as "a compassionate Conservative.") It also had been a militarily aggressive four-year period, with wars in Afghanistan and, most notably, Iraq. Each military foray—as with much of the foreign policy and domestic legislation passed by the Congress, or actions taken on presidential initiative alone—a direct consequence of the 9/11 attacks.[9]

9/11 Shapes an Administration

On September 11, 2001, two planes flew into the Twin Towers in New York City, causing explosions and, in short order, the buildings to collapse, trapping workers, firemen, police, and emergency personnel in the carnage. A third plane hit the Pentagon. A fourth plane, apparently also intended for Washington, D.C., and an attack on the White House or Congress (no one is totally sure of the destination), crashed in a field in Pennsylvania when the passengers attempted to overcome the hijackers. All on board were killed. Roughly three thousand people were to die in the attacks on the Twin Towers. The nation was stunned. Disbelief greeted the scenes of the burning and collapsing buildings, pictures of people jumping from skyscrapers, and fire and emergency workers sacrificing their lives to do what they could to save those they could.

To understand what was to follow in the administration and the 2004 campaign, it is necessary to comprehend the horror of 9/11 and its impact. No one had experienced anything remotely like it. A few accounts from the front pages of national newspapers convey the dimensions of the shock and the impact on the country. First, from the *Washington Post,* under the headline "Terrorists Hijack 4 Airliners, Destroy World Trade Center, Hit Pentagon; Hundreds Dead" and the subheading "Bush Promises Retribution; Military Put on Highest Alert":

> It was the most dramatic attack on American soil since Pearl Harbor, and it created indelible scenes of carnage and chaos. The commandeered jets obliterated the World Trade Center's twin 110-story towers from their familiar perch above Manhattan's skyline and ripped a blazing swath through the Defense Department's imposing five-sided fortress, grounding the domestic air traffic system for the first time and plunging the entire nation into an unparalleled state of anxiety.[10]

Second, from the *New York Times* under the headline "U.S. Attacked: Hijacked Jets Destroy Twin Towers and Hit Pentagon in Day of Terror" and the subheading "A Creeping Horror: Buildings Burn and Fall as Onlookers Look for Elusive Safety":

> The horror arrived in episodic bursts of chilling disbelief, signified first by trembling floors, sharp eruptions, cracked windows. There was the actual unfathomable realization of a gaping, flaming hole in first one of the tall towers, and then the same thing all over again in its twin. There was the merciless sight of bodies helplessly tumbling out, some of them in flames. Finally, the mighty towers themselves were reduced to nothing. Dense plumes of smoke raced through the downtown avenues, coursing between the buildings, shaped like tornadoes on their sides. Every sound was cause for alarm. People scrambled for their lives, but they didn't know where to go. Should they go north, south, east, west? Stay outside, go indoors? People hid beneath cars and each other. Some contemplated jumping into the river.[11]

Third, graphically and succinctly, the headline from the *New York Daily News:*

> "It's War."[12]

As these news stories would indicate, the emotional and psychological impact on the nation of the terrorist attacks was incalculable. This nation's response would form the context of the administration's policies and provide the dominant issue of the 2004 campaign.

On another level, there was a demand for an explanation for what had happened, as well as a need for the national government to act decisively. How it should respond and who was responsible for the acts of mass violence were far from clear.

9/11 and Its Consequences

As the days progressed, it became clear that a virtually unknown (by the American public) organization housed in Afghanistan, Al Qaeda, and led by a man named Osama bin Laden, a member of the extensive Saudi royal family, had planned and executed the bombings. While unfamiliar to the public at large, Al Qaeda had been involved in a number of terrorist attacks against American embassies abroad and in the explosion of the USS *Cole* in Yemeni waters. The terrorist organization had also masterminded a bombing in 1993 of the World Trade Center, although not at the level of devastation of the 9/11 attacks.

Initially also, the government was confused and unprepared for an effective response to the terrorist attacks. President Bush was in Florida and flew to various military bases as a security precaution. To the extent anyone was in charge, it was Vice President Cheney in Washington. The Congress, and most of the major government officials, operated from security bunkers in the D.C. area.

Bush first advised Americans to act normally, pursue their daily activities, and not give in to the terrorist agenda of fear. He promised repeatedly revenge against the groups that had planned and executed the attacks and an all-out "war on terrorism" that would include not only eliminating the terrorist threat but holding accountable all those who funded, supported, or actively sympathized with the terrorists' objectives.

The Congress was all too willing to turn the problem over to the executive branch. After less than two weeks of deliberations, it passed the Patriot Act, centralizing extraordinary powers in the executive, including the "strike-first" capability (the president did not have to wait for congressional approval for "preemptive" attacks on enemy nations). Bush was to use such powers in Afghanistan and, with less success and more controversially, in Iraq to unseat Saddam Hussein.

Additionally, the Patriot Act provided an indication of support for the wars' efforts and, more indirectly, addressed the level of fear and concern in the country more broadly (see Table 1.1).

The Patriot Act conferred a large and varied assortment of new powers on the administrative branch. Among its provisions were authorizations for:

- A reassessment of immigration standards and procedures.
- A "delayed" notice of search warrants if they might have "an adverse effect" on an investigation.
- The search of offices of businesses representing foreign countries.
- Government authority to obtain communication and computer records of individuals or corporations without notice to the consumer.
- Access to personal information on an individual by police, defense, intelligence, and security officials. This encompassed everything from prison to health, education, travel, and credit records.
- Requiring financial firms and other institutions to reveal to the government "suspicious" transactions without notifying their clients.
- Penalties and prisoner terms for terrorists and financiers of terrorism, and sanctions against countries involved in money-laundering or other forms of support for terrorist groups.

Table 1.1

Congressional Votes on Key Bush Administration Legislation, by Party

	Total vote	Democrat		Republican		Independent	
		Yea	Nay	Yea	Nay	Yea	Nay
USA Patriot Act (2001)							
Senate	96–1	49	1	46	0	1	0
House	357–66	146	62	211	3	1	1
Department of Homeland Security (2002)							
Senate	90–9	41	8	48	0	0	1
House	295–132	88	120	207	10	0	2
Iraq/Afghanistan Appropriations (2003)							
Senate	87–12	37	11	50	0	0	1
House	303–125	83	118	220	6	0	1

- Confiscation of the property of alleged terrorists.
- The sharing among security and intelligence agencies of once-secret grand jury testimony.
- And so on.

Some of the powers were justifiable, others questionable, and a number clearly eroded legal and constitutional protections of the citizenry.[13]

Second, the administration proposed, and the Congress voted to accept, a new Department of Homeland Security. It was to be the largest reorganization of the federal government since the creation of the Department of Defense in the post–World War II period. The intent was to better fight the war on terror.

The new department brought together a host of old and new agencies and departments, from the Coast Guard and previously largely independent immigration and border agencies to the creation of new departments to assess and execute chemical, biological, and nuclear countermeasures. Threat assessments, cybersecurity, and emergency preparedness and response were all listed as among its obligations. Its powers, much as with the Patriot Act's provisions, were inclusive. They ranged from the duty to collect and disseminate among all national, state, and local governing units information and preparedness warnings as to terrorist actions and threats; guidelines for and the supervision of the delivery of health services and emergency crews in responding to crises; authorization to collect and prioritize (in association with the Central Intelligence Agency) foreign intelligence; the power to coordinate antiterrorist training nationally; and the charge to protect the nation's critical infrastructure from attack. It was an ambitious and difficult-to-achieve agenda that would take years to implement. It also raised questions from congressional critics as to whether the resources put into the restructuring of government best served the nation's interests in fighting terrorism.

Curiously, one of the immediate fallouts during the campaign was the new department's charge to monitor the adequacy and availability of vaccine stockpiles (as well as other essential medicines). This became an issue in the election when the supply of flu vaccine fell far below that needed for the population. Access to flu shots was severely limited and, as an example, nurses in some states who administered unauthorized shots were threatened with legal penalties, fines, and up to six months' imprisonment. At the height of the controversy, it was revealed that members of Congress (and presumably other government officials) had quietly received such shots. The result was an issue of unexpected emotion from an angry citizenry, one that continued up to election day (and beyond).

The administration, while never making a clear projection as to the likely total costs for Iraq or the war on terrorism, asked the Congress to provide a supplemental appropriation of $87 billion to fund the continuing military efforts, which it did (although more voices in both parties began to be raised questioning the war in Iraq, in particular its cost in dollars and human lives and the necessity of such an occupation).

Taken together, the congressional votes on these three measures serve to indicate the level of support in the Congress, in both parties, and, more indirectly, in the country for the Bush administration's actions. The policies commanded a broad base of support, however controversial some were proven to be.

The acceptance of administration policies was not universal—some in the Congress criticized these bitterly—and by the time of the 2004 election they had become matters of national debate; the Democrats attacked, the Republicans defended the actions taken.

9/11 and the Bush II Presidency

President Bush had vowed revenge in the immediate aftermath of the 9/11 attacks and the war on terrorism had begun. A new era for the country and one with severe international, domestic, and human rights consequences, was to follow.

Using his new powers under the Patriot Act, Bush authorized a war in Afghanistan, the home base of those responsible for the attacks: Al Qaeda and Osama bin Laden, its leader. The war was quick. It overthrew the fundamentalist Islamic Taliban government that had provided refuge to bin Laden and his terrorist group and it destroyed many of Al Qaeda's mountain bases. It was hailed as an immediate success, although later problems in governing, instituting democratic reforms, selecting political officials, providing security to citizens, and controlling lawlessness in general would emerge.

Al Qaeda, it turned out, was far from disabled and may even have benefited (in recruitment, financing, and international attention in confronting the American giant) from 9/11 and the American response. The Taliban also, on a more limited basis, evidenced something of a resurgence as a guerrilla operation.

Bush's next priority, an invasion of Iraq, was considerably less successful and less well received. In fact, it has proved to be a prolonged and expensive (in financial cost and in American and Iraqi lives) operation with little evidence of an end in sight. The war seemed to provide a rallying point for Islamic extremists, and the postwar fighting and carnage (the war was declared officially over in May of 2003), including the mobilization and continued attacks by terrorist organizations within Iraq, resulted in the heaviest conflicts and most casualties of the war. Over 1,200 Americans died after the victory had been declared, a figure that would rise in the months and years to come. The death toll of Iraqis was uncertain.

The terrorist attacks against the U.S. military, American installations, foreigners in general, and Iraqis either part of the new government or sympathetic to the Americans have continued with success. In an unusually brutal series of killings, the terrorists kidnapped foreigners within Iraq and then televised their beheadings. The escalation of terrors appeared to have no limits. The United States had entered the war basically alone (except for the backing of Tony Blair, British prime minister, among major nations) and without the support of the international organizations such as the United Nations.

It was the administration's war to win or lose and, in association with the fallout over national security provisions and infringements on civil liberties domestically, provided the centerpiece for the general election campaign of 2004. The granting of military contracts in the restructuring of Iraq also proved to be controversial. The award of billions of dollars to corporations such as Halliburton, the politically connected Bechtel Corporation, and others, as well as the later charges of fraud, corruption, mismanagement, and overpricing, became issues in the campaign. The torture and humiliation of prisoners by American soldiers and privatized security personnel at Abu Ghraib prison in Iraq, with graphic pictures shown on national television in the United States and worldwide, shocked Americans. Reportedly, and rather than an isolated incident, however appalling, the use of torture more generally in interrogations represented an administration policy with roots in the highest levels of command.[14] The indefinite imprisonment of "detainees" at Guantanamo Bay, Cuba, and elsewhere, without trials or access to legal aid also became a conflictual issue in the fight over accountability in the wars under way.

Domestically the country was attempting to cope with the aftermath of 9/11 and the economic and social policies of the Bush administration, to a large degree reminiscent, and an expansion of, those followed in the Reagan presidency.

9/11: The Political Fallout

To a major degree, the terrorist attacks on September 11, 2001, defined both the presidency of George W. Bush and the campaign of 2004. Many voters were fearful of terrorism and for their own safety. Bush, whatever problems he faced in Iraq or elsewhere, was seen as a strong leader and the one best able to lead the country in a time of crisis. It was to be his biggest campaign asset.

Kerry, on the other hand, had to convince Americans that he had the necessary ability to serve as commander in chief and was better able than the incumbent to execute the duties of the presidency and to protect the nation and its people. It was Kerry's single biggest hurdle in the campaign.

The actions taken by the Bush administration post-9/11 provided the context and major themes for the 2004 presidential campaign. This book looks at the context of the election campaign, reviews the primaries and national conventions, the policy positions and strategies of the contenders, and the most significant developments of the general election campaign. The closeness of the race, the issues of greatest consequence, and the ferocity of the contest are hallmarks of a divisive, if unusually important, election. They all receive attention. It was to be a pivotal chance to decide the future course of America as a nation.

A Note on the Book

This book takes the events recounted up through the election of 2004. It assesses the campaigns of the two parties, the presentation of the Bush administration's record to the public, the choices offered by the Democratic candidate, John F. Kerry, the strategies and counter-strategies of the campaigns, and evaluations of the election results and their policy implications. The effort is to provide an understanding of these developments and the factors that influenced them and policy continuity in the unfolding events that occur, from the first four years of the Bush presidency to the beginning of its second term. The policy emphasis throughout and the effort to tie what took place to broader issues of democratic representation—from levels of political participation and the changing impact of reform on nominating processes to the relevance of campaign finance efforts, now over three decades old, and both the obvious and less obvious associations between economic, religious, and social transformation and their policy consequences—are all factors in the accounts to follow. It was an election full of drama, a clash of opposites, and an unusually close outcome. It was also an election of unusual significance in American politics.

The commitment to these objectives is clear in what follows. But this leads to another point. This is a book with a point of view. It includes contributions by authors of different political persuasions, but that is not the issue. All of the authors share one common assumption, regardless of how they approach the issue. The unifying belief is that the 2004 presidential election was extraordinarily important, nothing less than a marking point in American electoral history. Internationally there is the debate over terrorism, how best to handle it, the national resources to be committed, and the adequacy of the often-controversial approach the administration has followed. Seemingly, in an election fought most decisively over leadership, values, and international threats, the Bush presidency's policies had been approved by a majority of electors.

Election results are difficult to read, complex, and multifaceted. There is never the clear rendering of the verdict, as campaign strategists or the media would lead us to believe. Nonetheless, it would certainly appear that the president's program as presented in the campaign has received what is at least a general endorsement. Put another way, in international affairs, whatever the difficulties encountered, the Republicans' approach found more support than did the Democrats'.

In terms of domestic affairs, the results are likely to be equally important. The Bush campaign was clear in its priorities. Funds would be restricted to the degree possible for social, health, housing, and entitlement programs. Social Security, a popular program that could well test the administration's powers of persuasion on Capitol Hill, was to be largely privatized (young members of the workforce would be allowed to invest their retirement in stock market accounts). Government funding would be redirected from social benefits programs to the military and to fighting terrorism. Meanwhile, taxes would be cut ("reformed"), primarily benefiting the upper income earners and private corporations. The nation's debt and trade imbalance would continue to grow. The environment would be less important than oil exploration and economic development.

The 2004 election presented the nation with a clear, even stark, policy agenda. It is one with roots in the Reagan years in particular, and it could become—and this is the ultimate importance of its impact—a final death knell for the remnants of the New Deal agenda, presaging its place the substitution of another, quite distinctive governing philosophy.

The president has repeatedly argued in favor of what he terms "freedom." It applies domestically in relation to the freedom of individuals to fashion their own economic future with little interference or support from the government. Internationally, it involves the freeing by military force, if necessary, countries from authoritarian and nondemocratic rule. The promotion of the right of people to choose their government in such systems has become an ideology of liberation. It appears straightforward, but its enactment has proven challenging and the complexities and costs involved in its application have yet to be clearly established.

This, then, is the ideology of change, a transformation in how a government thinks and what it does. It is also the mapping of a new domestic policy and a unilateral approach to international policy. The president's action in foreign affairs and the fight against terrorism were bold. They included a rejection of a primary emphasis on the multilateralism that had defined American foreign policy since World War II.

A multitude of forces combined to establish the presidential election as "a defining moment" in the evolution of American politics and for public policy in the United States. It is a recognition of the special importance of the 2004 election that all contributors to this volume share.

Introducing the Chapters

This first chapter by William Crotty ("The Bush Presidency: Establishing the Agenda for the Campaign") has reviewed and assessed developments during the first four years of the Bush presidency, and in particular, the response to the terrorist attacks of 9/11. Those actions set the stage for the 2004 election campaign. For the Bush administration, the campaign was to be run on the administration's record and its victory signified a ratification of its policies. The chapter has also introduced the unifying themes in the chapters to follow, which include the policy implications for the country of the issue positions taken by the candidates and those endorsed by the public through its vote.

In Chapter 2 ("Constituencies and Consequences of the Presidential Vote"), Richard J. Powell and Mark D. Brewer present an overview of the campaign and its execution. Topics discussed include the strategy, issue differences between parties, and consequences of the Bush victory. Succeeding chapters develop from this base.

In Chapter 3 ("Political Participation in the 2004 Presidential Election: Turnout and Policy Consequences"), M. Margaret Conway explores various explanations of the election turnout and their applicability in explaining patterns of participation in 2004. Conway also assesses the dynamics that motivate people to turn out and vote, the manner in which these impacted the vote in 2004, and the policy implications of levels of turnout.

Christine L. Day, Charles D. Hadley, and Harold W. Stanley in Chapter 4 ("The Inevitable Unanticipated Consequences of Political Reform: The 2004 Presidential Nominating Process") review the primaries, the movement of an increasing number of states to the front of the prenomination calendar, the historic amount of funds expended, and, in broader relief, the consequences of the reform movement for parties, candidates, and American politics.

Chapter 5 by William Crotty ("Financing the 2004 Presidential Election") examines the extraordinary level of expenditures in the 2004 election and the staggering increases in the cost of campaigns in general. The 2004 presidential race witnessed the introduction of "527s," groups legally unaffiliated with the campaigns of the major candidates and therefore free to advance positions and air unrestrained television attacks against one party or candidate or the other without the restrictions normally placed on such advertising. The relevance of the campaign finance reforms meant to equalize the playing field and not force presidential candidates to rely on large donors in their election efforts are brought into question by the levels of funding experienced in the 2004 election.

In Chapter 6 ("The Presidential Race of 2004: Strategy, Outcome, and Mandate"), Patricia Conley assesses the claims of mandates for actions resulting from presidential elections. Roughly one-half the presidents since 1824 have claimed such mandates, as the Bush administration did in 2004 (and 2000). The basis for such mandates is explored, as are the political relevance and potential costs of such claims.

Jerome M. Mileur in Chapter 7 ("Incumbency, Politics, and Policy: Detour or New Direction?") places the Bush presidency and its reelection efforts in broader historical perspective, assessing the options open to incumbents and the strategies employed by both parties nationally and on the state level. The policy and future implications of the Republican Party's victory are discussed at length.

John S. Jackson III in Chapter 8 ("The 2004 Congressional Races") redirects attention to congressional races and the policy consequences of the Republican Party's ten-year control of the Congress, extended in the 2004 election. Jackson refers to this as a "semipermanent majority," which appears to be appropriate. The lack of attention given in the media and by the public to House and Senate contests is one indicator of the extent to which presidential politics have come to dominate the national agenda. Incumbency worked to the Republicans' advantage and the 2004 outcome dramatically reinforced their dominance. On both a political and policy front, the Democrats are in their worst condition since the New Deal, a sobering thought for those who believe in competitive two-party politics.

Thomas Ferguson in a more complex but rewarding analysis in Chapter 9 ("Holy Owned Subsidiary: Globalization, Religion, and Politics in the 2004 Election"), develops the root causes of Republican and Democratic Party voting. He ties these to economic conditions, especially when assessed on a state-by-state level (as opposed to relying on national averages, which tend to hide differences), and the effects of turnout on election results. When times are good, the Democrats do well. When times are not economically promising, many voters, and especially those of lower incomes, seek solace in religious absolutes. They also vote more Republican, thus providing an explanation for the fundamentalist and value-oriented explanations given for the vote in 2004 and other years. The essence, as Ferguson shows, can be traced to economic forces impacting the electorate.

John Kenneth White, who has written extensively on cultural forces and the values divide, in Chapter 10 ("The Armageddon Election") places the 2004 election in historical context. He reviews the structure of fundamentalist appeals put forward for the Bush campaign in particular and assesses the public's response to these. John Adams and Thomas Jefferson are presented as potential models for the president's second term, not bad company to find oneself in, but each pointing in quite different directions.

Finally, the concluding chapter ("Armageddon, Just Another Campaign, or Something In-Between? The Meaning and Consequences of the 2004 Election") by William Crotty reviews the Republican and Democratic responses to the election results. The Republicans felt triumphant and vindicated in their policy commitments, the Democrats morose and frustrated. The basic question, however, is how the power granted to the Bush administration will be used and whether its actions will build on its record in the first four years or if it chooses to seek an accommodation and an openness not always evident previously. The initial responses indicate a stronger commitment if anything to the policy and national directions internationally and domestically laid out in the first term.

As a whole, this book assesses an extraordinary campaign and its consequences. What happened and why are developed in explanatory detail as are the forces behind the campaign and the final vote. The policy differences between the parties and candidates in what was an unusually polarizing election, explored in each of the chapters, are the likely consequence for the nation's long-term political agenda.

Notes

1. Thomas George Weiss et al., *Wars on Terrorism and Iraq: Human Rights, Unilaterialism, and U.S. Foreign Policy* (New York: Routledge, 2004); William Crotty, ed., *The Politics of Terror* (Boston: Northeastern University Press, 2004); Jeremy Brown, *Warfare in the 21st Century* (New York: H.W. Wilson, 2003); Paul Krugman, *The Great Unraveling: Losing Our Way in the New Century* (New York: W.W. Norton, 2004).

2. *George Bush and Richard Cheney, Petitioners vs. Albert Gore, Jr. Et als.* 531 U.S. 98.

3. Cited in William J. Crotty, *America's Choice 2000* (Boulder, CO: Westview Press, 2001), 76.

4. Ron Fournier, "Kerry Looks to Avoid Gore Recount Errors," Associated Press, October 21, 2004. Available at www.aponline.com.

5. James Dao, "As Election Nears, Parties Begin Another Round of Legal Battles," *New York Times,* October 18, 2004, A1.

6. Ibid.

7. Benjamin Ginsberg and Matthew Crenson, *Downsizing Democracy: How America Sidelined Its Citizens and Privatized Its Public* (Baltimore, MD: Johns Hopkins University Press, 2002).

8. Dan Briody, *The Halliburton Agenda* (Hoboken, NJ: Wiley, 2004).

9. Crotty, *The Politics of Terror*; John S. Jackson III and Chris Barr, "The View from America," in *Democratic Development and Political Terrorism,* ed. William Crotty, 32–57 (Boston: Northeastern University Press, 2005); Irene Gendzier, "Who Rules the Middle East Agenda?" in Crotty, ed., *Democratic Development and Political Terrorism,* 58–72.

10. Cited in The Poynter Institute, *September 11, 2001* (Kansas City, MO: Andrews McMeel Publishing, 2001), 21.

11. Quoted in ibid., 71.

12. Quoted in ibid., 70.

13. William Crotty, "On the Home Front: Institutional Mobilization to Fight the Threat of International Terrorism," in Crotty, ed., *The Politics of Terror,* 191–234.

14. Seymour Hersh, *Chain of Command: The Road from 9/11 to Abu Ghraib* (New York: HarperCollins, 2004).

2

Constituencies and the Consequences of the Presidential Vote

Richard J. Powell and Mark D. Brewer

In May 2003, as President George W. Bush landed on the deck of the USS *Abraham Lincoln* in the copilot's seat of a navy fighter jet and thanked U.S. sailors for their efforts in Iraq under a large banner declaring "Mission Accomplished," most knowledgeable political observers felt that Bush would cruise to a second term in the next year's presidential election. However, circumstances have a way of changing quickly in contemporary American politics. The rapid and relatively painless removal of Saddam Hussein's regime in Iraq evolved into an ever-intensifying and increasingly violent insurgency that had cost the lives of over 1,100 Americans by Election Day 2004. The memories of 9/11 remained raw and salient, and Americans continued to be worried about terrorism and national security as fighting wore on in Afghanistan, major terrorist attacks took place in Spain and Russia, and, most important, Osama bin Laden remained on the loose and eventually on Americans' television screens. Growth of the American economy continued to lag behind what the president had promised when pushing for his tax cuts, as job growth sputtered and many Americans felt at least somewhat uneasy about the economic situation in the nation. These facts added up to a hard-fought and tightly contested race for the White House, one whose outcome remained up in the air even as the candidates cast their own ballots on the morning of November 2. In the end, Bush won reelection with a slim victory (in both the popular and electoral vote) over John Kerry in the closest election since 1916 involving an incumbent president who had been elected to his own term.

In the days immediately following the 2004 presidential vote, news stories were filled with quotes from voters in "red" (Bush) and "blue" (Kerry) states. Generally, these comments showed that voters in different regions felt increasingly alienated and unable to understand the perspectives of those in other areas of the country. With the prevalence of the dramatic red and blue electoral maps showing the results of each election, it has become commonplace to focus on the geographic divisions between the two parties. However, geographic differences are merely surface indicators of deeper group-based divisions among voters. During the campaign, Democratic vice presidential nominee John Edwards often talked about "two Americas" in reference to growing inequality between people from different economic classes. From an electoral standpoint, there are indeed two Americas, but the divisions run much deeper than socioeconomic class. They are also rooted in religion, race, ethnicity, marital and family status, and a wide range of social and cultural perspectives. These divisions are reinforced by the increasing ability of people to associate with others most like themselves, through geographic mobility, selective social interactions, and an explosion of targeted media on cable television, talk radio, and the Internet.[1]

American electoral politics has always been rooted in group conflict.[2] Political parties in the United States are coalitional parties, made up of loose combinations of the various social and demographic groups that exist in American society. This is not to say that all the members of a specific group support a particular party, but rather that there are many groups whose members tend to support one party more than the other on a regular basis. Both the Republican and Democratic parties are assembled from these group blocs, and each party has its own unique groups that make up their respective core constituencies. It is from these core constituency groups that the major political parties (and by extension their candidates) begin their attempts to fashion electoral victories. Not all groups, of course, find themselves firmly in the coalition of one party or the other. There are a number of groups that represent swing constituencies, and they are actively courted and wooed by both parties. There are also many groups whose group identification is not politically relevant, either on a regular basis or for a particular election. These latter groups will be ignored here. This chapter tells the story of the 2004 presidential election from a relevant group perspective. We will examine the core constituencies of the Republicans and Democrats, as well as the swing constituencies that both parties sought to attract. Analyzing the voting behavior of these groups will provide us with a much better understanding of this presidential contest.

In any election, a political party wants to activate and keep the support of its base, attract a larger percentage of support from swing groups than the opposition, and if possible at least chip away at the base of the other party. In the 2004 presidential election, Bush and the Republicans were able to achieve these three objectives to a much higher degree than were Kerry and the Democrats. Key components of the Republican base—evangelical Protestants, regular church attenders, white males, affluent voters, veterans, gun owners, and rural dwellers—strongly supported Bush for reelection. Bush also fared better than Kerry among swing constituencies like Roman Catholics, senior citizens, and suburbanites. Finally, while Kerry and the Democrats were able to hold strong levels of support from some groups in their base, such as less affluent voters, union households, African Americans, homosexuals, and, to a slightly lesser extent, Jews, significant numbers of individuals in other key groups in the traditional Democratic base, such as Latinos, women, and city dwellers, defected to Bush. Bush and the Republican Party received strong support from the groups in their base, attracted more voters from key swing groups than did their opponents, and peeled off some support from traditionally Democratic groups. That is why the GOP will control the White House for much of this decade.

Republican Core Constituencies

For most of the twentieth century, the Republican base consisted of affluent voters in the business and professional communities and nonsouthern white Protestants.[3] Regionally, these voters were concentrated in the Northeast and in the rural areas of the Midwest and Mountain West. However, the mid-1960s saw the beginning of a number of important social and political changes that would significantly reshape the Republican coalition. With the nomination of Barry Goldwater for president in 1964, the GOP clearly delineated itself as the conservative (economically and socially) option in America's two-party system. When this decision was combined with the often-turbulent events of the late 1960s and early 1970s, a number of social groups began to rethink their partisan attachments. Most notably, southern whites abandoned the Democratic Party in very high numbers and became reliable members of the Republican base.[4] Intertwined with this move, there was a dramatic increase in support for Republicans from religiously observant Protestants, especially evangelicals, owing to the cultural upheavals of the Vietnam era and controversial Supreme Court decisions on issues such as school prayer, birth control, and abortion rights.[5] Other key components of the Republican base in recent decades have been white men (especially white males in the South), active military personnel and veterans, and gun owners. The party has also been able to maintain, and even increase in some elections, the support of some groups in its traditional base, such as the more affluent and rural dwellers who live outside of the South.[6]

With a loss in the popular vote in 2000, a natural reelection strategy for Bush would have been to reach out to swing voters while maintaining support among his base. Although Bush pursued both of these strategies, he placed the most emphasis on energizing his political base. Following their razor-thin victory in 2000, Republican strategists, led by Karl Rove, were convinced that millions of would-be Republican voters failed to turn out on Election Day, with evangelical Christians believed to be the most important segment of this group (Rove regularly stated that Bush lost the popular vote in 2000 because 4 million evangelicals who should have voted did not do so).[7] Beginning in late 2000, Bush embarked on a four-year effort to mobilize those voters through a combination of initiatives designed to win their favor, such as the appointment of John Ashcroft as attorney general, proclaiming support for a constitutional amendment banning gay marriage, making vouchers available for attendance at religious schools, actively pushing through Congress a ban on so-called partial-birth abortions, and the pursuit of faith-based initiatives. This was accompanied by an ambitious grass-roots effort to build ties to a variety of religious groups. The 2002 midterm election, only the second midterm election since 1934 in which an incumbent president's party gained seats, was viewed as a successful test run of this new strategy.

As shown in Table 2.1, in 2004 Bush strengthened his support with the Republican base from 2000. A general indicator of Bush's strength with his party's core constituencies was his ability to win support from 93 percent of Republicans, exceeding his 2000 total of 91 percent. Undoubtedly, Bush's successful efforts to strengthen his ties with white evangelicals were a crucial element in shoring up the party base, and also a key part of his victory. After paying close attention to his religious base during his first three and a half years in office, President Bush did not forget them during the campaign. During his acceptance speech at the Republican National Convention, Bush spoke directly to religious conservatives:

Table 2.1

Social Groups and the Presidential Vote, 1996–2004

% of total vote in 2004	Social group	2004		2000		1996		
		Bush	Kerry	Bush	Gore	Clinton	Dole	Perot
	Sex							
46	Men	55	44	53	42	43	44	10
54	Women	48	51	43	54	54	38	7
	Race and ethnicity							
77	White	58	41	54	42	43	46	9
11	Black	11	88	9	90	84	12	4
9	Latino	44	53	35	62	72	21	6
	Sex and race							
36	White men	62	37	60	36			
41	White women	55	44	49	48			
10	Nonwhite men	30	67					
12	Nonwhite women	24	75					
	Age							
17	18–29	45	54	46	48	53	34	10
29	30–44	53	46	49	48	48	41	9
30	45–59	51	48	49	48	48	41	9
24	60 and over	54	46	47	51	48	44	7
	Party identification							
37	Republican	93	6	91	8	13	80	6
37	Democrat	11	89	11	86	84	10	5
26	Independent	48	49	47	45	43	35	17
	Ideology							
34	Conservative	84	15	81	17	20	71	8
45	Moderate	45	54	44	52	57	33	9
21	Liberal	13	85	13	80	78	11	7

	Region							
22	Northeast	43	56	39	56	55	34	9
26	Midwest	51	48	49	48	48	41	10
32	South	58	42	55	43	46	46	7
20	West	49	50	46	48	48	40	8
	Type of community							
25	Rural	57	42	59	37			
46	Suburban	52	47	49	47	47	42	8
30	Urban	45	54	35	61			
	Religious tradition							
54	Protestant (all)	59	40	56	42	41	50	8
23	Protestant (evangelical)	78	21					
27	Roman Catholic	52	47	47	50	53	37	9
3	Jewish	25	74	19	79	78	16	3
10	None	31	67	33	57			
	Church attendance							
16	More than weekly	64	35	63	36			
26	Weekly	58	41	57	40			
14	Monthly	50	49	46	51			
28	Few times per year	45	54	42	54			
15	Never	36	62	32	61			
	Family income							
8	Under $15,000	36	63	37	57	59	28	11
15	$15,000–30,000	42	57	41	54	53	36	9
22	$30,000–50,000	49	50	43	49	48	40	10
23	$50,000–75,000	56	43	51	46	44	48	7
14	$75,000–100,000	55	45	52	45	41	51	7
11	$100,000–150,000	57	42	54	43	38	54	6
4	$150,000–200,000	58	42	—	—	—	—	—
3	$200,000 and over	63	35	—	—	—	—	—

(continued)

Table 2.1 *(continued)*

% of total vote in 2004	Social group	2004		2000		1996		
		Bush	Kerry	Bush	Gore	Clinton	Dole	Perot
	Union household							
24	Yes	40	59	37	59	59	30	9
76	No	58	41	52	44			
	Served in military							
18	Yes	57	41					
82	No	49	50					
	Marital status							
63	Married	57	42	53	44	44	46	9
37	Not married	40	58	38	57	57	31	9
	Children under 18							
37	Yes	53	45	53	45	48	41	9
63	No	50	49	46	50			
	Sexual orientation							
96	Heterosexual	53	46	50	47			
4	Homo- or bisexual	23	77	25	75	66	22	7
	Gun household							
41	Yes	63	36	61	36			
59	No	43	57	39	58			

Sources: Figures for 2004 are taken from the national exit poll conducted by Edison Media Research and Mitofsky International for the National Election Pool (a consortium of ABC News, the Associated Press, CBS News, CNN, Fox News, and NBC News), as reported by CNN (available from www.cnn.com/ELECTION/2004/pages/results/states/US/P/00/epolls.0.html), and the *New York Times*, Marjorie Connelly, "How Americans Voted: A Political Portrait," November 7, 2004, section 4, p. 4. Figures for 2000 taken from the national exit poll conducted by the Voter News Service, as reported by CNN (available from www.cnn.com/ELECTION/2000/results/index.epolls.html), and the *New York Times*, Connelly, "How Americans Voted: A Political Portrait." Figures for 1996 taken from the national exit poll conducted by the Voter News Service, as reported by the *New York Times*, Connelly, "How Americans Voted: A Political Portrait."

Note: For church attendance, the category "Few Times Per Year" was "seldom" in 2000. For both 1996 and 2000 the top income category offered was "over $100,000."

> Our society rests on a foundation of responsibility and character and family commitment. . . . Because a caring society will value its weakest members, we must make a place for the unborn child. Because religious charities provide a safety net of mercy and compassion, our government must never discriminate against them. Because the union of a man and a woman deserves an honored place in our society, I support the protection of marriage against activist judges.

Bush did not end his appeals to this group when the GOP left New York City. During the second presidential debate in St. Louis, Bush explained his decision to allow only limited federal funding of embryonic stem cell research as based on the need to balance scientific progress and the respect for life. During this same debate, Bush made his position on abortion very clear. In response to a question from the audience on the use of tax dollars to support abortion, the president said: "My answer is, we're not going to spend taxpayers' money on abortion. . . . I signed the partial birth—the ban on partial-birth abortion. It's a brutal practice. It's one way to help reduce abortions. My opponent voted against the ban. . . . Culture of life is really important for a country to have if it's going to be a hospitable society." Bush repeated these same sentiments during the third debate. Also at the final debate, he was asked by moderator Bob Schieffer if he believed homosexuality was a choice. His response was, "You know, Bob, I don't know. I just don't know."

The above examples are a just a few of the most prominent appeals made to religious conservatives by Bush and his campaign. Somewhat below the radar of the major media's campaign coverage, but perhaps even more important, the Bush camp made intense efforts to contact evangelical Protestant ministers and work with them to increase voter turnout among their congregations.[8] The Republican National Committee even went so far as to distribute a mass mailing in Arkansas and West Virginia implying a Democratic victory would lead to the banning of the Bible and the allowance of gay marriage.[9] In the end, evangelical Protestants did not let the president down. He won 78 percent of the vote from these voters, his best showing among any group. Nevertheless, the impact of the evangelical vote was greatly overstated by the popular press in the weeks following the election. While this group did support Bush by a slightly higher margin than in 2000, there was no surge in the evangelical vote relative to other groups in the electorate. Turnout in 2004 increased across the board for nearly all types of voters, with evangelicals comprising about one-quarter of the electorate in both 2000 and 2004.[10] White evangelicals continue to be the most reliable voting group within the Republican coalition, but their importance in swinging the 2004 election to Bush has been greatly exaggerated by many in the media.

The Republicans' religious appeal to their base did not end with evangelicals. In recent years attendance at worship services has been closely aligned with vote choice, with the likelihood of supporting the GOP increasing with attendance.[11] Bush often talked openly about his faith during the campaign (and, indeed, throughout his first four years in the White House), and made no secret that his religious beliefs played a large role in shaping his political views and influenced how he governed.

On the other hand, the media often commented on how Kerry felt that his faith was a private matter, and that he remained somewhat aloof on the issue, at least in public.[12] Seemingly recognizing the importance of this issue late in the campaign, Kerry discussed the importance of religion in his life more frequently during the end stages of the race. During the third debate Kerry noted that "My faith affects everything that I do," and he delivered a speech on how his faith and religious values affected his policy positions on October 24 in Fort Lauderdale, Florida. For example, Kerry noted that his faith led him to "holding to a vision of a society of the common good."[13] In the end, however, Kerry's efforts to attract more religious voters fell short, with voters attending worship services on at least a weekly basis voting for Bush by a large margin.

While these results likely reflect the preference of religious voters for choosing a candidate for whom faith is also important, they are also perhaps indicative of the unexpected importance of moral issues for voters in the election. When asked which issue was most important to them in casting their votes, 22 percent of voters cited moral values, the highest of any issue in the election. In particular, the saliency of the same-sex marriage issue (the most prominent of the "moral values" issues in this campaign) was raised by the decision of the Massachusetts Supreme Judicial Court legalizing the practice, the presence of gay marriage bans on 11 state ballots, and news coverage of Kerry's comments in the final presidential debate that singled out Mary Cheney, the vice president's daughter, as a lesbian. This worked significantly to the Republicans' advantage since 80 percent of voters citing moral values as being most important backed the president.

It is important, however, not to overstate the significance of moral issues in deciding the election. Notably, the exit poll question that asked voters about the most important issue was poorly designed because it offered only closed-end, multiple-choice responses. In fact, Iraq and terrorism, which were presented as separate categories, dwarf the importance of moral values when taken together. Similarly, 25 percent of voters selected either the economy or taxes as the most important issue. Moreover, it is difficult to know exactly what the phrase "moral values" means. Conceivably, this could mean very different things to different people. According to the postelection punditry, the saliency of moral values among voters was interpreted to mean that there was a surge in the participation of socially conservative voters. However, the exit polls do not support this conclusion. Only 16 percent of voters said abortion should always be illegal, the same percentage as in 2000.[14] And, despite the supposed influence of the same-sex marriage issue in determining the outcome of the election, 60 percent of voters supported either legalization of marriage or civil unions for same-sex couples.[15]

Regardless of the role played by moral issues in this election, religious conservatives and regular church attenders were not the only part of the Republican core constituency to strongly back Bush. In keeping with a long historical tradition, more affluent Americans strongly supported the Republican Party's presidential candidate. Bush won at least 55 percent of the vote from every income group above $50,000 per year, with 63 percent of those making over $200,000 per year voting for the president. That this latter group supported Bush in such an overwhelming fashion is not surprising since Kerry vowed to raise their taxes if elected. For his part, the president regularly talked about how spending by individuals and businesses, rather than government, was the key to economic growth, and how important it is to keep money in the hands of the people who earned it rather than in government coffers by way of taxes. Three statements from the presidential debates illustrate Bush's position here quite well. During the second debate in St. Louis, the president said: "I think if you raise taxes during a recession, you head to depression. I come from the school of thought that says when people have more money in their pocket during economic times [*sic*], it increases demand or investment. Small businesses begin to grow, and jobs are added." Bush returned to this same theme during the third debate in Tempe, Arizona: "It's your money. The way my opponent talks, he said 'We're going to spend the government's money.' No, we're spending your money. And when you have more money in your pocket, you're better able to afford things you want." And finally, also from the third debate: "The way to make sure the economy grows is not to raise taxes on small-business owners. It's not to increase the scope of the federal government. It's to make sure we have fiscal sanity and keep taxes low."

President Bush also performed well with other groups that have traditionally voted Republican. A particular strength of Bush's was with those who have served in the military; he received 57 percent of the vote from that group. The president regularly portrayed Kerry as being unsupportive of the military, often presenting Kerry's vote against the $87 billion supplemental bill to fund the operations in Iraq as a prime example, as he did during the first presidential debate in Coral Gables, Florida:

> My opponent says [to American troops] help is on the way, but what kind of a message does it say to our troops in harm's way, 'wrong war, wrong place, wrong time'? . . . As well, help is on the way, but it's certainly hard to tell it when he voted against the $87-billion supplemental to provide equipment for our troops, and then said he actually did vote for it before he voted against it. Not what a commander in chief does when you're trying to lead troops.

Bush also took every opportunity to present Kerry as weak on national defense, and to make the case that this weakness would not only hurt the country in general, but would be particularly harmful to America's military personnel. Consider this comment by the president as he addressed the National Guard Association in Las Vegas: "Our troops, our friends and our allies, and our enemies, must know where America stands and that America will stand firm. We cannot waver because our enemies won't."[16] The Kerry campaign tried very hard to blunt Republican support among veterans and the active military. The Democratic National Convention was chiefly a paean to Kerry's service in Vietnam. Kerry surrounded himself with retired military personnel during campaign stops and repeatedly cited their support. At least once during each of the three debates Kerry talked about how either the active military or veterans were in some way getting a raw deal under the policies of the Bush administration. On the other hand, Kerry was on the defensive for most the final months of the campaign because of the ads run by the Swift Boat Veterans for Truth criticizing his Vietnam service record. In the end, Kerry's efforts were for naught, and Bush was able to keep the part of the GOP base rooted in the United States military.

The president's strong performance with the Republican base did not stop with the groups discussed above. Among two groups with a fairly high degree of overlap, Bush won 57 percent of the rural vote and 63 percent of voters in households with at least one gun owner. Kerry made strong plays for both of these groups—in Iowa promising to convene a "rural summit" within the first 100 days of his administration, his infamous goose hunting photo op in rural Ohio, discussing his favorite firearm with *Outdoor Life* magazine, and appearing all over the Midwest in his brown barn coat—but in the end he once again came up short. Kerry's record in the Senate of consistently voting in favor of gun control made him public enemy number one with the NRA, who officially endorsed Bush in mid-October, and spent $20 million to defeat Kerry.[17] The Bush campaign regularly mocked Kerry's attempts to appear friendly with gun owners. For example, senior campaign staff members Karl Rove and Karen Hughes exited the campaign plane one night clad in camouflage hunting gear similar to what Kerry had worn in Ohio on his goose hunting trip. Just hours after the pictures of Kerry in his camouflage gear with shotgun in hand splashed across television and computer screens across the nation, Vice President Cheney told a Toledo, Ohio, audience that Kerry's camouflage was "an October disguise—an effort he's making to hide the fact that he votes against gun owner rights at every turn. My fellow sportsmen, this cover-up isn't going to work. The Second Amendment is more than just a photo opportunity."[18] And it was not only the gun issue that hurt Kerry among rural voters; his stands on abortion and gay marriage were unpopular as well. Perhaps most important was a sense of inability on the part of rural Americans to relate to the Massachusetts senator. This feeling was neatly summed up by David Yespen, a veteran political analyst for the *Des Moines Register,* in a comment to the *New York Times.* Discussing Kerry's difficulties with rural voters, Yespen said "There's a cultural disconnect between the chainsaw gang and the windsurfer," referring to the now well known video of John Kerry windsurfing off the coast of Nantucket during a break from campaigning.[19] Many rural voters simply never came to feel that Kerry understood or even was capable of understanding their concerns, and thus voted for the president on Election Day.

Finally, white men have been a reliable part of the Republican base in recent decades.[20] This continued to be the case in 2004, with Bush receiving 62 percent of the vote from this group. Of course, white men comprise a large group, and one that has considerable representation in some of the other Republican constituencies discussed above, such as active military personnel, veterans, and gun owners. Bush's aforementioned appeals to these groups certainly helped him among white males. However, it is also the case that the president's constant tough talk on national security, Iraq, and military matters in general very likely worked to his benefit among white men. In a more impressionistic sense, Bush tended to present himself in ways that American culture would typically define as masculine. While this is of course difficult to document empirically, it is not farfetched to think this went far toward earning Bush strong support among white men.

All in all, the president was very successful in building support among the Republican base. With the ongoing threat of terrorism, the continuing war in Iraq, and his own liberal stands on some hot-button social issues, Kerry was unable to make any headway with groups that have traditionally voted Republican. Except for rural voters, which supported Bush by 2 percent less than in 2000, the Republicans increased their share of the vote with every segment of their base. The GOP achieved the first goal of a party contesting an election—they held onto and even increased the levels of support of their own voters. However, this alone was not enough to secure a second term for Bush. As we discuss in the following sections, the real success of the Bush campaign was in its ability to make significant inroads with swing voters and even parts of the Democratic base.

Democratic Core Constituencies

Despite the supposed demise of the New Deal coalition, a number of the groups that supported Roosevelt and Truman have continued to be reliable components of the Democratic Party base into the current era of American politics. Less affluent voters, union members, African Americans, urban dwellers, and Jews all remain core Democratic constituencies. In recent years, new groups such as Latinos, homosexuals, and, to a lesser extent, women have joined the Democratic fold. The Democrats have, however, suffered some erosion in the coalition that FDR built. Perhaps most important has been the loss of white southern males, who by and large have shifted their loyalty to the Republicans.[21] In the last two presidential elections, Roman Catholics have shifted as well, going from reliably Democratic to a key swing constituency.

It is important to note that Kerry's performance was not an electoral disaster on par with George McGovern's in 1972 or Walter Mondale's in 1984. Kerry won the vote of 89 percent of Democrats, and 85 percent of liberals. For the most part, Kerry was successful in garnering the votes of traditionally Democratic groups. However, Bush was able to make small inroads with some of these groups, and in an election as close as this one, small gains can make a big difference in the final outcome.

We start with the core groups among which Kerry was able to maintain support. Since the 1960s, no group in the United States has been more reliably Democratic than African Americans.[22] One can imagine Democrats' concern when in the weeks leading up to the 2004 election several public opinion polls showed President Bush nearly doubling his support with African Americans over what he received in 2000.[23] At this point the Kerry campaign went into overdrive in an effort to make sure black voters supported their candidate. During the last month of the campaign Kerry appeared at a different African American Protestant church every Sunday, speaking directly to congregants from the pulpit, often surrounded by prominent black clergymen such as Jesse Jackson and Al Sharpton. Kerry also appeared in an extended interview special on Black Entertainment Television (an invitation that Bush did not accept) in an effort to reach African American voters. In late October, former Vice President Al Gore visited six black churches in Florida on one Sunday morning in an effort to increase African American support for Kerry.[24] The Democrats even called in their biggest gun of all to appeal to the black community—Bill Clinton. Immediately after his return to the campaign trail (after heart surgury) in Philadelphia, Clinton participated in a conference call with Kerry and one thousand black ministers across the nation.[25] When all was said and done, African Americans stayed with their party and overwhelmingly supported Kerry. Bush received only 11 percent of this group's vote, an increase of 2 percent from the previous election but still much lower than some estimates a month earlier. Kerry's ability to maintain support among African Americans can be attributed to the significant appeals he made to this group in the final weeks of the campaign.

The have-nots in American society are another long-term component of the Demcoratic coalition.[26] And less affluent voters were another key component of the Democratic base that went solidly for Kerry. He won 57 percent of the vote among those with family incomes from $15,000 to $30,000 and 63 percent among those who earned less than $15,000. John Edwards was perhaps the campaign's most vocal and articulate spokesperson appealing to these voters. As noted in the introduction to this chapter, Edwards often referred to the "two Americas," pointing out the growing economic inequality in the United States at every opportunity. He was particularly pointed in his speech at the Democratic Convention:

> John Kerry and I believe that we shouldn't have two different economies in America: one for people who are set for life, they know their kids and their grandkids are going to be just fine; and then one for most Americans, people who live paycheck to paycheck.

And also:

> We can also do something about 35 million Americans who live in poverty every day. And here's why we shouldn't just talk about, but do something about the millions of Americans who live in poverty: because it is wrong. And we have a moral responsibility to lift those families up.

Kerry appealed to lower-income voters as well. He made it very clear that he was going to raise taxes on those wealthy Americans who earned over $200,000 per year in order to provide benefits to the lower and middle class. Kerry also emphasized the plank in the Democratic platform calling for raising the minimum wage to $7.00 an hour. Kerry and the Democrats appealed to their less affluent base, and they were rewarded with strong support among this group of voters.

Kerry also did well among other important groups in the Democratic base. Voters with at least one union member in their household once again came through in strong fashion for the Democratic candidate, with Kerry receiving 59 percent of their votes. Both Kerry and Edwards talked frequently about the outsourcing of jobs during their convention, the debates, and at campaigns stops. Kerry talked to locked-out workers at a picket line in rural Ohio, and voiced strong support for their cause. Despite frequent media reports in the weeks leading up to the election speculating that Bush's strong support for Israel and Ariel Sharon would cost the Democrats among Jewish voters, in the end Jews ended up giving Kerry 74 percent of their vote, only 5 percent less than this same group gave Gore in 2000. Again, while Bush did improve among Jews, his increase was not as large as had been predicted in the weeks leading up to Election Day. Finally, Kerry also did well among homosexuals, garnering 77 percent of their vote. While not supporting gay marriage, both

Kerry and Edwards very clearly stated that they supported full partnership rights for homosexual couples: Edwards during the vice presidential debate and Kerry during the third presidential debate. And while Kerry's comments relating to Mary Cheney at this same debate likely hurt him among some groups, his stance that homosexuality is an innate trait rather than a lifestyle choice likely helped him among homosexuals.

Despite his success among the Democratic core groups described above, there were some traditionally Democratic groups that supported Kerry at lower levels than they had other recent Democratic candidates. Latinos, a key Democratic constituency in recent elections, are one such group. Republicans have made very significant attempts to court this fast-growing group in recent years, and the Bush effort in 2004 represents the strongest (and most successful) effort to date. The campaign aired numerous ads on Spanish-language television and radio stations across the country. Bush and his strategists believed that Latino voters were especially open to Republican appeals because of their religiosity and social conservatism. Bush also regularly addressed Latino crowds in their first language. Attracting a fair share of the Latino vote has been of long-term interest to Bush, going back to his days as Texas governor. Kerry and the Democrats seemed to do little to directly court the Latino vote, outside of speaking in Spanish at a few rallies in Colorado and New Mexico. Although Kerry won among Latino voters with 53 percent of the vote, Bush increased his vote with this group by 9 percentage points over 2000, which translated into nearly 1 million additional votes.

In recent years the voting patterns of men and women have received considerable attention because of the emergence of a "gender gap" in their votes. Generally since 1980, women as a group have consistently voted Democratic, while men have voted Republican.[27] For instance, in 2000 Bush won 53 percent of the male vote, but lost 54 to 43 among women. In 2004, Bush increased his advantage with men, garnering 55 percent of their vote. Although Kerry won the female vote, Bush cut into the Democrat's advantage by winning 5 percent more among women than he had in 2000. However, focusing solely on gender obscures some important differences among women as a group. Kerry won significantly with nonwhite women and nonmarried women, but Bush won a majority of the vote from white women and married women. In sum, the gender gap is better understood when looking at the interaction between gender, race, and marital status.

Because they constitute such a large portion of the electorate, white women are an especially important group, especially those living in suburban areas with children under the age of 18. This group tends to be moderate on many issues, but they have been particularly motivated by family issues such as drugs, school safety, educational quality, family leave, and health care in recent years; they were a critical component of Clinton's electoral victories in 1992 and 1996. Clinton appealed to this group with his policy proposals on things such as school uniforms, television V-chips and ratings systems, an assault weapons ban, and family leave.

Like other recent Democratic candidates, Kerry put particular emphasis on appealing to women during his campaign through the issues of health care and the economy. For example, in September he held a town-hall meeting in Jacksonville, Florida, with women to discuss these issues. The next week he held a similar meeting in Davenport, Iowa, to discuss national security with an all-female audience. Kerry even made an appearance on the popular morning talk show, "Live with Regis and Kelly," where he talked about his early days as a prosecutor on rape cases.[28] Later in the campaign, Kerry frequently attacked Bush for not working to renew a federal law that banned assault weapons, in an effort to appeal to women worried about crime and school safety.

For his part, Bush also made extensive efforts to attract women voters. With polls showing that so-called security moms were very concerned about the threat of terrorism, Bush made national security the cornerstone of his pitch to women. In late October, for example, the Republicans purchased $14 million of advertising time for an ad that featured a teenager who lost his mother in the 9/11 attacks. In many of his campaign speeches, Bush highlighted his administration's record of liberating Afghan women from the oppression of the Taliban. The Bush campaign also held a series of campaign events and printed campaign materials using the theme "W stands for Women." Kerry responded to these appeals with similar ones of his own. For example, the Democrats produced an ad late in the campaign featuring Kristen Breitweiser, whose husband was killed on 9/11, saying that Kerry would make her daughter safer from terrorism.[29] In the end, Bush's appeals seemed to work. As mentioned above, one of the keys to Bush's victory in 2004 was in cutting into the Democrats' traditional advantage with women voters by 5 percentage points.

Finally, the president was able to significantly increase his support among a group that has been a crucial component of the Democratic coalition since at least Al Smith's campaign in 1928—urban voters.[30] While Kerry still won the majority (54%) of urban voters, Bush increased his share of the vote with this group by 10 percent over 2000. Neither candidate did very much in the way of making specific policy appeals to urban voters, reflecting the virtual disappearance of urban policy from the national agenda.[31] However, Bush's dominant focus on fighting terrorism and the perception that he was the candidate better able to defend against terrorism likely played a key role in attracting urban voters, who tend to feel more directly threatened by terror than suburbanites and rural dwellers.

In summary, Kerry performed well with most groups comprising the traditional Democratic base. However, Bush was able to make sizable inroads with many of these groups—specifically women, Latinos, and urban dwellers. This played a significant role in the president's reelection.

Swing Voters

In addition to performing well with his base and making meaningful inroads with elements of the Democratic core, the other key factor in explaining Bush's victory was his appeal to swing voters. Swing voters, who by definition are willing to vote for a candidate of either party depending upon the circumstances, played a pivotal role in deciding the outcome of the 2004 election. Over the past several years, pundits have tagged different groups of swing voters with catchy labels like angry white males, soccer moms, NASCAR dads, and security moms. Although these labels oversimplify large groups of people, they do tend to identify groups that have not found a natural political home with either major party.

The Catholic vote received an inordinate amount of attention in the 2004 campaign. Both candidates thought they could do well among this group. For most of the twentieth century Catholics were strongly Democratic,[32] and Kerry was the first Catholic presidential nominee since John F. Kennedy in 1960. Clinton had done well among Catholics in 1992 and 1996, and Kerry hoped to equal if not surpass these levels of success. However, the Republicans had high hopes on the Catholic front as well. Bush's political hero, Ronald Reagan, did very well with Catholic voters in 1980 (and to a lesser extent in 1984), and Bush turned in a relatively strong performance among Catholics in 2000. Since Catholics comprise about 25 percent of the electorate, both Kerry and Bush made extensive efforts to appeal to them. As mentioned above, this was a cornerstone of Bush's courting of Latino voters. Similarly, Kerry focused more and more on his faith as the campaign progressed. Kerry attended mass every weekend and Holy Day during the final months of the campaign. In October he also began delivering a number of speeches about his personal faith although he had been fairly private about this in the past. For example, on October 24 Kerry delivered a speech in Fort Lauderdale, Florida, in which he drew connections between his beliefs, the Bible, and economic justice.[33] Despite his efforts, Kerry was on the defensive on religious matters throughout much of the campaign, particularly after several Catholic bishops said that he should be denied communion for his pro-choice position on abortion. Archbishop Charles Caput of Denver attracted a considerable amount of press attention in October when he issued a thinly veiled endorsement of Bush by calling on voters to cast their vote on the issue of abortion.[34] Perhaps the greatest contrast on matters of concern to Catholics came on October 21, when Kerry appeared at an event to advocate embryonic stem cell research with the widow of Christopher Reeve, while Bush held a well-publicized meeting with Cardinal Justin Rigali of Philadelphia.[35] In the end, Bush prevailed with Catholic voters by a margin of 52 to 47 percent. This represented an improvement for Bush over his total of 47 percent in 2000. And, it showed that Republicans had made particularly strong gains with Catholics since 1996 when Dole won just 37 percent of the Catholic vote.

Senior citizens comprise another voting bloc that is part of the swing vote, going for Reagan in the 1980s but Clinton in the 1990s. In 2000, Gore beat Bush among this group by 51 to 47 percent. Although senior citizens are generally more conservative in many of their viewpoints, they have often been attracted to Democratic policies on Social Security and Medicare. Through his backing of the government's new prescription drug plan for seniors, Bush hoped at least to neutralize the Democratic advantage with this age group.

Both candidates made substantial appeals to senior citizens during the campaign. In particular, Kerry delivered numerous speeches in which he criticized Bush over the shortage of flu vaccine, including an address to the American Association of Retired Persons in Las Vegas on October 14.[36] He also warned publicly that Bush had a "January surprise" to cut Social Security benefits by 25–45 percent.[37] For his part, Bush touted his own prescription drug plan and criticized Kerry during the third debate as having a weak record on Medicare in the Senate. In the end, Bush reversed the trend of Democratic success with this group in recent elections, beating Kerry by a margin of 54 to 46 percent among senior citizens.

It is also important to note that some of the shift in voting patterns among senior citizens may be influenced by generational replacement. For many years, senior citizens consisted mostly of individuals who had lived through the Great Depression and fought in World War II, and had become politically aware during Franklin Roosevelt's tenure in office. By 2004 the youngest senior citizens were born in the 1940s and were primarily shaped by the Cold War with the Soviet Union and relatively robust economic times of the 1950s and early 1960s. As a group they tend to be less Democratic than the previous generation.

Another swing group that received a great deal of attention in 2004 was young people between the ages of 18 and 29. Young voters have not played an important role in recent elections because they have tended not to vote in very high numbers. In 2000, for example, fewer than 40 percent of these voters went to the polls.[38] When they have voted, young people have been the quintessential swing voters. In the 1980s they supported Reagan by wide margins over his Democratic opponents, but they switched their loyalties to Clinton in the 1990s. In 2000 they divided their vote almost evenly, giving 48 percent to Gore and 46 percent to Bush.

In 2004, a number of groups launched massive efforts to register young voters and encourage them to vote. Both parties ran youth registration drives, but it was the Democrats who were especially active in courting the youth vote. Democrats mobilized extensive campus networks, particularly around the issue of opposition to the war in Iraq. Organizations such as Rock the Vote and the New Voter Project claimed to have registered millions of new voters. Kerry courted this group through public appearances with well-known celebrities including Bruce Springsteen and Jimmy Buffett. In a number of speeches Kerry asserted that Bush would be likely to institute a military draft in a second term, a charge Bush strenuously denied.

In the end, young voters supported Kerry by a margin of 54 to 45 percent. The campaign's efforts at increasing support among young voters did pay off, as Kerry improved on Gore's performance by 6 percentage points. However, those aged 18–29 did not provide the winning margin the Democrats had expected. Although turnout among young voters increased in 2004, so did turnout among most other groups. They constituted 17 percent of the electorate in both 2000 and 2004, meaning that Kerry got a boost here, but not the push over the top that many analysts had been speculating about in the weeks prior to Election Day.

In summary, a significant factor in Bush's victory in 2004 was his ability to appeal to swing voters. Although Kerry managed to increase the Democratic share of the youth vote, Bush made very significant gains with Catholics and senior citizens, both of which comprised larger shares of the electorate than young people.

Policy Implications for George W. Bush's Second Term

The old adage "to the victor goes the spoils" has a long and storied tradition in American politics. In a quadrennial November ritual, those groups whose support helped the winning presidential candidate achieve his success begin to make rumblings (some loudly and some quietly) about what they expect from the administration in return for their support. Based on the record of his first term, Bush is not likely to by shy in rewarding groups that were important to his reelection. Bush typically has governed in a style that rewards friends (and sometimes punishes foes), and his second four years as chief executive figure to follow this same pattern. After all, Bush pursued policies during his first term as if he had won a landslide victory, not as a president who had lost the popular vote. Armed this time with victories in both the popular and electoral votes, most believe that Bush will aggressively seek to accomplish his policy goals. As Vice President Cheney said as he introduced the president for his victory speech to the nation the day after Election Day, "President Bush ran forthrightly on a clear agenda for this nation's future, and the nation responded by giving him a mandate."[39] If the administration's plan of attack needed any further clarification, the president provided it during his victory address as he discussed his second-term agenda: "I earned capital in the campaign, political capital. And now I intend to spend it."[40] This final section of this chapter will briefly address some of the possible policy implications of the 2004 election for Bush's second-term agenda. This examination will not be a comprehensive look at the Bush agenda, but rather a particular focus on the parts of this agenda that relate to the Republican-supporting groups that we have discussed in this chapter.

Religious conservatives were the group receiving the most attention in the weeks immediately following the 2004 presidential election, and they are also the group with the longest list of demands. High on this list are restrictions on abortion, a federal amendment banning gay marriage, holding the line on stem cell research and banning human cloning, and tougher obscenity laws. The lynchpin of their demands is a call for more conservative federal judicial appointments from the Supreme Court on down. Many religious conservatives are tired of what they see as unfulfilled promises from the Republican Party in the past, and view Bush's second term as the time for their rewards. As the Free Congress Foundation's Paul Weyrich said, "We're not going to be trotted out every four years and then get kicked in the teeth afterwards."[41] Early indicators suggest that Bush will try to deliver on many of the items on the religious right's agenda. Bush has made his support for the amendment banning gay marriage very clear, and he most certainly is opposed to human cloning and increasing federal funding on stem cell research. His constant references to the importance of a "culture of life" bode well for religious conservatives on the abortion issue, as do his railings against "activist judges" on the matter of judicial appointments. If religious conservatives do not get much of what they want from Bush's second term, it is not likely to be due to lack of effort on the president's part.

While religious conservatives and their policy goals have been most prominently discussed, they are not the only group hoping their support of Bush translates into policy success. Affluent Americans are another group who will likely benefit from Bush's reelection. The president has consistently expressed his desire to make the tax cuts of his first term permanent, and also has spent considerable time since the election discussing his desire to flatten and simplify the tax code. Similarly, gun owners will continue to see their positions championed by the Bush administration. Having already let the assault weapons ban expire during his first term, it is highly improbable that Bush will pursue any policy that would raise the ire of Second Amendment activists. Barring an unforeseen national tragedy involving firearms, the issue of gun control is dead at the national level, at least through the next presidential election.

While their policy preferences have received much less attention from the press, rural voters likely also expect some rewards from the Republicans. While Bush's conservative stands on social issues and guns will sit well with a large segment of rural America, it is certain that these voters will be watching the president closely for more particularized benefits, possibly dealing with agriculture. Bush pushed hard for an incentive-laden farm bill during 2004, and rural voters will expect a similar effort with the next round of agriculture legislation. There are also significant matters relating to agriculture and trade that have to be dealt with during Bush's second term, and policy-savvy farm interests will be closely monitoring the administration's performance here.[42]

Another group expecting to cash in on their reelection support for Bush is Latinos. Already Latinos have seen the nomination and appointment of Alberto Gonzales as attorney general, the first member of their community ever selected for this position. A far bigger policy prize relates to immigration reform. Renewing calls he made in the early months of his first term, Bush has talked about the need to reform immigration laws to allow undocumented individuals to hold steady employment in the United States. While the details of Bush's plan are not yet known, some of the ideas that have been floated include temporary, renewable work visas, assistance to those who qualify for such visas in gaining citizenship, and even a form of amnesty for at least some of the undocumented workers already in the United States. In the week after the election, Karl Rove, Colin Powell, and Tom Ridge all spoke publicly about such possibilities, a sign that this issue could be important in Bush's second term.[43]

The potential policy benefits for some of the other groups that supported President Bush are less clear, but a few possibilities can at least be mentioned here. For those individuals who voted for Bush because of his stands on the military and national security—groups such as veterans and active-duty military personnel, white men, white women with children under 18, and urban voters—they will likely be rewarded with more of the same from the president on these fronts. The positions and actions of the first term will carry over into the second.[44] Those Roman Catholics who voted for Bush for his stands on abortion and stem cell research are also likely to be rewarded, as discussed above. And senior citizens will get the full benefit of the president's prescription drug plan in 2006, and at least an attempt at Social Security reform, whether they like it or not. It is of course a certainty that additional unforeseen events and issues will arise, and these phenomena will have a major impact on Bush's second-term actions. However, at this point the policies discussed above represent a reasonable projection for how the president will endeavor to reward the groups that supported him at the ballot box in 2004.

The 2004 presidential campaign was certainly interesting to observe. There were important issues under discussion, the candidates had clear differences on many of these issues, and the electorate was at its most highly engaged in years. The final outcome was close, but unlike 2000 it was also clear. President George W. Bush won a second term in office. What he does with this new term will go a long way toward setting the stage for the next presidential election in 2008.

Notes

1. See Cass Sunstein, *republic.com.* (Princeton, NJ: Princeton University Press, 2001).

2. Paul F. Lazarsfeld, Bernard Berelson, and Hazel Gaudet, *The People's Choice,* 2nd ed. (New York: Columbia University Press, 1987); Bernard R. Berelson, Paul F. Lazarsfeld, and William N. McPhee, *Voting* (Chicago: University of Chicago Press, 1954); Donald Green, Bradley Palmquist, and Eric Schickler, *Partisan Hearts and Minds* (New Haven, CT: Yale University Press, 2002).

3. Everett Carll Ladd, Jr., with Charles D. Hadley, *Transformations of the American Party System* (New York: W.W. Norton, 1975).

4. Earl Black and Merle Black, *The Rise of Southern Republicans* (Cambridge, MA: The Belknap Press of Harvard University Press, 2002).

5. Kenneth D. Wald, *Religion and Politics in the United States,* 4th ed. (Lanham, MD: Rowman & Littlefield, 2003).

6. Jeffrey M. Stonecash, Mark D. Brewer, and Mack D. Mariani, *Diverging Parties* (Boulder, CO: Westview Press, 2003).

7. Rove first made this statement publicly at an American Enterprise Institute seminar in 2001. Julia Duin, "Evangelicals Urged to Vote and 'Shape Public Policy,'" *Washington Times* (online), June 22, 2004 (accessed November 16, 2004, www.washingtontimes.com/national/20040622–122338–9915r).

8. Alan Cooperman and Thomas B. Edsall, "Evangelicals Say They Led Charge for the GOP," *Washington Post,* November 8, 2004, A01.

9. David Welna, "RNC Mailing Claims Democrats Seek to Ban Bible," National Public Radio, "Morning Edition" (online), October 1, 2004 (accessed November 19, 2004, www.npr.org/templates/story/story.php?storyId=4056255).

10. Data from 2000 taken from Voter News Service (VNS) exit polls.

11. Geoffrey Layman, *The Great Divide* (New York: Columbia University Press, 2001).

12. Jodi Wilgoren and Bill Keller, "Kerry and Religion: Pressure Builds for Public Discussions," *New York Times,* October 7, 2004, A23; Jim VandeHei, "Faith Increasingly Part of Kerry's Campaign," *Washington Post,* October 18, 2004, A1.

13. David M. Halbfinger and David E. Sanger, "Kerry's Latest Attacks on Bush Borrow a Page from Scripture," *New York Times,* October 25, 2004, A17.

14. Data from 2000 taken from VNS exit polls.

15. Data from 2004 exit poll results as reported by CNN. Available at www.cnn.com/ELECTION/2004/pages/results/states/US/P/00/epolls.0.html.

16. Associated Press, "Bush Salutes National Guard," CNN.com (online), September 14, 2004 (accessed September 14, 2004, no longer available on World Wide Web).

17. Jodi Wilgoren, "Kerry on Photo-Op to Help Image," *New York Times,* October 22, 2004, A18.

18. Ibid.

19. Quoted in R.W. Apple, Jr., "Kerry Pins Hopes in Iowa on Big Vote from Absentees," *New York Times,* September 28, 2004, A18.

20. Paul R. Abramson, John H. Aldrich, and David W. Rohde, *Change and Continuity in the 2000 Elections* (Washington, DC: CQ Press, 2002).

21. Ibid.; William H. Flanigan and Nancy H. Zingale, *Political Behavior of the American Electorate,* 10th ed. (Washington, DC: CQ Press, 2002); Warren E. Miller and J. Merrill Shanks, *The New American Voter* (Cambridge, MA: Harvard University Press, 1996).

22. Abramson, Aldrich, and Rohde, *Change and Continuity in the 2000 Elections;* Edward G. Carmines and James A. Stimson, *Issue Evolution: Race and the Transformation of American Politics* (Princeton, NJ: Princeton University Press, 1989).

23. See, for example, the results of the *New York Times*/CBS News Poll, as reported in *New York Times,* October 19, 2004, A20.

24. Jim Dwyer and Jodi Wilgoren, "Gore and Kerry Unite in Search for Black Votes," *New York Times,* October 25, 2004, A17.

25. John Whitesides, "Clinton and Kerry Team Up on Bush," Reuters (online), October 26, 2004 (accessed October 27, 2004, http://olympics.reuters.com/newsArticle.jhtml?type=topNews&storyID=6606230§ion=news).

26. Jeffrey M. Stonecash, *Class and Party in American Politics* (Boulder, CO: Westview Press, 2000).

27. Abramson, Aldrich, and Rohde, *Change and Continuity in the 2000 Elections;* Center for the American Woman and Politics, "The Gender Gap: Voting Choices, Party Identification, and Presidential Performance Ratings," *Fact Sheet.* Eagleton Institute of Politics, Rutgers University, July 1996.

28. Katherine Q. Seelye, "Kerry in a Struggle for a Democratic Base: Women," *New York Times,* September 22, 2004, A1.

29. Katharine Q. Seelye, "Polls Show Gains for Kerry Among Women in Electorate," *New York Times,* October 20, 2004, A23.

30. Stonecash, Brewer, and Mariani, *Diverging Parties;* Samuel Lubell, *The Future of American Politics,* 2nd ed., revised (Garden City, NY: Doubleday Anchor Books, 1956).

31. Dennis R. Judd and Todd Swanstrom, *City Politics*, 4th ed. (New York: Pearson Longman, 2004).

32. Mark D. Brewer, *Relevant No More? The Catholic/Protestant Divide in American Electoral Politics* (Lanham, MD: Lexington Books, 2003).

33. Halbfinger and Sanger, "Kerry's Latest Attacks on Bush Borrow a Page from Scripture," A17.

34. David D. Kirkpatrick and Laurie Goodstein, "Group of Bishops Using Influence to Oppose Kerry," *New York Times,* October 12, 2004, A1.

35. David Espo and Scott Lindlaw, "Bush Courts Catholics as Kerry Hunts Goose," *Bangor Daily News,* October 22, 2004, A5.

36. Elisabeth Bumiller and David M. Halbfinger, "Bush and Kerry, Feeling Like Winners, Go to Las Vegas," *New York Times,* October 15, 2004, A21.

37. CBS News, "Kerry Wary of 'January Surprise,'" CBSNews.com (online), October 18, 2004 (accessed November 18, 2004, www.cbsnews.com/stories/2004/10/18/politics/main649861.shtml).

38. Timothy Egan, "Vote Drives Gain Avid Attention of Youth in '04," *New York Times,* September 15, 2004, A1.

39. Associated Press, "Bush Prepares to Lay Out Agenda," CNN.com (online), November 11, 2004 (accessed November 15, 2004,www.cnn.com/2004/ALLPOLITICS/11/04/bush.cabinet.ap/index.html).

40. Jonathan Weisman, "Domestic Issues on the Front Burner," *Washington Post,* November 7, 2004, A08.

41. Quoted in Debra Rosenberg and Rebecca Sinderbrand, "Of Prayer and Payback," *Newsweek* (online), November 22, 2004 (accessed November 22, 2004, www.msnbc.msn.com/id/6479271/site/newsweek).

42. Associated Press, "Agriculture Agenda to Focus on Trade," CNN.com (online), November 12, 2004 (accessed November 15, 2004, www.cnn.com/2004/ALLPOLITICS/11/12/bush.agriculture.ap/index.html)

43. *Newsweek,* "Immigration: A Hot Topic (Now That the Election's Over), *Newsweek* (online), November 14, 2004 (accessed November 15, 2004, www.msnbc.msn.com/id/6479335/site/newsweek/); Alan Elsner, "Bush Could Use Political Capital on Immigration," Reuters (online), November 11, 2004 (accessed November 15, 2004, http://news.yahoo.com/news?tmpl=story&u=/nm/20041111/us_nm/politics_immigration_dc_4).

44. Glenn Kessler, "President Signals No Major Shift in Foreign Policy," *Washington Post,* November 7, 2004, A1.

Part II

The Presidential Campaign and Congressional Races

3

Political Participation in the 2004 Presidential Election

Turnout and Policy Consequences

M. Margaret Conway

Why do individuals vote? Rational choice theory suggests that the probability that any one individual can affect the outcome of an election is so small that it is irrational to vote.[1] Modifications of rational choice theory attempt to explain why some vote. One alternative is that individuals consider the effect that a group of which they are members can have on the outcome if a significant number of the group's members participate.[2]

Other theories provide alternative explanations for deciding to vote in elections. Socioeconomic status theories suggest that those who are more likely to vote tend to perceive themselves as effective in influencing political outcomes and to have more of the resources necessary to be effective. For example, those who participate more tend to have higher levels of education, higher levels of income, and to be older. Those who are older tend to have acquired more information about government and politics and perhaps have more time to participate in elections.[3]

Civic volunteerism theory combines elements of these theories as well as mobilization theory to explain patterns of participation in politics. It emphasizes that resources (time, money, and skills) as well as recruitment to participation are the keys to understanding who participates.[4] Political mobilization connects resources with motivation to participate in an election. The motivation may be concerned with an issue, liking or disliking a candidate, commitment to a political party, or social pressure to participate. Although the resources necessary to vote are minimal to most citizens, mobilization reduces the cost to participate by helping unregistered citizens register and by providing targeted potential voters with information that connects their personal and group interests and issue concerns to the act of voting.

Mobilization theories suggest that who is mobilized, when, and how is the consequence of the decisions made by political elites in their efforts to build a winning coalition of supporters. When election outcomes in an area are dominated by one party, that party has no incentive to increase turnout for local elections. When elections are competitive, each party has an incentive to increase turnout by those who will vote for its candidates. In the 2004 presidential election, both major parties and the groups that supported each candidate had an incentive to win enough popular votes to win the Electoral College vote in closely contested states. Thus mobilization theory suggests that political elites would identify potential supporters and try to stimulate them to vote.[5]

This chapter discusses who the mobilizing elites were in the 2004 presidential election, the targets of their efforts, the methods used to maximize turnout, who voted, and the policy consequences of the patterns of voter turnout that occurred.

The November 2004 election stimulated one of the most extensive and perhaps the most expensive get-out-the-vote efforts in American history. Political parties, political organizations known as 527 committees, and groups representing a variety of economic, social, environmental, and other interests are estimated to have raised and spent record amounts to organize and carry out voter mobilization drives.[6] They recruited and deployed armies of campaign workers to conduct voter registration drives and to ensure that those registered actually voted. Mobilization efforts used door-to-door canvassing, mass mailings, telephone solicitations, television advertising campaigns, pre–Election Day personal contacts with registered voters, Election Day monitoring of turnout, and service provision to potential voters. The result was the highest level of voter turnout since 1968.

Historical Patterns of Voter Turnout

A major emphasis in 2004 was on personal contacting to register and turn out voters, a return to traditional voter mobilization methods. In many parts of the United States in the latter half of the nineteenth century and the first half of the twentieth century, effective local political party organizations identified the party's supporters though personal contacts with local residents, made sure the party's supporters were registered to vote, and got them out to vote on Election Day. During the second half of the twentieth century, changes in employment and residential patterns, lifestyles, and laws and regulations affecting government employment and the granting of government contracts resulted in weakened local party organizations. Higher-level party organizations and a myriad of interest groups assumed a greater role in political mobilization, but used different methods. Political messages were communicated through impersonal means, with television ads, recorded phone calls from telephone banks, and campaign literature dropped on the doorstep replacing personal contacts from local political party activists.

Voter turnout in presidential elections has varied substantially over time. Since the end of World War II in 1945, it reached a high in 1964 when 61.9 percent of the voting-age population voted, but declined until 1992 when 55.1 percent voted. Because the voting-age population includes a significant proportion of noncitizens, a better base of analysis is turnout by citizens. In 2000, 55.7 percent of the citizens voted but only 69.9 percent of citizens were registered to vote. Among those who were registered, 85.4 percent voted.[7] In 2004, an estimated 58.8 percent of the eligible electorate voted.[8]

Voter Mobilization

Drawing lessons from labor unions' success in mobilizing members and their families through personal contacts and from research demonstrating the effectiveness of personal contacts in voter mobilization, in 2004 the political parties and other organizations emphasized personal contacts with individuals to increase voter registration. Their next task was to get the newly registered voters and infrequent voters among their supporters to cast their ballots. Each party also sought to persuade undecided voters to support its candidates. And of course, both parties focused on mobilizing their existing base of supporters. Furthermore, the political parties, 527 committees, and other groups saturated television in competitive contests with attack ads in attempts to decrease turnout among the opposition party's weak supporters and to reinforce the commitment of their supporters.[9] During the last 72 hours of the campaign, the political parties, 527 committees, and other groups concentrated on the "ground game," with volunteers and hired campaign workers personally contacting targeted supporters among potential voters. The emphasis was on contacting new registrants and those previously registered who had not consistently voted in past elections to make sure they voted.

Early in 2004, the presidential campaigns focused on 18 battleground states in which the outcome of the presidential race was uncertain. As the election neared, the emphasis narrowed to 11 states in which surveys of likely voters indicated the outcome of the presidential election was still in doubt.

Voter mobilization drives can be effective, but at a price. Research by Donald Green and Alan Gerber indicates that successful voter activation drives are costly. The most effective technique is door-to-door canvassing, with a cost of between $7 and $17 per vote, and only one additional vote is gained for each 14 contacts. Leaflets are not as effective as door-to-door contacting, with one registered potential voter stimulated to vote for each 66 leaflets left on the doorstep and at a cost of $14 to $42 per vote. Direct mail delivered to potential voters and telephone calls to their homes are even less successful, with a higher cost per additional vote obtained.[10]

The presidential contest was not the sole focus of voter mobilization efforts. Elections were also being held for one-third of the U.S. Senate and all members of the House of Representatives, and in 11 states elections for governor and other statewide offices. A number of states were also electing state legislators and local officials. In addition, 34 states had initiatives and referenda on the ballot, with many of these commanding the electorate's attention and contributing to higher turnout among some groups.[11]

Actors in the Voter Mobilization Process

Several types of groups and committees other than the political party organizations played a major role in campaign activities and voter mobilization efforts in the 2004 elections. The 527 committees, named after the provision in the federal law that permits their creation, sponsored ads that presented positive portrayals of their candidate and attack ads that conveyed negative messages about the opposition candidate. Among the 527 committees playing a prominent role in the campaigns were America Coming Together (ACT) and Media Now (which shared fund-raising activities and opposed the policies of the Bush administration), Progress for America (supporting Republican candidates), and Swift Boat Veterans for Truth (a conservative group attacking Democratic presidential candidate John Kerry's record of service in Vietnam). By the end of the 2004 campaign season, the 527 committees had raised a total of

$469 million, with $357 million being raised by committees focusing on national elections. Some 49 of the 527 committees had raised more than $1 million each, and three had raised more than $50 million.[12]

In addition, political action committees formed by groups not affiliated with political parties—such as business interests, organized labor, medical professions, social activists, and environmental groups—collected vast sums from donors. The funds raised were used in efforts to identify potential supporters of each group's preferred party or candidates and register them to vote. The primary goal of these groups was to stimulate voting turnout among carefully targeted segments of the electorate.[13] Many political action committees active in the 2004 campaigns increased their efforts to stimulate turnout among targeted groups. For example, the Business Industry Political Action Committee (BIPAC) increased its spending tenfold from the 2000 election to the 2004 campaign, from $500,000 to $5 million. BIPAC helped companies and associations in swing states encourage their employees to vote for probusiness candidates.[14]

Tax-exempt charities, including several focusing on social issues, also engaged in get-out-the-vote activities. For example, the Pew Charitable Trusts created the New Voters Project in an effort to increase participation in the election by younger persons, allocating $9 million to the project.[15]

Religious leaders played a major role in increasing participation by evangelical Christians and Catholics. In hotly contested states such as Ohio, many members of the clergy attended meetings to learn how they could discuss the election in church services without endangering their church's tax-exempt status. Religious leaders distributed voter registration forms to their members, encouraging them to register and vote.[16] Voter guides were distributed after church services by religious groups and others such as antiabortion groups. According to national exit polls, Bush received 78 percent of the votes cast by evangelical Christians and 52 percent of the votes cast by Catholics. In 2000, Bush obtained 50 percent of the Catholic vote.[17]

The Role of Ballot Initiatives in Voter Mobilization

Ballot initiatives frame issues and facilitate distribution of messages to targeted segments of the electorate. Candidates' issue stands and their expressed or implied support of or opposition to ballot measures help the electorate distinguish among candidates. In addition, the process of gaining access to the ballot through the signature-gathering process energizes political activists.

How can the effect of ballot initiatives on voter turnout be explained? Ballot initiatives generate activities by groups to persuade others to their views and to rally the initiative's supporters. Of course, ballot measures may also galvanize opponents. They also receive media coverage, enhancing the educative effect deriving from group efforts to pass or defeat ballot initiatives. Campaign expenditures in support of or opposition to ballot propositions cannot be limited, as such restrictions would be a violation of free speech provisions in federal and state constitutions. Therefore, placing initiatives on the ballot in key states provides a way to use unrestricted funds that cannot be used by a political party or its candidates for federal office. Ballot measures may appeal to potential voters supporting one candidate or party; thus one consequence of ballot initiative campaigns would be increased turnout.[18]

Although research demonstrates that ballot issues are more effective in stimulating turnout in midterm than presidential elections, ballot issues were perceived to be a useful voter mobilization tool by both Republican and Democratic strategists in the 2004 election. White House political strategist Karl Rove believed that 4 million evangelical Christians had not voted in the 2000 election. He was encouraged by leaders of conservative Christian groups to support the placing of controversial bans on gay marriage on state ballots and to encourage Republicans in several states to place the ban on state ballots with the goal of stimulating turnout among religious conservatives.[19] Initiatives to ban same-sex marriage were on the ballot in 11 states in the November election, including three considered to be swing states (Michigan, Ohio, and Oregon).

Other ballot initiatives were expected to increase turnout. For example, initiatives to increase the state minimum wage were placed on the ballots in Florida and Nevada, also considered swing states. This issue was used in both states to increase voter registration and turnout among targeted groups—including the working poor, women, African Americans, and Hispanics—thought likely to vote Democratic. The goal of the minimum-wage ballot drives was to increase turnout among those groups by 6 to 8 percent.[20]

Research indicates that the larger the number of initiatives on the ballot, the higher the level of turnout in both midterm and presidential elections. Examining the impact of ballot initiatives on turnout in elections between 1980 and 2002, Caroline Tolbert and Daniel Smith found that turnout among the electorate increased by 0.7 percent for each initiative on a state's ballot in presidential elections after controlling for the effects of several political and state contextual variables. In midterm elections, each additional initiative on a state's ballot increased turnout by 1.7 percent.[21]

The signature-collection process used to get initiatives on a state's ballot can be combined with a voter registration drive. For example, in Florida prior to the 2004 election, ACORN, a grassroots activist group, registered 155,000 new voters while gathering signatures to place the state minimum wage increase initiative on the ballot. In Nevada, the AFL-CIO's signature-collection drive in support of the minimum wage increase initiative also resulted in adding 21,000 new Hispanic citizens on the voter registration rolls. Both Nevada and Florida were expected to be very competitive states in the 2004 presidential election.[22]

The Effects of Voter Mobilization Efforts

Perceptions of a close presidential race stimulated the electorate's interest in the 2004 election and voter registration increased in several states. The closeness of the 2000 presidential election outcome demonstrated to many citizens that people like themselves could have a significant impact on an election's outcome. Interest- and issue-based appeals by candidates, organized interest groups, the political parties, and other political organizations enhanced this perception. An appeal to interests shared by group members enhances the sense of political involvement that can stimulate voter participation. Furthermore, controversial ballot measures in a number of states also increased attentiveness to the 2004 campaigns among targeted groups.

Voter registration varies substantially with a number of social-demographic characteristics. In 2000, for example, only 36 percent of those aged 18 to 24 were registered to vote, compared to 50 percent of those 25 to 34 and more than 60 percent of each of the older age categories.[23] In 2004, political involvement among younger citizens (ages 18 to 29) was greater than in any election since 1972. However, the level of attentiveness among younger citizens varied with their issue concerns. When asked whether Iraq or the economy was of greater concern to them and how much attention they were paying to the campaign, 72 percent of younger voters more concerned with Iraq reported paying some or a great deal of attention to the campaign. In contrast, only 48 percent of those more concerned with the economy reported paying some or a great deal of attention to the campaign. [24]

Even in the early stages of the 2004 campaign, citizen attentiveness to election news was substantially higher than in 2000. In the week of the Super Tuesday primary contests in early March, attentiveness was substantially higher than in 2000. For example, younger potential voters reported higher levels of attention to news (49% in 2004 v. 36% in 2000), talking with other about the campaign (39% in 2004 v. 29% in 2000), and thinking about the campaign (43% in 2004 v. 26% in 2000). What explains this increased attentiveness? In 2004, three-fifths of young adults believed that the election would have a great deal or quite a bit of impact on the country's future. Young adults were more likely to believe this than older adults (51% v. 33%).[25]

A national poll of college students conducted by Harvard University's Institute of Politics provides additional evidence of increased political involvement among younger persons. A high 84 percent indicated they would "definitely be voting." Only 26 percent of the students believed that political involvement only rarely had tangible benefits. In 2000, in contrast, 51 percent of students surveyed believed that only rarely does political involvement have tangible benefits.[26]

The targeting of unregistered citizens has the potential to increase voter registration, but by how much? In 2004 voter registration data from 26 states compiled after the close of registration indicate changes in levels of voter registration occurred since 2000. However, voter registration changes varied greatly from state to state. Voter registration increased in 18 of the 26 states and decreased in 8 states. In Alaska, registration declined by 23.3 percent but still exceeded the estimated number of eligible citizens by 4.3 percent. Missouri reported a 10.9 percent increase in registration, with 99.2 percent of the estimated eligible voting-age population being registered. Registration levels in those two states led some to suggest that fraudulent registrations had occurred. In most of the swing states contested in the presidential election, registration increased, but it dropped in two (Hawaii and Nevada). Two of the battleground states (Minnesota and Wisconsin) permit voter registration on the day of the election.[27]

In 2004 the methods used to mobilize members of the electorate and the targets of mobilization efforts were carefully identified to maximize the effect of mobilization efforts. Political mobilization activities by political parties, 527 committees, and interest groups increased, with each focusing on a narrowly targeted set of citizens who supported the group's position on a specific set of issues or the group's preferred candidate. Steven Schier argues that such narrowly focused mobilization, which he labels activation, is a rational response not only to the decline of local party organizations but also to changes in mass communications, the multiplication of communications channels, and increases in the number of political advocacy organizations and organized special interests operating at the national, state, and local levels.[28] In activation the goal is to increase turnout only among the party's or group's supporters. Prior to 2004, highly targeted voter activation relied heavily on the impersonal communications techniques previously discussed. For example, television ads focusing on particular candidates or issues appeared during programs popular with the targeted segments of the electorate. However, these impersonal methods of communication with potential voters are less effective than the personal contact methods formerly used by local party organizations.

Political Profiling and Voter Mobilization

In the aftermath of the 2000 election, recognition that personal contacts were more effective resulted in a significant change in voter mobilization methods. The Republican National Committee developed a systematic plan to implement more personalized methods of contacting, tested it in some state elections in 2001 and in selected 2002 congressional contests, and implemented it in battleground states for the 2004 election. One component of effective voter registration efforts is careful targeting of potential supporters based on political profiling.

In political profiling, data are collected from a variety of sources and combined into a data file on each person. Not only is basic information collected about individuals—such as their place of residence, age, and occupation—but also information that indicates their views and interests. That information is collected from a variety of sources, such as church membership lists, lists of donors to various charities, state records of licenses to hunt and fish, drivers' license records, motor vehicle records that indicate the types of vehicles owned and their costs, magazine subscription lists, and memberships in organizations. Of course, other important information included in political profiles is whether or not each individual is registered to vote, and if so, whether they are registered as a Democrat, Republican, or Independent. If registered, also contained in the profile is the regularity of their voting turnout. A number of different general lifestyle profiles—from 45 to 70 or more—can be developed, with several subgroups within each type. Data collected from surveys and information obtained through focus-group studies enable political consultants to match political attitudes, beliefs, and concerns to lifestyle types and to add that information to political profiles. From the patterns identified, political strategists can identify specific citizens to target for voter registrations drives and voter mobilization efforts.

Political profile databases are compiled and sold by marketing firms to candidates, political parties, and interest groups. A political profile database facilitates more efficient targeting of potential party and candidate supporters. In 2000 the Republican National Committee's (RNC) voter profile database contained information about 165 million Americans. The RNC could sort the list to provide information about the electorate in a specific area to assist Republican Party organizations in their campaign work as well as a candidate running in a particular city, county, state, or congressional district.[29] In 2004 the Democratic National Committee also used an extensive political profile database. Political profile data were also used by 527 committees, such as ACT, and political action committees (PACs) in their campaign efforts. The national Democratic Party organization lacked the funds to sponsor a massive voter registration effort of the size carried out by the Republican National Committee. However, organizations supporting Democratic candidates worked to increase Democratic voter registration using political profiling techniques to identify potential Democratic supporters.

For example, a 527 committee could use political profile data to target specific individuals to persuade them to register and to vote. Campaign workers could be provided with information about each citizen they are to contact and, if the campaign were well funded, with Palm Pilot or other brands of hand-held devices containing the relevant information. These memory banks could even be loaded with a series of short (less than one minute) videos from which could be selected the one that would best appeal to the political attitudes, beliefs, and concerns of each individual contacted. The appropriate video to display to each person contacted would be included in the information provided to the campaign workers.

The Republicans' carefully planned get-out-the-vote campaign established quotas for electoral units as small as the election district. The goal was to expand the Republican Party's base of supporters. Early in the campaign it assigned campaign volunteers and paid workers to contact targeted individuals to persuade them to register if not registered and to vote. Assistance was provided to those needing absentee ballots. In states that permit early voting, registered voters were encouraged to vote early. In the 72 hours beginning the Saturday before Election Day, the party's volunteers began to execute systematic, carefully structured efforts of frequent contacts with targeted individuals to get out the vote.

In contrast to the Republican Party's centralized voter mobilization program, the Democratic Party relied heavily on the voter mobilization efforts of other organizations. Because of federal laws and regulations, the efforts of the Democratic Party and supporting groups could not be systematically coordinated. For example, one of the largest efforts in support of Kerry was that of America Coming Together, which used 45,000 volunteers and paid workers. Other 527 committees as well as PACs used both volunteers and paid workers to mobilize Kerry supporters.

The Bush campaign's budget for voter mobilization was estimated to exceed $125 million, triple the amount spent in 2000. Declining to accept federal funding, the Bush campaign could receive contributions in excess of the limit imposed by federal election laws on those accepting federal funding. In contrast, Kerry accepted federal funding for his campaign, and his campaign operated on a more limited budget. The Kerry voter mobilization budget was estimated to be nearly $60 million, less than half that spent by Republicans in 2004 but double the amount the Democrats spent in 2000. The Democratic Party and other organizations supporting Kerry depended more on paid workers, the Republicans more on volunteers in staffing their get-out-the-vote campaigns. Federal laws regulating campaign expenditures prohibit formal coordination of campaign activities between a political party and either 527 committees or PACs. The Republicans were able to control and coordinate voter mobilization activities, while groups supporting Kerry could not. That resulted in less systematic and less cost-effective voter mobilization efforts by the Democratic Party and its supporters. Republican volunteers are estimated to have numbered 1.4 million by election day, with the Democratic Party's volunteers estimated to be one-quarter of that number.[30]

Message Content and Political Mobilization

The narrowcasting of campaign messages, as opposed to more traditional broadcasting, is a more cost-effective form of political persuasion. It targets the individuals most receptive to a particular message. Unlike commercial advertising, which is regulated by laws that set standards for truth in advertising, no such requirements exist for campaign ads. Half-truths and even outrageous lies can be broadcast or narrowcast. One defense against such campaign messages is a well-prepared "rapid response" team that can provide counterinformation from the candidate about whom the half-truths and outrageous lies are distributed. Of course, if the messages are being delivered through individual contacts with potential voters by campaign workers, it is more difficult to counter the damaging information without contributing to its further distribution. Such efforts can be made, although they may not be effective. For example, the candidate who is alleged to support gun control can be shown returning from a hunting trip with a shotgun over his shoulder. In the future, political parties and campaign groups that can afford narrowcasting through contacts with individual voters are likely to devote more of their resources to that campaign method. Political campaigns may then become even more divisive and contribute further to making governing processes that require cooperation across political parties and diverse groups difficult.

Turnout tends to be lower among nonunion blue-collar workers, the less educated, persons with lower levels of income, younger persons, racial minorities, and single women. For a variety of reasons, members of these groups might be expected to be more likely to vote for Democrats. In 2004, increasing the registration and turnout of targeted members of these groups was a major goal of political mobilization efforts by the Democratic Party and other organizations backing Democratic candidates. However, although turnout increased among those groups, it also increased among groups more likely to support Republican candidates. In a postelection interview, Kerry Donley, Democratic State Party Chair in Virginia, said "One of the things we saw is [the] conventional wisdom about increased turnout benefiting Democrats tossed out the window. We didn't see it in Virginia and we didn't see it nationally."[31] The Republican Party demonstrated that higher turnout benefits the party that is most successful in applying effective political mobilization techniques both to expand its base and to capture the votes of swing voters.

Among the targets for the Republican Party's political mobilization efforts, in addition to its traditional base of supporters, were rural voters, evangelical Christians, and residents of the outer suburbs of large cities in the Midwest and South.[32]

Legal Controversies About Registration and Voting in 2004

In late October, the *Economist* magazine expressed a widely shared view of the coming American election: "Combine a tight election, millions of newly registered voters, confusion about new electoral procedures, and a heavy dose of partisan passion—-and you have a recipe for plenty of election day wrangling."[33] Wrangling over election procedures actually began weeks before the election in many states and continued over disputed ballots after the election. Preelection legal conflicts in many states occurred over the rules relating to voter registration, the identification to be required of voters at the polling places, and making provisional ballots available to persons whose rights to vote were challenged at the polling place. Both parties recruited a large number of poll watchers to monitor voting at the polling places and attorneys to challenge election administration activities and decisions believed harmful to their political party's interests.

In 2002 the Congress enacted a law, the Help America Vote Act, regulating voting procedures in federal elections in an effort to avoid a repeat of problems that occurred in the 2000 election. Those problems included an estimated 1.5 million ballots not being counted, disputed votes in Florida and other states, ballots being denied to many who believed they were registered to vote, and allegations that intimidation prevented many minority race members from voting. The act requires that individuals who are not listed on the election district or precinct voter registration list but who believe they are registered to vote must be given a provisional ballot. After being cast, a provisional ballot is set aside, to be counted if the voter's registration can be verified.

Must individuals who vote using provisional ballots vote in the precinct to which they are assigned? The law is vague on that issue, and the states differed in 2004 in their interpretation of the law. In 28 states, a provisional ballot could be considered a valid vote only if it were cast in the precinct to which the individual is assigned. In 17 states, the ballot would be counted if cast in the correct county.[34] The remaining states allow voter registration on the day of the election.

Confusion about where to vote was expected among some newly registered voters and in areas where precinct lines had been redrawn but some voters had not received notification of the change in their polling place location. Others affected by this problem were residents of areas heavily damaged by hurricanes; either their homes were destroyed or their regular precinct polling place had been destroyed. In Florida, hammered by four hurricanes during a six-week period in August and September, Secretary of State Gloria Hood, appointed to office by Republican Governor Jeb Bush, ordered that provisional ballots be counted only if cast in the voter's assigned precinct.[35]

Prior to November 2, court cases focusing on provisional ballot issues were filed in several states in which the outcome of the presidential election was expected to be close. In Ohio and Michigan, federal district judges decided against a narrow interpretation of the provisional ballot section of the Help America Vote Act, ruling that the ballot must be counted if cast in the correct county. However, the Sixth U.S. Court of Appeals overturned the federal district court ruling. On election eve, U.S. Supreme Court Justice John Paul Stevens, on the basis of practical considerations, refused to set aside the Court of Appeals decision.[36]

Republican fears of fraudulent registration led to legal challenges of new registrants in several states. In Cleveland, Republicans asked the county election board to disqualify more than 20,000 newly registered voters; many were registered in voter registration drives sponsored by pro-Democratic groups. Challenges were made to their registration after campaign materials mailed to them were returned by the U.S. Postal Service as undeliverable. Republicans in Ohio also planned to challenge many new registrants at the polls on Election Day. Democrats recruited lawyers to monitor precincts where a number of challenges by Republicans to newly registered voters were expected.[37]

In states that permit voter registration on Election Day and do not use electronic voting machines, the possibility of an inadequate supply of ballots at the polling places exists. One state that permits Election Day registration is Wisconsin. In that state prior to the election, a Republican elected official, Milwaukee County Executive Scott Walker, cited voting fraud fears and refused to provide the number of ballots requested by the election supervisor in the City of Milwaukee. That raised the fear that the city could run out of ballots on election day. The ballot controversy escalated when Governor Jim Doyle called for a state probe of the county executive's refusal to provide the requested ballots. The county then agreed to provide 679,000 ballots, below the number requested by the city elections supervisor but more than County Executive Walker initially offered to provide.[38] Furthermore, in Wisconsin, challenges by Republican poll watchers to many of the 100,000 newly registered voters were expected; in response, the Democratic Party recruited 500 lawyers to work in the precincts to defend those challenged by the Republicans.

Who Voted?

Postelection estimates of turnout ranged from 117.8 million, which excluded uncounted mail ballots and absentee ballots in many states, to 120 million. Total votes cast in the presidential election exceeded 118.7 million. The latter would be the largest proportion of citizens voting since 1968.[39] Six southern states set records for the number of votes cast.[40]

Surveys of voters exiting the polling places on Election Day provide a snapshot of who voted. Voter turnout patterns exhibit some similarities and also some differences with voter turnout patterns in 2000. Women were 54 percent of the electorate in 2004, compared to 52 percent in 2000. Both African Americans and Latinos were a slightly larger share of the electorate in 2004, each group increasing its share of the electorate by 1 percent (see Table 3.1).[41]

Although major efforts were made to increase voting turnout by younger voters in 2004, according to the exit polls citizens aged 18 to 29 were the same proportion of the electorate as they had been in 2000. However, preliminary estimates indicate almost 21 million members (or 52%) of that age group voted, compared to 42 percent in 2000. While the absolute number and the proportion of the young adult group voting increased in 2004, so did the number and proportion of older voters. Turnout among younger voters is estimated to have been highest in ten of the states in which outcome of the presidential election was closest. The Washington, D.C.–based Youth Vote Coalition, composed of more than 100 groups cooperating in increasing voting among younger adults, reported that more than $100 million was spent in an effort to increase the youth vote.[42] Concern with the war in Iraq and the economy and the multiple methods used to register and mobilize younger voters contributed to the increased number of younger citizens voting. The proportion of first-time voters increased from 9 percent

Table 3.1

Social Characteristics and Political Attitudes of the Voters, Comparing 2004 to 2000

	Percentage of voters with these characteristics in 2004	Percentage of voters with these characteristics in 2000
Gender		
Male	46	48
Female	54	54
Race		
White	77	81
African American	11	10
Latino	8	7
Asian	2	2
Other	2	1
Age		
18–29	17	17
30–44	29	33
45–59	30	28
60 and older	24	22
Income		
Under $15,000	8	7
$16,000–30,000	15	16
$30,000–50,000	22	24
$50,000–75,000	23	25
$75,000–100,000	23	13
More than $100,000	18	15
Union member	14	16
Union household	24	26
Education		
No high school	4	5
High school graduate	22	21
Some college	32	32
College graduate	26	24
Postgraduate study	16	18
Employed full time	60	67
Have you lost a job: Percent yes	17	—
First-time voter	11	9
Gun owner in household	41	48
Religion		
Protestant	54	56
Catholic	27	25
Jewish	3	4
Other	7	5
None	10	9
Frequency of attendance at religious services		
More than weekly	16	14
Weekly	26	28
Monthly	14	14
A few times a year	28	28
Never	14	14

(continued)

Table 3.1 *(continued)*

	Percentage of voters with these characteristics in 2004	Percentage of voters with these characteristics in 2000
Married	63	65
Married with children under 18	37	39
Size of community where resident		
Big city	13	9
Small city	19	20
Suburb	45	43
Small town	8	5
Rural	16	23

Source: The data were obtained from reports of exit polls in 2000 and 2004, available at the website www.CNN.com.

in 2000 to 11 percent in 2004. Undoubtedly the increased numbers of younger voters contributed to that.

Voters surveyed in the 2004 exit poll were equally divided between Democrats and Republicans (37% each), with 26 percent identifying themselves as independents (see Table 3.2). In 2000, 39 percent were Democrats, 35 percent were Republicans, and 27 percent were Independents. Ideologically, in 2004, 21 percent identified themselves as liberals, 45 percent as moderates, and 34 percent as conservatives, compared with 20 percent liberal, 50 percent moderate, and 29 percent conservative in 2000. Perhaps two of the most significant outcomes of the 2004 election are the increase in the proportion of voters who identify as Republicans and as conservatives.

When asked in 2004 "Would you describe yourself as a born again or evangelical Christian?" 23 percent answered yes. Because of differences in the wording of the question, responses in 2004 cannot be compared with 2000. When asked "Which one issue mattered most in deciding how you voted today?" the most frequent response was moral values, with 22 percent providing that answer; 20 percent indicated the economy was the most important. Two issues related to international affairs were also the most important for a significant portion of the electorate, with 19 percent responding terrorism and 15 percent responding Iraq. Smaller groups identified taxes (5%), education (4%), and health care (8%) as the one issue that had most influenced their vote choice.

As Table 3.2 illustrates, issues cited as those that mattered most in voters' presidential vote choice differed substantially between the 2004 and 2000 elections. Social Security and Medicare/prescription drugs, frequently cited in 2000, did not rank among the top seven mentions in

Table 3.2

Political Orientations of the Voters, Comparing 2004 to 2000

	Percentage of voters with these characteristics in 2004	Percentage of voters with these characteristics in 2000
Party identification		
Democrat	37	39
Republican	37	35
Independent	26	27
Ideology		
Liberal	21	20
Moderate	45	50
Conservative	34	29
What issue matters most in vote choice		
Taxes	5	14
Education	4	15
Iraq	15	—
Terrorism	19	—
Economy/jobs	20	18
Moral values	22	—
Health care	8	8
Medicare/rx drugs	—	7
Social Security	—	14
World affairs	—	12
Family's financial situation		
Better	32	50
Worse	28	11
Same	39	38
Abortion should be		
Always legal	21	23
Mostly legal	34	33
Mostly illegal	26	27
Always illegal	16	13

Source: The data were obtained from reports of exit polls in 2000 and 2004, available at the website www.CNN.com.

2004. Both education and taxes declined substantially in mentions as the most important issue in vote choice. Only the economy and jobs maintained their relevance as the most important issue for voters.

Other survey data also indicate that a concern with issues stimulated the high levels of turnout in the 2004 election (see Table 3.3). The Vanishing Voter survey found that 92 percent of first-time voters and 86 percent of repeat voters cited election issues as a major factor in their

Table 3.3

Political Beliefs and Attitudes, 2004

	Percent
Policy toward same-sex couples	
Legally marry	25
Civil union	35
No legal recognition	37
Decision to go to war in Iraq	
Strongly approve	29
Somewhat approve	23
Somewhat disapprove	19
Strongly disapprove	31
How things are going for U.S. in Iraq	
Very well	11
Somewhat well	34
Somewhat badly	20
Very badly	33
Worried about terrorism	
Very worried	22
Somewhat worried	53
Not too worried	19
Not at all worried	6
Compared to four years ago, U.S. is	
Safer from terrorism	54
Less safe	41

Source: The data were obtained from reports of exit polls in 2000 and 2004, available at the Web site: CNN.com.

decision to vote. However, liking or disliking a candidate also played a major role in generating turnout. First-time and repeat voters differed in the impact of disliking a candidate, with almost two-thirds of new voters and one-half of repeat voters really disliking a candidate being one reason for voting.[43]

Of course, issues, party identification, and ideology may not be the principal motivating factors in turnout. Approval or disapproval of the president's job performance may also stimulate turnout in a presidential election. In the 2004 exit poll, 53 percent of those voting approved how President Bush was handling his job, while 46 percent disapproved. When asked if their vote for president was mostly for their candidate or against his opponent, 69 percent said it was for their candidate, while 25 percent said it was against his opponent.

Political mobilization agents in the 2004 campaign emphasized personal contacts with potential voters. To what extent did those who voted receive such contacts? When asked if they were contacted by the Bush campaign, 24 percent said yes; 26 percent reported that they had been contacted by the Kerry campaign. Many voters may have been contacted by other groups involved in trying to stimulate voting in support of a presidential candidate. A substantial amount of the contacting in support of Kerry was carried out by groups such as America Coming Together, Women Vote, and labor unions. Furthermore, contacts by campaigns for congressional, senatorial, state, and local candidates were not measured in the exit polls. Highly contested races for many of those offices also contributed to higher levels of turnout in several states.[44]

Personal contacts from friends and family were also three times more likely to motivate turnout among first-time voters than among those who had voted in a previous election; 14 percent of first-time voters indicated that they voted because a group or individual had helped them to register to vote; 7 percent of first-time voters also indicated that they were influenced to vote by appeals from celebrities. Among those who had been eligible to vote before 2004 but had not voted, 14 percent said celebrity appeals influenced their decision to participate.[45]

More voters resided in the suburbs (45%), small towns (8%), and rural areas (16%) than resided in the big cities (13%) and small cities (19%). Some observers asserted that it was the unusually high turnout of small-town and rural voters that enabled Bush to carry some of the battleground states.[46]

The Bush campaign sought to increase the number of registered Republicans by 3 million. The Republicans were successful in that effort; they registered 3.4 million. That expansion of the Republican base and the issues his campaign emphasized enabled Bush to gain more support from a number of sociodemographic groups. Republican support increased among married women, Catholics, Hispanics, and African Americans. The ultimate Republican goal is a slow gradual change in the political party identification patterns in the nation—a secular realignment.[47]

Policy Consequences of Voter Turnout Patterns

What are the implications for public policy of voter turnout patterns in the 2004 elections? In a press conference on the day after the election, President Bush declared that the outcome of the election provided him with political capital and that he intended to use it to enact his policy agenda. Results of elections to the U.S. House and U.S. Senate enhanced the probability that he would be successful, with Republican majorities increased by four members in each chamber of the Congress.

The issues related to moral values were framed in narrow terms,[48] appealing to conservatives, with implications for several policies. Appointment of more conservative judges to the Supreme Court could result in overturning a number of court decisions, including those relating to abortion and same-sex marriage. A federal constitutional amendment banning same-sex marriage was endorsed by President Bush but not enacted by the Congress prior to the election. With larger Republican majorities in both the U.S. House of Representatives and the U.S. Senate after the 2004 elections, and with 41 states having either state laws or constitutional provisions banning same-sex marriage, the chances for passage of such an amendment and its ratification by the states were enhanced by electoral outcomes. Another item on President Bush's agenda, obtaining more domestic energy sources, included drilling for oil and gas on federal lands such as Alaska's National Wildlife Refuge. Many environmental groups actively opposed Bush's reelection, but oil companies and other business interests that supported his reelection favored that policy. Environmental concerns were not among the seven issues cited in exit polls as the most important issue influencing presidential vote choice.

Also on the Bush agenda was making tax cuts enacted during his first term permanent. Critics argued that earlier tax cuts disproportionately reduced taxes paid by the highest income earners. In addition, a tax bill enacted prior to the election included $157 billion in tax cuts for corporations. A majority of the upper-income beneficiaries of these tax cuts supported Bush. The proportion of voters having incomes in excess of $75,000 increased from 28 percent in 2000 to 41 percent in 2004.

The Bush reelection coalition included significant numbers of Catholics and evangelical Christians whose parochial schools would benefit from an expanded, federally funded voucher system that would enable children in failing schools to receive federal funding to attend alternative schools. The increase in votes from evangelical Christians and Catholics contributed to the Bush victory.

Although Hispanics made up only a small part of the Bush reelection coalition and many of those who would benefit from changes in immigration policy are not citizens, changes in immigration policy would benefit Hispanics as a group. In his first term, President Bush proposed laws that would enable undocumented immigrants to become legal residents and to establish a national guest worker program.

In his advocacy of an ownership society, Bush also proposed changes to the Social Security System that would enable individuals to divert part of their Social Security tax payments into retirement savings accounts that could be controlled and invested by each individual. Those who might benefit most from this are younger persons and those among the more affluent who would prefer to manage their retirement funds themselves.

Conclusion

In the 2004 campaigns, both the Democratic and Republican parties applied sophisticated methods of identifying those who would be likely to vote for their candidate and party. Then, aided by technology, both used the old-fashioned political mobilization techniques of personal contacts for voter registration and voter mobilization. The battle for the presidency was won by the candidate and political party with the best-organized get-out-the-vote campaign, with Bush's campaign winning the "ground game" of increasing Republican voter registrations among targeted segments of the electorate. His campaign was more successful in getting newly registered voters, swing voters who were persuaded to support Bush, and his preexisting base of supporters to the polls.

Notes

1. William H. Riker and Peter C. Ordeshook, *An Introduction to Positive Political Theory* (Englewood Cliffs, NJ: Prentice Hall, 1973), 62–69; M. Margaret Conway, *Political Participation in the United States,* 3rd ed. (Washington, DC: CQ Press, 2000), chap. 6.

2. Carole J. Uhlaner, "Political Participation, Rational Actors, and Rationality: A New Approach," *Political Psychology* 7 (1980): 551–57; Carole J. Uhlaner, "'Relational Goods' and Participation: Incorporating Sociability into a Theory of Rational Action," *Public Choice* 62 (1988): 253–85; Carole J. Uhlaner, "Rational Turnout: The Neglected Role of Groups," *American Journal of Political Science* 33 (1989): 390–442; Margaret M. Conway, "Fostering Group Based Political Participation," in *Political Socialization, Citizenship Education and Democracy,* ed. Orit Ichilov, 297–312 (New York: Teachers College Press, Columbia University).

3. Conway, *Political Participation in the United States,* chap. 2.

4. Sidney Verba, Kay Lehman Schlozman, and Henry E. Brady, *Voice and Equality* (Cambridge, MA: Harvard University Press, 1995); Nancy Burns, Kay Schlozman,

and Sidney Verba, *The Private Roots of Public Action* (Cambridge, MA: Harvard University Press, 2001).

5. Steven J. Rosenstone and John Mark Hansen, *Mobilization, Participation, and Democracy in America* (New York: Macmillan, 1993); Kay Lehman Schlozman and John T. Tierney, *Organized Interests and American Democracy* (New York: Harper and Row, 1986); John H. Aldrich, "Rational Choice and Turnout," *American Journal of Political Science* 37 (1993): 261–63.

6. Political parties and PACs have to identify their contributors through registering with the Federal Election Commission and filing financial reports. A 527 committee must file regular disclosure reports if it is a creation of a political party or PAC that campaigns for or against a candidate for federal office or engages in electioneering communications. Otherwise it must file with the state government in the state where it is located or with the Internal Revenue Service. Data on funds raised and spent are available at www.opensecrets.org.

7. United States Department of Commerce, Bureau of the Census, "Voting and Registration in the Election of November, 2000," Table C, p. 12, "Reported Voting in the Presidential Election Years by Region, Race, Hispanic Origin, Sex, and Age, November 1964 to 2000."

8. This proportion was calculated from estimated turnout of 120 million and an estimated eligible electorate of 203.9 million. For details on the estimated eligible electorate, see "2004 Voting-Age and Voting-Eligible Population Estimates and Voter Turnout." The estimated eligible electorate data are available at a website created by Michael MacDonald: http://elections.gmu.edu/Voter_Turnout_2004.htm.

9. John Harword, "As a Final Gambit, Parties Are Trying to Damp Turnout," *Wall Street Journal,* October 27, 2004, A1.

10. Donald P. Green and Alan S. Gerber, *Get Out the Vote!* (Washington, DC: Brookings Institution Press, 2004).

11. Ballot Initiative Strategy Center, "Ballot Initiative and Referendum," Washington, DC: October 2004.

12. These data were compiled by the Center for Responsive Politics, Washington, DC, from records released by the U.S. Internal Revenue Service. Several groups developed multiple organizations to permit them to separate activities as a 527 committee and as a PAC. The 527 committees engage in issue advocacy and voter mobilization efforts and are legally allowed to raise unlimited amounts of money, including from wealthy contributors and corporations. PACs operating at the federal level advocate the election or defeat of particular candidates. Federal laws restrict how much individuals may contribute and prohibit contributions from corporations in federal elections. See www.opensecrets.org/527s, November 8, 2004.

13. Michael Moss and Ford Fessenden, "Interest Groups Mounting Costly Push to Get Out Vote," *New York Times,* October 20, 2004, A1.

14. Ibid.

15. Pew Charitable Trusts, "A Briefing on Young Voters 2004: Motivating Younger People to Vote," www.pewtrusts.org.

16. Alan Cooperman and Thomas B. Edsall, "Evangelicals Say They Led the Charge for the GOP," *Washington Post,* November 8, 2004, A1.

17. The impact of the religious conservative vote rests not only on the percentage of support but in the numbers voting. Evangelicals are estimated to have cast 27 million votes. In contrast to earlier elections, local churches and activists re-

ceive some of the credit for stimulating higher levels of turnout and higher levels of support for Bush.

18. Ballot Initiative Strategy Center, "Ballot Initiative and Referendum."

19. Cooperman and Edsall, "Evangelicals Say They Led the Charge for the GOP."

20. Alexandra Starr and Richard S. Dunham, "Stirring the Passions of Apathetic Voters," *Business Week,* September 20, 2004, 49.

21. Caroline J. Tolbert and Daniel A. Smith, "The Educative Effects of Ballot Initiatives on Voter Turnout," *American Politics Research* 33 (March 2005: 283–309).

22. Ballot Initiative Strategy Center, "Ballot Initiative and Referendum," 8.

23. Bureau of the Census, "Voting and Registration in the Election of November, 2000," Table B, p. 6. "Reported Voting and Registration by Selected Characteristics, November, 2000." Others less likely to vote include individuals who are single, divorced, or widowed, renters, persons with lower levels of income, and individuals who have lived in their residence for less than five years. See Conway, *Political Participation in the United States.*

24. Vanishing Voter Project, "Iraq Issue Propels Election Interest: Young Voters Affected Most." Press release, September 17, 2004, www.vanishingvoter.org/releases/release091704. Cambridge, MA: Joan Shorenstein Center for the Press, Politics, and Public Policy, John F. Kennedy School of Government, Harvard University.

25. Vanishing Voter Project, "Election Interest Among Young Adults Is Up Sharply from 2000." Press release, March 12, 2004, www.vanishingvoter.org/releases041204. Cambridge, MA: Joan Shorenstein Center for the Press, Politics, and Public Policy, John F. Kennedy School of Government, Harvard University.

26. Joshua Partlow, "More College Students Taking Their Vote Seriously," *Washington Post,* October 23, 2004, B5.

27. "A Slight Rise in Registration," *Washington Post,* November 1, 2004.

28. Steven E. Schier, *By Invitation Only* (Pittsburgh: University of Pittsburgh Press, 2000), chap. 1.

29. John Mintz and Robert O'Harrow, Jr., "High-Tech Political Profiling," *Washington Post National Weekly Edition,* October 16, 2000, 13.

30. Dan Balz and Mike Allen, "Four More Years Attributed to Rove's Strategy," *Washington Post,* November 7, 2004, A1.

31. Cameron W. Barr and Eric Weiss, "Voter Turnout Either Sizzled or Fizzled," *Washington Post,* November 4, 2004, B1.

32. Paul Farhi and James V. Grimaldi, "GOP Won with Accent on Rural and Traditional," *Washington Post,* November 4, 2004, A01.

33. "Worse Than Last Time?" *The Economist,* October 30, 2004, 32.

34. Ibid.

35. James Dao and Ford Fessenden, "Ohio Court Battles Flare over Challenges to Voters," *New York Times,* October 29, 2004, www.nytimes.com/2004/10/29/politics/campaign/; Michael Moss, "Big G.O.P. Bid to Challenge Voters at Polls in Key States," *New York Times,* October 23, 2004, www.nytimes.com/2004/10/23/politics/campaign/.

36. James V. Grimaldi, "Court in Ohio Clears Way for Voting Challengers," *Washington Post,* November 2, 2004, www.washingtonpost.com/wp-dyn/articles/A17931-2004Nov2.html; James Dao and Terence Neilan, "Justice Ends Effort to Stop G.O.P. Challenges in Ohio," *New York Times,* November 2, 2004, www.nytimes.com/2004/11/02/politics/campaign/.

37. James Dao, "As Election Nears, Parties Begin Another Round of Legal Battles," *New York Times,* October 18, 2004, www.nytimes.com/2004/1018/politics/campaign; Moss, "Big G.O.P. Bid to Challenge Voters at Polls in Key States"; Dao and Fessenden, "Ohio Court Battles Flare over Challenges to Voters."

38. Dave Umhoefer and Greg J. Borowski, "City, County Spar over Ballot Supply," *Milwaukee Journal Sentinel,* October 12, 2004, www.jsonline.com/news/metro/oct04; Dave Umhoefer and Steve Schultze, "Doyle Joins Rift over Ballot Supply," October 14, 2004, www.jsonline.com/news/metro/oct04/266863.asp.

39. Calculated from estimates of eligible electorate and presidential election results reported by the *Washington Post*, November 16, 2004, www.washingtonpost.com/wp-srv/elections/2004/page/29500.

40. Exit poll data reported by CNN, November 3, 2004, www.cnn.com.

41. The discussion that follows is based on exit polls from 2000 and 2004. Several problems could cause estimates based on exit polls to be incorrect. One is that in some areas persons attempting to survey voters could not gain access to voters; efforts to prevent electioneering could in some voting districts have prevented access. Another potential factor skewing exit polls is that some individuals (such as conservatives) may be more reluctant to participate in the survey. See "How the Poll Was Conducted," *New York Times,* November 4, 2004, www.nytimes.com/2004/11/04/politics/campaign; Jim Rutenberg, "Report Says Problems Led to Skewed Surveying Data," *New York Times,* November 5, 2004, www.nytimes.com/2004/11/05/politics/campaign/.

42. Katherine M. Skiba, "Get-Out-Vote Blitz Boosted Youthful Turnout by 4.7 Million," *Milwaukee Journal Sentinel,* November 6, 2004, www.jsonline.com/news/nat/nov04/273047.asp.

43. Vanishing Voter Project, "First Time Voters Propelled to Polls by Personal Contact: Non-Voters Discouraged by Election Procedures." Press release, November 10, 2004, www.vanishingvoter.org/releases/release111004. Cambridge, MA: Joan Shorenstein Center for the Press, Politics, and Public Policy, John F. Kennedy School of Government, Harvard University.

44. In Ohio, the Bush campaign's 85,000 volunteers (four times the number active in 2000) succeeded in increasing Republican vote margins over those of 2000 in exurban and rural counties. Farhi and Grimaldi, "GOP Won with Accent on Rural and Traditional," A1.

45. Vanishing Voter Project, "First Time Voters Propelled to Polls by Personal Contact: Non-Voters Discouraged by Election Procedures."

46. Farhi and Grimaldi, "GOP Won with Accent on Rural and Traditional."

47. Balz and Allen, "Four More Years Attributed to Rove's Strategy," A1.

48. Confronting Christian conservatives' framing of morality issues in terms of banning same-sex marriage, stem cell research, and abortion, moderate and liberal Christians argued against shrinking Christian ethics to those three issues. In post-election interviews, leaders of the Interfaith Alliance and the National Council of Churches believed one consequence of the election would be to stimulate a discussion on the nature of values. That dialogue would focus not only on issues of personal piety, such as values related to civil unions, abortion, and stem cell research, but also on social or public values, such as poverty, the environment, and the peaceful resolution of conflicts. Larry B. Stammer, "Moderates, Liberals Hear Call to Morality Debate," *Los Angeles Times,* November 10, 2004, A 29.

4

The Inevitable Unanticipated Consequences of Political Reform

The 2004 Presidential Nomination Process

Christine L. Day, Charles D. Hadley, and Harold W. Stanley

Two continuing trends from past elections marked the presidential nomination season of 2003–4. First, states scrambled to move up their primaries, resulting in the early emergence of winning nominees; second, previous fund-raising records were smashed following major campaign finance reform. What set this season apart from past years was the rapid rise of a front-runner for the Democratic nomination after the early collapse of the previous front-runner.

President George W. Bush enjoyed the enviable position of not being challenged for the 2004 Republican nomination. For Senator John Kerry (D-MA), ultimately the Democratic presidential nominee, the path to the nomination seemed promising in early 2003, but turned perilous as former Vermont Governor Howard Dean's campaign took off. With the Iowa caucuses win on January 19, 2004, Kerry revived his campaign, surging through the primaries and caucuses to wrap up the nomination by early March.

The official nominations would come at the party conventions in late July and August, but the general election campaign between Bush and Kerry began in earnest once Kerry could claim the nomination. As polls revealed, neither candidate established a lasting, sizable lead over the other. The contest, widely anticipated to be closely competitive, remained close throughout the months leading up to and through the national nominating conventions and the general election.

Discussion of the defining moments in the 2004 presidential nomination process tracks the chronology. Consideration of the initial stages of the Democratic nomination contest contrasts with Kerry's sweep of the primaries and caucuses. The early start of general

election campaigning in March made the national nominating conventions less of a political coming-out party for Kerry, less of a reelection campaign launch for Bush, and more of a continuation of an already long campaign.

The Very Visible "Invisible Primary" of 2004

The "invisible primary" refers to the months of campaigning for the presidential nomination before the primary and caucus voting begins (Hadley, 1976; Buell, 1996). The significance of this period, evident in 1976, is even more important in today's nomination process because of front-loading, which became apparent as early as 1992 (Hadley and Stanley, 1993).

The reforms of the presidential nomination process since 1968 have increased the number of presidential primaries and lengthened the campaign for the nomination (Stanley and Niemi, 2003, 66–68; Busch and Mayer, 2004). States have jostled for greater influence by moving up to the beginning of the nomination calendar. The resulting "front-loaded" nomination process is practically shorter since so many convention delegates are at stake, a candidate can clinch the nomination in the opening weeks, as Kerry did in 2004. Although Democratic primaries and caucuses ran for more than four months from mid-January to early June, Kerry's campaign won the support of a convention majority in little more than eight weeks.

This front-loading has the effect of making the months before the voting starts all the more critical to establish support, particularly in the crucial initial states of Iowa and New Hampshire. Doing well early is essential, so presidential candidates spend months visiting Democratic activists and potential voters in Iowa and New Hampshire, raising funds across the nation, and seeking to garner favorable media attention.

Before the voting begins, Hadley (1976) noted that pundits and journalists assess candidates by considering (1) whether candidate psychology indicates the "fire in the belly" needed to endure the arduous process, (2) whether the candidate's staff reflects successful managerial abilities, (3) whether the candidate has a plausible strategy for capturing the nomination, (4) whether the candidate can raise the sums needed to compete, (5) whether the candidate can capture media attention, and (6) whether the candidate can secure enthusiastic supporters committed to his candidacy.

By each measure, Dean appeared to lead the pack in late 2003. Exceeding expectations works wonders for presidential candidates. Expectations for this unknown, small-state governor were virtually nil at the start, but his campaign outperformed presumably stronger candidates, capturing media coverage, voter support, prominent endorsements, campaign funds, and momentum. Claiming to represent "the Democratic wing of the Democratic Party," Dean energized Democrats with positions critical of the Bush administration and the war in Iraq. To rally supporters and capture media attention, Dean conducted a "Sleepless Summer Tour" in August of 2003. Dean surged into the lead in the polls for the Democratic nomination during fall 2003. Dean's antiestablishment campaign relied in large part on the Internet to rally supporters, targeting disaffected voters opposed to the war in Iraq (Simon, 2004). Dean captured the mood among Democrats: discontent with President Bush was acute and partisan polarization high after the 2000 election—especially the Bush victory resulting from Supreme Court resolution of the Florida vote count fiasco.

Dean decisively led the Democratic candidates in fund-raising, on track to raise $50 million by the first primary (Thomas et al., 2004, 49). He raised most of his money over the Internet in small contributions; only about 13 percent came from donors who gave the legal maximum of $2,000. The Kerry campaign, second among Democrats in fund-raising, had raised $29 million in 2003. President Bush, meanwhile, raised well over $100 million during 2003, more than the two top Democrats combined (Justice, 2004).

Dean's fund-raising success enabled him to forego public financing in November 2003. Bush had done the same in 2000, raising record amounts, and sought to do the same in 2004, exploiting a presumed Republican fund-raising edge. Although a candidate would pass up the additional cash such matching funds would offer, a candidate not taking public funding could ignore the state-by-state and national spending limits that came with the public funding. Once Dean passed up public funding, Kerry followed, although the state of Kerry's campaign organization and finances was not strong. Indeed, Kerry announced on November 14 that he, too, would pass up public funding. Four days earlier he had fired his campaign manager (Halbfinger and Nagourney, 2003; Cardwell and Weiser, 2003). Kerry's campaign had started with promise but stumbled throughout 2003, lingering in the shadow of a surging Dean.

By the end of 2003, Dean appeared to be leading the pack among rank-and-file Democrats, among Democratic contributors, and among party elites. More superdelegates had committed to him than to any other candidate. He received important labor support with the endorsements of the American Federation of State, County and Municipal Employees and the Service Employees International Union. On December 9, Al Gore endorsed Dean. Dean seemed to be not only the front-runner but peaking (Bernstein, 2004, 3).

Yet, hindsight would show the best days of the Dean campaign were behind him. Later reporting would reveal what was not evident at the time: Dean and his campaign manager seldom spoke; Dean's Iowa support was soft and hyped; would-be supporters attracted by Dean's anti-establishment positions resented the Democratic establishment's embrace of Dean; and Dean's candidate skills did not match his front-runner status (Simon, 2004).

As 2003 came to a close, Dean seemed gaffe-prone—gaffes that echoed with the media spotlight that came with front-runner status. When the capture of former Iraqi president Saddam Hussein on December 13, 2003, dominated the news, Dean claimed the United States was not safer as a result. Critics pounced. Dean's statements had previously given critics cause to question his judgment. For instance, perhaps seeking to make the sensible point that Democrats should not write off the South, Dean said, "I still want to be the candidate for guys with Confederate flags in their pickup trucks." Critics assailed the statement as insensitive and racist, leading to a later Dean apology (Balz, 2003; VandeHei, 2003).

Kerry Becomes the Presumptive Nominee

Major party nominations since 1976 had nearly always gone to the candidate leading in fund-raising and in the polls before the primaries and caucuses began (Mayer, 2004), and Dean had been the front-runner in both. This election, however, saw a break in the pattern.

News coverage prior to Iowa's caucuses often framed the contest as a battle between Dean and Representative Dick Gephardt (D-MO), the winner of the 1988 Iowa caucuses. Polling in the days before the caucus indicated four candidates—Dean, Gephardt, Kerry, and Senator John Edwards (D-NC)—were close and competing for the top spot (Moore and Newport, 2003, 3–5).

The caucus results were a surprise. Kerry won handily with 38 percent, Edwards placed second with 32, Dean managed only a distant third with 18, and Gephardt soon exited the race with a fourth-place finish at 11 percent. Dean the front-runner had lost badly in the first actual voting. Dean made losing badly even worse with a defiant concession speech that seemed over the top. "The Scream" was repeatedly and endlessly replayed over the next few days on news shows, giving voters just focusing on the presidential campaign reason to wonder if Dean had the temperament to be president.

How did Kerry revive his campaign to win Iowa? In September Kerry had pulled most campaign resources out of other states, even early-voting New Hampshire, to roll the dice on Iowa. Kerry lagged far behind Dean in New Hampshire and nationally. Kerry mortgaged his house for $6.4 million to loan much-needed cash to his campaign. Seen as a desperate act by a failing campaign at the time, this financial move later seemed a very decisive moment as Kerry turned his campaign around (Edsall and Cohen, 2004). Kerry's Iowa organization was experienced and methodical, standing in sharp contrast to Dean's reliance on political newcomers to find and turn out supporters. As Dean's candidacy sagged in December and early January, Kerry was best positioned to benefit. Kerry had "electability," voters told pollsters, presumably meaning he was fit to take on and defeat Bush in the general election (Simon, 2004).

After winning the Iowa caucuses, the New Hampshire primary, and six of seven events on February 3, Kerry seemed unstoppable. He ultimately won the primaries and caucuses in every state except four. Edwards won both the North Carolina caucus and the South Carolina primary; Clark edged out Edwards and Kerry in Oklahoma; and Dean, in the end, won only in his own state of Vermont. Beginning with the January 19 Iowa caucuses and ending with the March 16 Illinois primary, voters in 32 of the 50 states selected 2,733 delegates to the Democratic National Convention. Kerry had seized the Democratic presidential nomination having won 1,844 delegates to his closest competitor Edwards with 478 (see Table 4.1).

Throughout the process Kerry continued to set new fund-raising records among presidential challengers. He also continued to broaden his appeal to various groups and to luminaries associated with the Democratic Party. His endorsements eventually included not only the AFL-CIO but also those of other presidential candidates as they dropped out of the race. He also persuaded many of the best-known campaign professionals in the party to join his campaign (Bernstein, 2004, 10).

In the end, many primary and caucus voters may have flocked to Kerry as the candidate who would have the best chance of beating Bush.

Table 4.1

Democratic Delegate Counts by Collective Contest Dates

Contest date	Total delegates	Clark	Dean	Edwards	Kerry	Others
January 19	45	0	7	18	20	0
January 27	22	0	9	0	13	0
February 3	269	28	4	67	152	1
February 7	204	0	53	6	138	7
February 8	24	0	9	0	15	0
February 10	151	18	0	48	85	0
February 14	50	0	3	0	29	0
February 17	72	0	13	24	30	0
February 24	61	0	0	15	26	8
March 2	1,151	0	9	277	774	8
March 9	465	0	0	22	375	0
March 13	33	0	1	0	32	0
March 16	186	0	0	1	155	30*
Total	2,733	46	108	470	1,844	54

Source: Compiled from "Where Kerry Won the Nomination," *CQ Democratic National Convention Guide* (Washington, DC: CQ Press); "Illinois Democrats," www.greenpapers.com/Po4/IL-D.phtml, accessed December 16, 2004.

Note: The Democratic presidential nomination was won with 1,760 delegates.

*Uncommitted Illinois delegates.

Kerry's appeal was sufficiently broad, not factional, and in Iowa he had proven to be a winner—even winning the antiwar vote there (Simon, 2004; Bernstein, 2004). Kerry's voting record in the Senate was that of a loyal Democrat: *Congressional Quarterly* party unity scores placed him in the top 10 percent of Democrats every year since 1990. As a decorated veteran who had voted with most other Democrats and all Republicans in the Senate to authorize the war in Iraq, Kerry was seen as a candidate who would be less vulnerable than others to charges of being soft on defense and to public fears of changing leadership in the middle of a war (Nather, 2004).

The General Election Campaign Begins Eight Months Before the Vote

In the previous reelection bid by an incumbent president, Bill Clinton in 1996, the challenger, U.S. senator Robert Dole (R-KS), took public funding and sewed up the nomination only to find himself essentially unable to spend for months before the convention. President Clinton's campaign, flush with cash, having no opponent for the Democratic nomination, seized the advantage with campaign spending on advertising to solidify and increase Clinton's support.

This situation was not repeated in 2004. Kerry, as did Dean and Bush, turned down public funding, so he could spend whatever he could raise in the run-up to the convention. And given the intensity of anti-Bush sentiment, fund-raising took on a record-setting pace for a challenger, allowing him to amass $233,985,144 (91.8 percent of it from individuals) to begin the election campaign in earnest. At the same time, Bush more than doubled the $94,466,341 (96.7 percent from individuals) he raised in 2000 to $258,939,099 (98.4 percent from individuals) (see Table 4.2). Raising such astronomical sums was made possible by the Bipartisan Campaign Reform Act (BCRA), which doubled from $1,000 to $2,000 the amount individuals could contribute to federal election campaigns. Moreover, BCRA had revised campaign finance law to outlaw the raising of "soft money" by political parties (Malbin, 2003).

Advocacy groups, nicknamed 527s from the section of the federal tax code that governs their activities, independent by law from a candidate's campaign, sprang up to fill the void, raising and spending vast sums as shown in Table 4.3. Such groups favorable to Bush and the Republican Party lagged on the understanding that such tactics had perhaps been made illegal by BCRA and the climate of Enron, Tyco, and other corporate scandals dampened corporate enthusiasm for undertaking questionable political fund-raising. When the legal challenges were not resolved favorably to Republicans and their allies, Republican-friendly 527s entered the scene late and scrambled to catch up, the only major players being Progress for America, Swift Boat Veterans for Truth (later renamed the Swift Vets and POWs for Truth), and Club for Growth. As a result, for the months before the conventions, not only did the Kerry campaign and Democrats raise and spend large sums, but the 527s, tilting in favor of Democrats and Kerry, compared very favorably with the Bush campaign, the Republican Party, and Republican advocacy groups (Edsall, 2004a, 2004b). For example, the 527s that were classified "major players" by The Center for Responsive Politics, spent nearly $258 million in the 2004 federal elections, and nearly three quarters (72.5%) was used against Republican candidates, 59 percent alone against President Bush. In fact, America Coming Together ($76 million) and MoveOn.org ($21 million) worked to defeat the president while the Media Fund ($54 mil-

Table 4.2

Presidential Prenomination Campaign Receipts Through August 31, 2004 (in dollars)

	Federal matching funds	Contributions from individuals	Contributions from committees	Contributions and loans from the candidate	Transfers from previous campaigns	Other receipts	Total
Republicans							
Bush	**0**	**$254,817,068**	**$2,633,400**	**0**	**0**	**$817,531**	**$258,939,099**
Democrats							
Clark	7,615,360	17,321,849	45,950	0	0	90,371	25,073,530
Dean	**0**	**51,083,674**	**15,300**	**0**	**0**	**27,854**	**51,126,828**
Edwards	6,604,769	21,636,492	2,000	0	962,908	0	29,206,170
Gephardt	4,104,320	14,263,715	406,462	0	2,403,521	25,120	21,203,139
Kerry	**0**	**214,898,596**	**146,269**	**0**	**16,754,000**	**2,186,279**	**233,985,144**
Kucinich	2,847,080	7,803,394	16,000	0	0	2,813	10,669,287
LaRouche	1,408,993	8,193,775	2,798	0	0	1,074	9,606,640
Lieberman	4,267,797	14,052,813	214,320	2,000	0	0	18,536,930
Mosley Braun	0	526,426	41,273	14,848	0	0	582,547
Sharpton	0	512,736	4,200	77,500	0	0	589,866
Other							
Nader*	547,097	1,455,069	0	40,544	86,628	0	2,373,338

Source: www.fec.gov/Campaign Finance Reports and Data/Presidential Campaign Finance Summaries/Activity Through August 31/ Receipts of Presidential Campaigns Through July 31, 2004. Accessed December 11, 2004.

* Nader also received "Other Loans" totaling $254,000.

Table 4.3

Expenditures of 527 Committees Reported as Major Players in the 2004 Federal Elections by The Center for Responsive Politics (by political party candidate supported)*

527 Committee	Party candidate supported	Expenditures ($)
America Coming Together**	Democrat	76,270,921
Media Fund**	Democrat	54,429,053
MoveOn.org	Democrat	21,205,288
New Democrat Network	Democrat	12,194,451
Voices for Working Families	Democrat	6,809,102
Sierra Club#	Democrat	6,147,176
Partnership for America's Families	Democrat	2,880,906
Grassroots Democrats	Democrat	2,468,622
America Votes	Democrat	2,533,523
Americans for Jobs, Healthcare and Values	Democrat	994,137
Natural Resources Defense Council	Democrat	971,193
Total		**186,904,371**
Progress for America	Republican	35,437,204
Swift Vets & POWs for Truth	Republican	22,424,420
Club for Growth	Republican	13,204,800
Total		**71,066,424**

Source: Compiled from "527 Committee Activity: Top 50 Federally Focused Organizations," www.opensecrets.org/527s/527cmtes.asp?level, accessed December 11, 2004.

*The committees were classified by party from the description for each one provided by The Center for Responsive Politics.

**America Coming Together and Media Fund jointly ran Victory Campaign 2004 and divided the proceeds between them; Victory Campaign 2004 reported expenditures of $72,347,983, but it would be double-counted money to include them as a separate organization.

#Expenditures coordinated with America Votes.

lion) worked to elect Kerry and the Swift Vets and POWs for Truth ($22 million) worked to defeat him (cf. Wayne, 2005, 8–11).

Beginning in March, the Bush campaign began running its advertisements. The first ads were positive ones praising Bush's presidency. Soon, however, the thrust of the ad campaign turned negative. The intended contrast was strong, steady leadership from Bush against inconsistent dithering from Kerry; "flip-flops" became a Bush campaign buzzword for Kerry's supposed inconsistencies. Kerry aided the Bush effort with a single sentence that Republicans gleefully repeated: "I actually did vote for the $87 billion before I voted against it" (Thomas et al., 2004, 70). Kerry was explaining his support for authorizing the president to wage war on Iraq coupled with his later refusal to support the president's appropriations request to support a faltering war effort. But the statement fueled the "flip-flop" charge.

The president, meanwhile, had his own problems. Events in Iraq proved volatile and the war on terrorism in Afghanistan ran short of resources, both raising questions about the wisdom of the war in Iraq and imperiling Bush support. News over misconduct by U.S. military personnel at the Abu Ghraib prison in Iraq had the same effect (Nagourney and Elder, 2004). Similarly, economic news over the growth or loss of jobs punctuated the campaign, providing talking points for one side or the other depending on the state and spin of the news (Porter, 2004). Some Democrats felt Kerry was not capitalizing effectively on his opportunities, given that the contest remained so close (Nagourney and Elder, 2004).

Kerry wondered out loud whether he should defer accepting the nomination at the Democratic Convention in late July in order to be able to continue to spend freely. The Republican Convention would nominate Bush a month later. Once candidates become the party nominee, acceptance of public funding for the general election campaign (which both candidates ultimately accepted although foregoing those public funds was considered) precludes the candidate's campaign from spending any other funds. Ultimately Kerry decided to accept the nomination at the convention. This had repercussions once the Swift Vets and POWs for Truth 527 began their attacks on Kerry after the Democratic Convention.

For his vice presidential running mate, Kerry conducted a very discreet search, avoiding the leaking of telling information. While the final field was known, the actual selection of Edwards remained secret until shortly before Kerry's announcement. Edwards brought to the ticket an optimistic, upbeat energy that complemented Kerry's more serious senatorial presence. The selection of Edwards, a southerner, also added regional balance to the ticket in what had become a Republican Party presidential stronghold (Black and Black, 2002). At the same time, the two senators' voting records were strikingly similar on nearly all major issues (Cochran, 2004). Thus, as the two major-party national conventions approached, each party ticket was characterized by a high degree of ideological harmony.

The National Conventions

Party national conventions ceased decades ago to serve as true nominating conventions; the presidential candidates are known long before the conventions take place. Thus the conventions serve primarily to showcase the candidates and their parties through a series of staged events.

At the Democratic National Convention in late July, Kerry and his advisers used the publicity primarily to debate the Republicans on their own terms: security and values. Emphasizing his foreign policy experience and his military service during the Vietnam War, Kerry promoted his ability to defend the country and keep it safe. Hoping to preempt a Republican monopoly on moral values rhetoric, Kerry also invoked symbols of patriotism, faith, and national unity. Kerry and other convention speakers took few opportunities to attack the Bush administration on Iraq, or to criticize the administration in general and persuade the public on the need for regime change (Balz, 2004).

The decision to play up his military service may have left Kerry more vulnerable to attacks on his military record from Vietnam veterans who resented Kerry's antiwar activism. The Swift Vets and POWs for Truth formed as a 527 organization in order to pay for ads challenging Kerry's war record and suggesting that accounts of Kerry's heroism were untrue or exaggerated. Contradictory accounts of the events that led to Kerry winning a Bronze Star, a Silver Star, and three Purple Hearts are caused in part by conflicting memories of those who were present and by ambiguous military archival evidence. But they also stem from partisan differences fueled by Kerry's antiwar activities after he returned from Vietnam in 1969 (Dobbs, 2004). Meanwhile, Bush's own military record as a member of the Texas Air National Guard also came under scrutiny but was overshadowed by the Republican National Convention and later by conflicting news accounts (Rutenberg and Zernike, 2004).

The Republican National Convention in August was more tumultuous than the Democratic Convention had been outside the convention hall, where crowds of demonstrators protested Bush administration policies and nearly 2,000 were arrested. Inside, however, the convention was dominated by "glowing testimonials" about President George W. Bush, conveying a positive message of partisan unity as well as effectively criticizing the Democratic opponents (Purdum, 2004, A1).

Conclusion: Unanticipated Consequences of Reform?

As the final party convention came to an end, and as the general election campaign officially began, party officials and political observers once again questioned the value of the evolving and much-reformed nomination process. The upside is that the process facilitates a quick selection of presidential nominees so that the party can unify around them early.

The downside is that the long-drawn-out campaign continues to test voter interest after major party nominees are known (cf. Patterson, 2002). As the events of the 2004 nomination process remind us, well-intended reforms lead to unpredictable results. Regulating political party soft money moves it to different venues like the 527 advocacy groups and 501(c)(4) groups. Coupled with the apparent ease of raising hard money from individuals, it leads to ever more expensive and extensive political campaigns.

References

Balz, Dan. 2003. "Dean Is Criticized over Remark on Confederate Flag." *Washington Post,* November 2, A5.

———. 2004. "A Challenge to the GOP on Values, Security." *Washington Post,* July 30, A1.

Bernstein, Jonathan. 2004. "The Rise and Fall of Howard Dean and Other Notes on the 2004 Democratic Presidential Nomination." *The Forum* 2, no. 1, Article 1. http://www.bepress.com/forum.

Black, Earl, and Merle Black. 2002. *The Rise of Southern Republicans.* Cambridge, MA: The Belknap Press of Harvard University Press.

Buell, Emmett H., Jr. 1996. "The Invisible Primary." In *In Pursuit of the White House: How We Choose Our Presidential Nominees,* ed. William G. Mayer, 100–41. Chatham, NJ: Chatham House.

Busch, Andrew E., and William G. Mayer. 2004. "The Front-Loading Problem." In *The Making of Presidential Candidates 2004,* ed. William G. Mayer, 1–43. Lanham, MD: Rowman and Littlefield.

Cardwell, Diane, and Benjamin Weiser. 2003. "Kerry, Following Dean, Rejects Public Financing for Primaries." *New York Times,* November 15, A1.

Cochran, John. 2004. "Contrast and Commonality." *Congressional Quarterly Weekly Report: CQ Democratic Convention Guide* 62 (July): 18–26.

Dobbs, Michael. 2004. "Swift Boat Accounts Incomplete." *Washington Post,* August 22, A1.

Edsall, Thomas B. 2004a. "Pro-GOP Groups Outpaced in Funds; Pro-Democratic '527s' Far Ahead." *Washington Post,* July 16, A9.

———. 2004b. "Fundraising Doubles the Pace of 2000." *Washington Post,* August 21, A1.

Edsall, Thomas B., and Sarah Cohen. 2004. "Kerry's Loan Was Key to His Revival." *Washington Post,* February 2, A06.

Hadley, Arthur. 1976. *The Invisible Primary.* Englewood Cliffs, NJ: Prentice Hall.

Hadley, Charles D., and Harold W. Stanley. 1993. "Surviving the 1992 Presidential Nomination Process." In *America's Choice: The Election of 1992,* ed. William Crotty, 31–44. Guilford, CT: The Dushkin Publishing Group.

Halbfinger, David M., and Adam Nagourney. 2003. "Kerry Dismisses Campaign Chief." *New York Times,* November 11, A1.

Justice, Glen. 2004. "The 2004 Campaign: Fund-Raising; Kerry Aides Say His Finances Have Been Improving Rapidly." *New York Times,* January 28, A-18.

Malbin, Michael J. 2003. *Life After Reform: When the Bipartisan Campaign Reform Act Meets Politics.* New York: A Campaign Finance Institute Book published by Rowman & Littlefield.

Mayer, William G. 2004. "The Basic Dynamics of the Contemporary Nomination Process: An Expanded View." In *The Making of the Presidential Candidates 2004,* ed. William G. Mayer, 83–132. Lanham, MD: Rowman and Littlefield.

Moore, David, and Frank Newport. 2003. "Dean Takes Front-Runner Status Nationally for the First Time." *Gallup News Service,* December 9, 1–5.

Nagourney, Adam, and Janet Elder. 2004. "Bush's Rating Falls to Its Lowest Point, New Survey Finds." *New York Times,* June 29, A1.

Nather, David. 2004. "A Long, Nuanced Paper Trail." *Congressional Quarterly Weekly Report: CQ Democratic Convention Guide,* 62 (July), 8–17.

Patterson, Thomas E. 2002. *The Vanishing Voter: Public Involvement in an Age of Uncertainty.* New York: Alfred A. Knopf.

Porter, Edwardo. 2004. "U.S. Job Growth for June Shows Steep Slowdown." *New York Times,* July 3, A1.

Purdum, Todd S. 2004. "Upbeat Republicans Revive Bush Theme of Convention." *New York Times,* September 1, A1.

Rutenberg, Jim, and Kate Zernike. 2004. "The 2004 Campaign: The Military Record; CBS Offers New Experts to Support Guard Memos." *New York Times,* September 14, A21.

Simon, Roger. 2004. "Turning Point." *U.S. News & World Report,* July 19, 34 ff.

Stanley, Harold W., and Richard G. Niemi. 2003. *Vital Statistics on American Politics, 2003–2004.* Washington, DC: CQ Press.

Thomas, Evan et al. 2004. "How Bush Did It." *Newsweek,* November 15, 34–127.

VandeHei, Jim. 2003. "Dean Seeks to Silence Critics with Apology for Flag Remark." *Washington Post,* November 6, A6.

Wayne, Stephen J. 2005. *The Quest for the Nomination and Beyond.* Belmont, CA: Thompson Wadsworth.

5

Financing the 2004 Presidential Election

William Crotty

The god of politics is money. The key to winning an effective national campaign is financing. Without adequate funding, consultants are not hirable, television ads are limited, critical response times to opponents' attacks are not possible, travel for the candidate's entourage is restricted, the mobilization of the necessary tens of thousands of ground troops with their computers, voting lists, and organizational costs are beyond a campaign's ability to subsidize, and the legal and professional teams committed to monitoring elections and challenging the results as needed are not likely to be fielded. Money is the key. Without it in abundance, a campaign is crippled, an election conceded before it begins.

Financing Presidential Elections

It is a crude assessment, yet an accurate one. Without proper financing there is no serious campaign. Candidate after candidate (Howard Dean in 2004 being the latest) has proved the axiom. But accepting this premise, the questions then are: How much money is needed? Where does it come from? Does it enter into or influence public policy decision making? And what are the consequences for the broader democratic system of money's role in elections?[1]

The questions are not new, nor is the concern with the potential abuse, or undue influence, of financial resources. Money and politics, and the rewards conferred by backing the right candidate, have been subjects of controversy, and congressional legislative efforts at control, for well over 130 years.

Most campaign reform efforts were weak intentionally, more an acknowledgement of public concern than an effort to regulate funding. The candidates (as was intended) could easily avoid the restrictions imposed and continue with business much as usual. The laws on the books were ineffective, rarely if ever enforced, and served the codependent political and money-laden world well.

All of this appeared to change in the immediate post-Watergate era with the adoption of a series of strict regulations on campaign expenditures. There were regulations as to its accounting, allocation as to what could (or could not) be spent in specified subareas of the campaign budget (the proportion allowed for media advertising as an example). The Federal Election Commission (FEC) was established and it was charged with monitoring election expenditures, and establishing formulas for the allocation of public funds to campaigns and for the dispensing of such funds. The FEC could bring administrative or judicial action against those who failed to comply with the reporting provisions of the law, misused funds, or otherwise abused the process. The FEC was intended to serve as a repository on behalf of the media and the public for campaign financial records. The latter charge to the FEC alone represented a quantum leap forward in developing a realistic assessment of the actual costs of campaigns and in introducing serious efforts at financial regulation into the political system. For the first time, reasonably accurate estimates of the costs of campaigns for office along with an identification of the sources that supported candidate efforts would become public knowledge.

The most revolutionary feature, however, of the new laws, given the country's previously ineffective efforts at campaign finance regulation, were the provisions providing for the introduction of public funding into presidential election contests, both in the primaries and general election contests.[2] In each of these regards—funding supplements, expenditure restrictions, and the archiving of campaign records—there was a seismic break with past practices. It appeared a new, reform-initiated era had been born in American politics. Anthony Corrado sums up the intent of the laws in this manner:

> The program was designed to promote most of the objectives sought by the advocates of reform. In theory, public financing reduces the emphasis on fundraising and allows candidates to devote more time to the substantive aspects of a campaign by replacing private monies with public resources. The law seeks to diminish or eliminate the need to rely on wealthy donors and interest groups, thus minimizing the opportunities available to donors to influence candidates. . . . [it] helps guard against public perception of favoritism and the appearance of corruption in the political system, which can lead to public cynicism and alienation.

> Public financing also helps to equalize the potential resources available to candidates so that serious challengers will have the funds needed to present themselves and their ideas to the electorate. The program is designed to broaden political participation by opening the process to candidates without ready access to personal resources and wealthy donors, and by encouraging candidates to solicit small contributions and expand their base of donors. Further, it provides an inducement to help control campaign spending by tying eligibility for subsidies to the acceptance of spending limits, a link that was reaffirmed by the Supreme Court's 1976 decision in *Buckley v. Valeo,* 424 U.S. 1, which declared that spending limits were constitutional when imposed on candidates receiving public subsidies.[3]

It was an ambitious agenda.

The requirements contained in the campaign finance reform laws are extensive. Among their major provisions are the following:

- A maximum contribution of $2,000/election (primary and general elections are considered separately).
- A total contribution to federal candidates not to exceed $25,000. An amount of $20,000/year may be given to the national committees of the parties; $5,000 to a political action committee (PAC) or other political committee.
- Limits on the amounts national committees or congressional campaign committees can give to individual candidates.
- PACs and other such committees are limited to contributing $5,000/year to a candidate.
- Candidates are allowed to spend a stipulated amount in primary elections (an original amount of $10 million plus cost-of-living adjustments that came to over four times that amount in 2004).
- Major party candidates who accept federal matching funds are limited in what they can spend in the general election ($20 million originally, adjusted for inflation, coming to over four times that amount in the 2004 general election).
- Presidential and vice presidential candidates are limited in the amount of personal funds they can put into their campaigns ($50,000).
- A national party can spend two cents/voter on behalf of its presidential candidate.
- The national party and congressional campaign committees can also donate funds to congressional candidates.

- There are no limits on what House or Senate candidates may collect or spend on their campaigns (from *Buckley v. Valeo*).
- There are no limits on the amounts individuals or independent groups (those not formally affiliated with the candidate or the campaign) can spend (from *Buckley v. Valeo*).
- Political parties can also make unlimited independent expenditures on behalf of their candidates (from *Colorado Republican Federal Campaign Committee v. FEC,* 518, U.S. 604, 1996).
- Presidential candidates can opt to receive federal election funds (or not so choose).
- The money for the public financing of elections would be drawn from a federal taxpayer voluntary checkoff account.
- Prenomination candidates who do not receive at least 10 percent of the vote in two consecutive primaries forfeit their eligibility for additional public funds.
- Federal subsidies are given to the parties for their national conventions.
- A six-member board, half Republican and half Democratic, would supervise financial distributions, campaign compliance with FEC rules, and mandate other judgments and provisions within their authority as needed
- All campaign contributions and expenditures have to be reported to the FEC.[4]

The early hopes of the reformers were obviously high. The effort was an inclusive one, revolutionary actually, and rewrote the federal landscape as to the controls imposed on election funding. The euphoria did not last long. The campaign reform acts began their life under attack (the initial controversies underlying their operations continue to this day). They became the target of a number of lawsuits by opponents hoping to declare them unconstitutional or, secondarily if this line of attack faltered, severely weaken their provisions, handicap the FEC in fulfilling its duties, and underfund the amounts needed for a serious presidential campaign. It all worked.

The most influential event in the antireform campaign was the Supreme Court's 1976 decision in *Buckley v. Valeo*. As mentioned by Corrado, while reaffirming parts of the reform legislation, the Court decided that limitations on spending by an individual or a candidate or those whose spending on behalf of a candidate is independent of the campaign, violated the First Amendment's free speech provisions of the Constitution and were therefore unconstitutional. Limits on contributions to campaigns, mandated disclosure requirements, and, if agreed to by the candidates, public funding were legal.

Effectively, according to the Supreme Court, money equated to free speech. It was a form of free expression. Placed in this context, any restrictions adopted by the Congress would of necessity have to pass court review as to their constitutionality and would be scrutinized under the most severe tests as to individual freedoms. The beginnings of the disassembling of the public finance impetus can be found in this decision and the criteria the Court applied.

There were other problems, however. There was an inflationary factor built into the funds to be made available to candidates. It proved to be far from adequate, and in recent elections (2004, 2000) the cost of campaigns exceeded by a factor of three or four the amount of money available. The system was to be financed by a voluntary income tax checkoff by taxpayers. Unfortunately this was not adjusted for inflation, limiting the amount of money available to subsidize presidential candidates. Another problem has been the unpredictable number of candidates who run in a given year in a party's primaries. Anyone can qualify for fund-raising stipulated sums through donations of $250 or less in contributions dispersed among the states. It is not a formidable barrier and is one that has served to further weaken both parties' (but especially the Democrats') control over its own nominating processes.

The number of taxpayers participating in the checkoff has been in general decline. At the same time, the dollars made available for public funding have declined in value, a dynamic that has also contributed to the major increases in the total costs of the campaign itself. It could be argued that a voluntary tax checkoff system does not adequately work for the purposes intended.

Candidates have circumvented the spending limits, ignored filing deadlines, and submitted partial reports as to their spending. The FEC has been slow to react to alleged abuses and even slower to bring any type of formal administrative or legal action. A consequence is that accountability within the present financing system is, at best, inconsistent and, more often than not, is not a major concern in campaign decision making.

A final point: corrections could be made in the financing and regulatory provisions of the campaign reform acts by the Congress if it so wished. Such talk is a staple of every presidential campaign and most candidates' platforms. It is not an issue that moves the public or wins or loses elections. In addition, the Congress is not sympathetic to the campaign regulations or to the FEC. Most members in both parties believe they can do better on their own and resent having to file detailed reports as to their expenditures and their supporters with an independent body. The original campaign reform came in the midst of a crisis. It is likely something of this magnitude would need to occur again to bring about substantial and fundamental changes attuned to the needs of contemporary presidential campaigns. Even then, the pattern has been for the candidates and the parties to find their way around any provisions or restrictions that might be adopted (as with the 527 groups in 2004).

A major objective of the original campaign reform laws was their intention to control election costs. The introduction of PACs, "soft money" (intended for "party building" rather than overt candidate support), the 527s (as noted), and the declaration of individual or group spending to be protected by free speech guarantees have all added substantially to campaign expenditures (and what could be called "uncontrolled expenditures"; that is, funding not accountable to FEC restrictions and allegedly independent of the candidate and the campaign).

The rise of election costs in today's political marketplace has far outstripped the amount of public monies available and therefore their attractiveness to the principal contenders. As shown in 2004, each party can raise funds far in excess of those granted by the FEC. For such candidates, opting out of the public matching fund program is the intelligent approach. Such candidates also opt out of complying with many of the restrictions on spending that accompany the receipt of such funds.

A curious pattern, evident in the 2004 election year, may be emerging. What the federal funding of elections has accomplished is to allow less-favored and even insurgent candidates (as indicated in the regulations, as long as they win two primary or caucus races in a specified period of time) to compete with the front-runners. Like much of the campaign reform acts themselves, this is not an aspect of the reforms that the professionals in either party welcome.

In broader terms in the primaries, however, much the same dynamic that has shaped funding a presidential contest appears to be in play. The Campaign Finance Institute reported that large donations to primary candidates rose to $88 million, small donations to $40 million in 2004 compared with 2000. The increase in contributions came to 72 percent, from a healthy $184 million in the 2000 primaries to a much healthier $316 million in 2004. It seems hard to believe, but public matching funds amounted to only 6 percent of the receipts.[5] It could be argued with credibility that such figures are skewed by the fact that the major party candidates (Bush and Kerry) and Howard Dean in the early Democratic Party contests did not opt to receive federal matching funds. It could also be argued that this set of choices makes the point: the heaviest and most influential money is private and goes to those with the greatest chance of winning.

By this account, what was referred to earlier as revolutionary is decidedly of less importance than its sponsors had intended and more a mechanism (the FEC) for a repository of records than a dynamic force in subsidizing elections and deescalating campaign costs.

The Basics: Funding the 2004 Presidential Races

In 2004, both campaigns had more than adequate funds at their disposal. In fact, it would appear that one candidate (John Kerry) had more than he could manage to spend (mysteriously, and to the annoyance of many Democrats, he wound up with a surplus of $14 million). Kerry's surplus was a point of contention among Democrats, creating "one more fissure in [a] . . . party . . . struggling to find new leadership and direction after losses to the Republicans on November 2."[6] Donna Brazile, who had managed Al Gore's race in 2000, was not pleased: "Seeing money left on the table put me in a state of shock. I got over my depression long enough to feel anger."[7] Her views represented those of many in the Democratic Party who felt the funds should have been used in the final days of the campaign to counter the Republicans' advertising blitz, or to be put into voter mobilization efforts, or used to help Democrats in other races. The Kerry camp admitted it had held onto the funds intentionally (it was not an oversight) to pay for any recounts or legal challenges, such as occurred in Florida 2000. Many of the Democrats who had experienced the loss of two close presidential races in a row were unconvinced.

Not only did the candidates have the financing available to run high-profile, comprehensive (and intensive) campaigns, each individually had more money donated to their campaigns than in any previous election. Taken together, the two parties easily ran the most expensive campaigns in American history. In addition, and it is difficult to find a precedent for this in the modern era, the Democrats actually drew in at least as much as, and actually in projection, more funds than, their Republican oppo-

Table 5.1

Top Five Expenditures in Candidates' Primary Campaigns 2004
(in dollars)

Bush / Cheney '04	
Media	118,984,473
Credit card payments	14,145,439
Postage	10,771,976
Payroll	8,918,775
Printing	7,253,578
John Kerry for President, Inc.	
Media	91,433,986
Travel expenses	19,301,270
Salary	9,840,955
Other itemized expenses	7,931,487
Fundraising expenses	5,797,358
Edwards for President	
Consulting / Media	10,113,105
Salary	3,900,168
Airfare / Travel	2,410,281
Payroll taxes	1,944,369
Direct mail expense	1,439,882

Source: Federal Election Commission. Data also available at www.opensecrets.org.

nents (although the final totals for the parties were close). The richest presidential campaign in history basically allowed both camps to run as serious and forceful a campaign as they chose. Money was not to be the limiting factor it had been in many previous contests.

Statistics tell the story. In the primaries, the successful candidates (Bush and Cheney; Kerry, Edwards) spent over $300 million (roughly $160 million by the Bush-Cheney campaign, winning without opposition; and for the Democrats, Kerry $134 million and Edwards $20 million) (see Table 5.1). The figures are impressive, multiples of what once financed presidential campaigns.

In the general election campaign, and using the last reporting period prior to Election Day, Bush-Cheney took in about $81 million and had spent 94.6% percent of it; Kerry-Edwards had total receipts of $84 million of which they had spent almost 98.5% percent. A comprehensive accounting, which could take years, is likely to be considerably higher in both campaigns. Later returns, while demonstrating both candidates had access to substantial financing, moved the Bush campaign ahead in the final count (Table 5.2).

Table 5.2

Candidate Financing, 2004 Presidential General Election (in dollars)

Candidates	Party	Receipts	Expenditures
Bush-Cheney	Republican	81,207,996	76,793,336
Kerry-Edwards	Democrat	84,665,576	83,408,246

Source: Political Money Line, www.fecinfo.com.

Of the expenditures, in the primaries between one-half and three-quarters of the money went into media buys and related consultant services (Bush-Cheney, 74%; Kerry, 68%; Edwards, 50%). During the general election period, 89 percent of the Bush-Cheney expenditures went for media as against 56 percent of the Kerry-Edwards campaign's outlays. Media unquestionably is the most effective and, despite the costs, efficient way to reach a broad electorate. In this regard and in relation to candidate expenditures, Bush outspent Kerry by approximately 50 percent ($46.5 million to $30.4 million).[8] In addition, the Center for Public Integrity found that 527 groups that could raise and spend unlimited "soft" funds (minimal accounting or regulation of expenditures) amassed at least $175 million.

These figures are one index of the escalation of political costs. Another is the increase in the amounts spent in congressional races. The Campaign Finance Institution found the winners in House races exceeded an average $1 million and the expenditures of incumbents in close Senate races rose from $4.5 million in the 2002 election to $7.8 million in 2004. Challengers for Senate seats in these contests went from $2.8 million in 2002 to $3.6 million in 2004.

The most effective of the television commercials were the earlier indicated "Swift Boat" ads. Some 75 percent of those polled by a Republican-affiliated firm recalled the ads. In second place was another Bush-Cheney ad showing a 15-year-old girl (called Ashley) crying for her mother killed in the 9/11 bombings and being consoled by President Bush.

The Kerry campaign and the groups supporting it basically matched the Bush campaign in media expenditures during the summer of 2004 and up to the final month of the election. In the final three weeks of the campaign, the ones most strategically important for reaching the undecideds and winning the swing states, "independent 527 groups backing President Bush bought nearly $30 million worth of television and

Table 5.3

Top Ten 527 Committees

Committee	2004 Contributions ($) Monies raised	Expenditures	Support of committee
Joint Victory Campaign 2004*	41,685,706	35,780,404	Democratic
Media Fund	28,127,488	27,208,905	Democratic
America Coming Together	26,905,450	24,196,532	Democratic
Service Employees International Union	16,652,296	8,817,805	Democratic (89%)
American Federation of State, County & Municipal Employees	13,658,207	13,285,839	Democratic (97%)
MoveOn.org	9,086,102	17,435,782	Democratic
New Democrat Network	7,172,693	6,970,070	Democratic
Club for Growth	6,301,037	8,698,440	Republican
Sierra Club	4,491,180	1,601,731	Democratic
EMILY's List	4,162,226	4,070,369	Democratic (Pro-Choice Women)

Source: Federal Election Commission. Data also available at www.opensecrets.org.
*Joint fund-raising committee of Media Fund and American Coming Together

radio ads, three times what their Democratic counterparts spent."[9] Strategically, it was money well invested.

As to where the money came from, the top ten 527s (the label comes from the tax code authorizing them) were primarily Democratic and spent most of their funds on behalf of Kerry-Edwards. The amounts ranged from $4 million (EMILY's List) to $35.8 million (Joint Victory Campaign 2004, a union of the Media Fund and America Coming Together) (see Table 5.3).

Among the top individual contributors to the 527s were George Soros, Peter Lewis, Alex Spanos, Steven Bing, T. Boone Pickens, and any number of other leaders of financial, entertainment, investors, and business corporations (see Table 5.4). The money spent by these contributors ranged from $1 million to $19 million.

Among the top 20 PACs, the funds invested in the campaign ranged from $1.4 to $3.7 million with a clear division of contributions to the parties in most cases. The labor unions supported the Democrats, at times giving them 90 percent or better of their funds. Auto dealers, beer wholesalers, UPS, the American Medical Association, and Wal-Mart decisively favored the Republicans.

With the cost of presidential campaigns now running into the billions

Table 5.4

Top Contributors to 527 Committees

Contributor	Total ($)
Joint Victory Campaign 2004	56,654,391
Service Employees International Union	30,308,194
American Fedn of St/Cnty/Munic Employees	24,262,816
Soros Fund Management/George Soros	23,731,000
Peter B. Lewis/Progressive Corp	22,730,000
Shangri-La Entertainment/Steve Bing	13,550,164
Golden West Financial	7,482,059
AFL-CIO	7,221,114
Sustainable World Corp/Linda Pritzker	6,625,000
Ameriquest Capital	5,000,000

Source: Open Secrets, www.opensecrets.org.

of dollars, it is difficult to see where the average voter fits in beyond providing a target audience for the candidates and their messages.

The 2004 election hit a new level of expenditures for a presidential (or any other) contest. Both camps did exceedingly well in collecting funds, as was to be expected. More surprising was the exceptionally high level of contributions to the campaigns by individuals, PACs, and, more indirectly through their advertising promoting one candidate or the other, the 527s. A second surprise was in the success enjoyed by the Democrats, normally a party falling well behind Republicans when it came to fund-raising. The Kerry campaign and the Democrats and their support groups at least equaled the Republicans in this regard. Both of the parties did well, serving to drive the costs of future campaigns up substantially and to raise the bar for potential candidates for 2008 and thereafter who wish to run in presidential elections. It is likely that future campaigns will equal or exceed the historic levels of expenditures found in 2004.

The End of a Reform Era

Another point, one with long-run consequences and little discussed in the postelection assessments: Should both the manner and extent of fund-raising extend into future elections, which is likely (and symbolized by the 2004 presidential contest), it may effectively condemn the reform-oriented public financing (and more rigorous control of and accounting for costs) in elections to extinction. The 2000 campaign notably began the process. The 2004 and 2000 elections taken together demonstrate the benefits of seeking private funding: minimizing scrutiny by the Federal Election Commission, and permitting a freedom in allocations and the use of subsidiary support groups that both campaigns employed effectively in the 2004 race.

Public funding of presidential campaigns has not kept up with either inflation or the times. The amounts supplied to candidates who agree to accept such funds (and the accounting procedures that go with them) are not attractive for those attempting to run a competitive race in the contemporary era. And, in fact, there is little incentive to qualify for such grants.

The public funding of presidential campaigns has been under sustained assault since its inception. To recapitulate: The intent of the reform legislation was to even the playing field between the parties, to closely monitor and restrict the cost of campaigns, and to relieve candidates of the necessity for spending large proportions of their election campaign funds in seeking out donors to finance their races.

It has never worked as effectively as intended. The 1976 Supreme Court ruling *Buckley v. Valeo*, as indicated, limited the applicability of the then recent laws, legally authorized PACs, providing the public funds only if agreed to by candidates, and reduced the requirements as to extensive campaign documentation. This did not help the system gain the control over campaigns or the supervisory powers in relation to expenditures it had originally sought. The Congress, while passing the campaign reform acts in the aftermath of the reaction to the Watergate break-ins, the abuses of authority, and the imprisonment of members of President Nixon's campaign team and cabinet, was never enthusiastic about the public financing system. Consequently, over the years the Congress and successive presidential administrations have done what they could to appoint partisan members to its governing board; restrict the FEC's funding, staff, and authority; and generally work to lessen its impact. Both parties have endorsed such an approach and, in terms of the FEC's organizational resources and its monitoring of presidential campaigns, they have largely succeeded.

The 2004 campaign may well mark the end of the Federal Election Commission as a primary force in presidential campaigns and its avowed role as an agent and surrogate for the American people in supervising presidential contests.

As a player of consequence in presidential politics, its best days may be behind it. Its limited role, and the lack of attention given it in 2004, effectively predicts what upcoming campaigns will likely reflect and the path to be taken in future contests.

The Policy Consequences of Campaign Funding

There are winners and losers in policy terms just as there are winners and losers in the election. How this all plays out is not always immediately clear. The relationships and interactions are complex. Simple associations between campaign donations by groups or individuals and the introduction or passage of a piece of legislation can be oversimplified, although not necessarily incorrect. In gross terms, the policy agendas of the major candidates for president had little, if anything, in common. The selection by the voting public of one candidate and one party and its priorities over the other clearly resulted in the adoption of positions that reward the winning coalition. This is obvious to all who take sides in electoral contests.

In 2004, unlike many other years, the future directions of administration policy are not difficult to predict. The president had a four-year record that he unequivocally ran on and that would set the stage for the next four years. In turn, the groups that benefited the most from the Bush administration's tax, economic, environmental/developmental, petroleum exploration, health and pharmaceutical, and faith-based initiative programs as well as the domestic and foreign contracts awarded by government contributed heavily to the president's campaign. They are the winners. The expectation is that similar to the first four years of the administration they will be rewarded. Such rewards can be substantial: favorable policy promotions of their interests, weakened government regulation of their activities, bureaucratic favoritism, federal contracts, sympathetic tax policies and interpretations, selective presentation of alleged legal violations, and the rest of the very considerable patronage that comes with holding the presidency and, not to be ignored, majorities in both houses of the Congress. The possibilities are virtually unlimited; the policy paybacks are well worth the campaign donations invested. The expectations of the pro-Bush heavy spenders are likely to be rewarded.

Politics, money, elections, policy, and private interests blend together in a fundamentally intrinsic interrelationship that both rewards those who choose to give and, on a broader canvas, determines the distribution of the nation's resources. As others have pointed out, this is how policy is made. An "investment theory" of democratic policymaking as developed by Thomas Ferguson is very much on target.[10]

In one sense, the funding of political campaigns represents a stream outside of (although critical to) the campaign and its target audiences and well beyond the understanding or participation of the voters who turn out in elections. It represents millions of dollars invested by corporations, professional lobbying groups, labor unions, and individuals in candidates, and more to the point, policy agendas that are favorable to their interests. Few such sums are given to promote the public's interest (however defined). Also, the giving and cultivation of political officeholders and parties does not begin or end with the campaign period. It is a year-round "permanent campaign" activity, part of a concerted and well-thought-out drive to achieve the policy objectives held important by the group or association in question. In effect, as noted, it is grafted onto the body politic and, more directly, electioneering. It most frequently has little to do with voters or mass interests on any broad social scale. Yet, under present conditions, campaigns cannot be run without the volume of funds supplied by privately oriented policy interest groups.

Such approaches have consequences for the electorate and for the representation of its interests. If the funding of politics and promoting of issues is a professionalized, year-around activity (and it is), then an increasingly fragmented and bypassed electorate experiences a continual diminution of its power over policy ends, regardless of what it does (or does not) do in elections. Decisions are being made elsewhere and the cord that ties these together is the availability of funding to facilitate the implementation, through campaigns or Washington-based lobbying efforts, of the objectives the group wants achieved and, most important, is willing to pay for. It is a crass calculus, but one that appears to be of relevance to today's politics.[11] The key resource in achieving one's political ends is financing. The 2004 election took this influence model to new heights. On Washington interests and their year-around representation, Matthew Crenson and Benjamin Ginsberg write:

> The proliferation of opportunities for individual access to government has substantially reduced the incentives for collective mobilization. For ordinary Americans, this means that it has become standard practice to deal with government as an individual customer rather than as a member

> of a mobilized public. . . . Americans of more than ordinary political status find that they can use courts, administrative procedures, and other political channels to achieve their ends without organizing a political constituency to support them and their aims . . . . Elites have fewer incentives to mobilize non-elites; non-elites have little incentive to join together with one another. The two circumstances have operated in combination with one another to produce a new politics of individualized access to government and a new era of *personal democracy* [italics in original].[12]

Popular expression and participation in policymaking continue to decline. It would appear that mass electorates are the passive recipients of superbly well financed campaigns during election periods. In the interelection intervals between campaigns, they play little to no role of consequence. The implication of such forces for a democratic society is not encouraging: the approach to government and its powers is individualized by group or audience and is multifaceted, expanding beyond elections to nonelection access points in an effort to achieve the legislative and political goals of individual groups and associations.

> [T]he population of Washington lobbyists and interest groups has grown rapidly . . . some of the newest interest groups have begun to target ever-narrower interests . . . contemporary interest groups tend to concentrate more on litigation, research, polling, fund-raising, and media relations and less on mobilizing popular support. The handful of Washington-based interest groups that have extensive grassroots memberships, such as the National Rifle Association and AARP, are connected with the vast majority of their constituents only by mail. . . . The interest group struggle in Washington, like the clash of party elites in Congress, becomes increasingly disconnected from the mobilization of citizens, and the scope of citizenship itself narrows.[13]

The glue in all of this would be the availability of the financing to pursue alternative avenues of influence or to hire the professional consultants, lobbyists, lawyers, and what have been referred to as "influence peddlers" to achieve the ends desired.

Ferguson (represented in this volume, see Chapter 9) refers to this as "the investment theory of politics." His position is unequivocally clear: "The American political system is not essentially driven by votes. Public opinion has only a weak and inconstant influence on policy. The political system is largely investor-driven, and runs on enormous quantities of money."[14] Ferguson illustrates what he means by an extended analysis of the tobacco industry in appearances before congressional committees and its claims, in the face of evidence to the contrary (and namely that "companies had calibrated levels of nicotine in cigarettes to keep smokers hooked"), that "nicotine levels are adjusted solely to enhance cigarette flavor and they [the tobacco executives] didn't think nicotine was addictive."[15] The industry's efforts were directed toward minimizing Federal Drug Agency, or congressional, control over the contents or merchandizing of tobacco products.

There are several ways to look at this. One is that there was a large degree of innocence manifested by the representatives of the tobacco industry. Another is that they had the millions of dollars needed to fight the adoption of hostile legislation and they used it. A third is that the exact same approach had been used successfully (combined with the financed support given candidates in elections) for generations, although in recent years the tide had turned and restrictions were imposed.

What is of interest about the tobacco industry is the amount of giving in which it involves itself (few other industries could equal it). It directs a full-time push in promoting its image and its product. Its manifest willingness to move beyond immediate political targets in elections, the administration, or the Congress (although it never forgets its basic objective), sets it apart, at or near the top consistently of corporations investing in politics, directly and indirectly. According to Darrell West and Burdette Loomis,

> A classic illustration of successful image enhancement over a long period of time is the tobacco industry. For years, tobacco companies have relied on well-connected agencies in order to sway reporters, run ads, sponsor sporting events, and underwrite cultural activities. Through its unique combination of public relations and philanthropy, tobacco has been more single-minded in its pursuit of public goodwill than perhaps any other industry. . . . Philip Morris . . . has sponsored a wide range of events including tennis tournaments and automobile races. The company has contributed generously to a range of philanthropic causes. It runs ads featuring company efforts to make the world a better place.[16]

The industry also gave handsomely in the 1990s to "the American Red Cross as part of tobacco's long-term goodwill campaign. Perhaps it was no accident that the head of the Red Cross was Elizabeth Dole [later Senator Dole from North Carolina and] the wife of [the then] Senate Majority Leader Robert Dole."[17] West and Loomis continue:

> At the same time, Philip Morris and other industry groups engaged in traditional lobbying tactics. . . . [T]obacco companies were the top "soft money" contributors to the national parties, giving . . . to the Republican and Democratic national committees for party-building activities. . . . The industry also contributed hundreds of thousands of dollars directly to congressional candidates around the country.[18]

Most (approximately 70 to 75%) of the tobacco industry's election funding went to the Republican Party. The Democrats received substantial amounts from labor and a number of 527s and PACs, virtually all of the monies these groups invested in races. Industry groups, corporations, unions, and others who give to candidates and campaigns are not shy about their intentions. They focus on election seats and contests of importance, candidates they wish to promote, and the major players in the policy areas of greatest importance to them for their particular attention.

William Keefe writes:

> Political action committees target their gifts carefully, taking into consideration such key factors as incumbency, party, and legislative position. . . . Committee chairs and party leaders are major beneficiaries of interest group largesse. Committee membership is also taken into consideration. Members of the tax and commerce committees . . . invariably receive more PAC money than members of the judiciary or foreign policy committees. The pattern of contributions is illustrated by these observations:
>
> "The main goal is to support our friends who have been with us most of the time." (An official of the UAW [United Auto Workers])
>
> "The prevailing attitude is that PAC money should be used to facilitate access to incumbents." (The director of governmental and political participation for the Chamber of Commerce of the United States)
>
> "We're inclined to support incumbents because we tend to go with those who support our industry. We are not out looking to find challengers. Our aim is not to change the tone of Congress." (A spokesperson for the Lockheed Good Government Program)
>
> "We're looking especially for members who serve on key committees, and people who help us on the floor." (A spokesperson for the Automobile and Truck Dealers Election Action Committee)
>
> Political action committees spread money around. Parties as well as candidates depend on them. . . . PACs have been a significant factor in the weakening of American parties and in the emergence and consolidation of candidate-centered politics.[19]

Reforming Campaign Financing

For some, the key to regaining control of election costs, and group and private contributions to candidates, is the reversal or severe modification of *Buckley v. Valeo.* It would not be easy. The Supreme Court of the mid-1970s was more receptive (however antagonistic it might have been) than the contemporary, highly conservative balance of the Court at present would likely be, to the public regulation of election costs. Nonetheless, advocates of this avenue of reform have argued that "*Buckley* emerged out of a political crisis that was different from the crisis we face today. We should not be limited in perpetuity to yesterday's solutions if today's problems are different," and that "the *Buckley* experience provides us with some object lessons about how to proceed next time around."[20] This, of course, assumes there will be a "next time around" in mounting a serious attack on the *Buckley* ruling.

Should there be, advocates recommend the following:

> [I]f the legislatures and initiative drafters wish to move the Court, they must identify clearly the evils they are addressing and the way in which their solutions address the harms. Reformers must develop a clear idea of the values they wish to advance and generate a compelling factual record to document the vices they are trying to cure. . . . [D]rafters must incorporate those values into forceful statements of purpose and develop a factual record that includes a compelling set of findings and prognostications as to how the reform effort would enhance our democracy. As the Court recently reminded us—in the context of a case full of knotty First Amendment questions—"courts must accord substantial deference to the predictive judgments" embodied in a law. Still, courts are more willing to defer to "unusually detailed statutory findings."[21]

Under any conditions, it is an optimistic scenario.

For others seeking campaign reform, the preferred approach is to concentrate on incremental pieces of legislation to meet each new challenge as it arises (PACs, "soft money," 527s). This is the avenue currently followed. Even then, it demands enormous amounts of political capital to achieve the most limited of results.

For yet others desiring reform, the most effective means of controlling campaign costs is to inaugurate a totally new and comprehensive campaign reform system. They may be right, but it takes a crisis of national proportions to initiate any such type of all-encompassing reform program. Even under these conditions, it does not come easily.

It should be added that a significant number of political figures, beyond giving lip service to reform in their campaign rhetoric and with the groups and private interests involved in the election process and in lobbying the Congress and the administration, would much prefer to see no restrictions on funding or provisions for accountability at all. These, of course, include all of those political officeholders who would have to develop and shepherd such a new system to fruition and the groups that provide the dominant amount of campaign funding and are representing their interests and views to legislators and policymakers year around.

Finally, there are the professional observers who believe such a battle on behalf of campaign regulation is excessively, if not prohibitively, costly and that no reform approach has a chance of achieving its ends, regardless of what is eventually implemented. The candidates, parties, and their support groups would quickly find their way around any restrictions or reform applications. This certainly has been the history of the legislative attempts to control campaign financing, from their inception in the late 1800s to the present, post-Watergate era.

Conclusion

All of this provides a context for the extraordinary election expenditures in 2004 in which new levels were reached. A number of issues are raised: Who can afford such political investments? Are such sums of money devoted directly to obtaining policy outcomes? Do they buy access, influence, and results? Where do they leave the individual voters? What are these voters' roles in such lavishly funded campaigns? Do such expenditures advance democratic politics? What can be done (or should anything be done) about the problem? Such questions are not readily answered.

What we do know is that the financing of the 2004 presidential election campaign lived up to form (and then some), setting new highs for expenses, fund-raising totals, and media costs, in addition to organizational canvassing, get-out-the-vote drives, and legal expenses. More than likely, if nothing else, it will be seen as a significant marking point in the escalation of campaign costs.

Notes

1. Robert L. Dudley and Alan R. Gitelson, *American Elections: The Rules Matter* (New York: Longman, 2002); Victoria A. Farman-Myers and Diana Dwyre, "Parties and Campaign Finance," in *American Political Parties: Decline or Resurgence?* ed. Jeffrey E. Cohen, Richard Fleisher, and Paul Kantor (Washington, DC: CQ Press, 2001), 138–161; A. James Reichley, ed., *Elections American Style* (Washington, DC: Brookings Institution, 1987); Larry Sabato, "Real and Imagined Corruption in Campaign Financing," in *Elections American Style,* ed. A. James Reichley (Washington, DC: Brookings Institution, 1987).

2. In 2004, the total sums of matching federal funds available to candidates who qualified in the primaries were $37 million and in the general election $74 million. (Federal Election Commission, available at: www.fec.gov/pages/brochures/pubfund_limits_2004.html).

3. Anthony Corrado, *Paying for Presidents: Public Financing in National Elections* (New York: Twentieth Century Fund Press, 1993), 9–10.

4. William Keefe, *Parties, Politics, and Public Policy in America* (Washington, DC: CQ Press, 1998), 155–157; Federal Election Commission, "2004 Presidential Spending Limits."

5. Campaign Finance Institute, "CFI Analysis of the Presidential Candidates' Financial Reports Filed March 20 [2004]" (Washington, DC: Campaign Finance Institute, March 24, 2004; available at www.cfinst.org/pr/032404.html).

6. Glen Justice, "Kerry Left $14 Million Unspent in Campaign," *New York Times,* December 4, 2004, A15.

7. Ibid.

8. Federal Election Commission, "Disclosure Reports," October 13, 2004; available at www.fec.gov/disclosure.shtml.

9. Jeffrey Birnbaum and Thomas Edsall, "At the End, Pro-GOP '527s' Outspent Their Counterparts," *Washington Post,* November 6, 2004, A06, A11.

10. Thomas Ferguson and Joel Rogers, *Right Turn: The Decline of the Democrats and the Future of American Politics* (New York: Hill and Wang, 1986); Thomas Ferguson, *Golden Rule: The Investment Theory of Party Competition and the Logic of Money Driven Political Systems* (Chicago: University of Chicago Press, 1995); Thomas Ferguson, "Blowing Smoke: Impeachment, the Clinton Presidency, and the Political Economy," in *The State of Democracy in America,* ed. William J. Crotty. (Washington, DC: Georgetown University Press, 2001), 195–254.

11. R. Kenneth Godwin, *One Billion Dollars of Influence: The Direct Marketing of Politics* (Chatham, NJ: Chatham House Publishers, 1988); Charles Lewis, *The Buying of the President, 2004: Who's Really Bankrolling Bush and His Democratic Challengers—and What They Expect in Return* (New York: Perennial, 2004); Greg Palast, *The Best Democracy Money Can Buy: The Truth About Corporate Cons, Globalization, and the High-Finance Fraudsters* (New York: Plume/Penguin Books, 2003).

12. Matthew Crenson and Benjamin Ginsberg, "Party Politics and Personal Democracy," in *American Political Parties: Decline or Resurgence?* ed. Jeffrey E. Cohen, Richard Fleisher, and Paul Kantor (Washington, DC: CQ Press, 2001), 87.

13. Ibid., 79.

14. Ferguson, "Blowing Smoke," 235.

15. Ibid., 207.

16. Burdett Loomis and Darrell West, *The Sound of Money: How Political Interests Get What They Want* (New York: W.W. Norton, 1998), 49.

17. Ibid.

18. Ibid., 49–50.

19. Keefe, *Parties, Politics, and Public Policy in America,* 142, 143, 145.

20. E. Joshua Rosenkrantz, *Buckley Stops Here: Loosening the Judicial Stranglehold on Campaign Finance Reform* (New York: The Century Foundation, 1998), 29.

21. Ibid.

6

The Presidential Race of 2004

Strategy, Outcome, and Mandate

Patricia Conley

President George W. Bush claimed a mandate for his political agenda immediately after the 2004 election returns were in. "When you win, there's a feeling that the people have spoken and embraced your point of view, and that's what I intend to tell the Congress," Bush said. "I earned capital in the campaign, political capital, and now I intend to spend it."[1]

Mandate claims are not unusual in the wake of a presidential contest. After every presidential election, politicians, journalists, and scholars eagerly discuss whether or not the new president has a mandate. Not all presidents claim a mandate for the policies put forward by them in their election campaign. President Bush did not claim a mandate after the 2000 presidential election contest. In 2000, Bush did not win the popular vote. He won half of the Electoral College votes only after the Supreme Court stepped in to resolve the dispute in Florida. In contrast, Lyndon Johnson (1964) and Ronald Reagan's (1980 and 1984) electoral victories were landslides and public opinion polls showed broad support for their policy agendas. They claimed mandates to justify substantial changes in policy direction.

How do we make sense of George W. Bush's claim to a mandate in 2004? His reelection was not a landslide and for that reason many Democrats are outraged that he would dare use mandate rhetoric. But Bush's behavior is not totally unexpected given that American presidents typically use mandate rhetoric fairly liberally. This chapter views the 2004 presidential election results in terms of presidential mandates. I examine how the 2004 campaign set the stage for postelection interpretations and put Bush's claim in the context of past electoral victories.

What Constitutes a Mandate

In theories of representation, a "mandate" refers to a command or instruction from voters to elected officials. With the presidency of Andrew Jackson in 1828, politicians and voters started viewing the American president as a representative of the people, and presidential elections as vehicles for the expression of the will of the people.[2]

Political scientists, however, often dismiss presidential mandate claims as meaningless because of the informational shortcomings of voters and the logical problems of identifying the collective preferences of the electorate.[3] But presidential mandate claims are not meant to be statements of fact about fully formed public preferences. Presidents use mandate rhetoric to signal that it is worth their while to put major policy changes on the national agenda. A president claims a mandate when he sees an opportunity to shift the status quo in the direction of his policy preferences.[4]

Elections constrain politicians by signaling the boundaries of public opinion. Though they do not have the individual-level survey data available to scholars, politicians act as if it is meaningful to think of policies favored by majorities of voters. They pay attention to election outcomes, and believe that elections provide useful information. For instance, the interpretation of elections affects how members of Congress construct their policy agendas, committee preferences, staffs, and provisions of constituency services.[5] Politicians make inferences about elections by relying on evidence such as patterns of party support across demographic groups, the magnitude of victory, and comparisons with elections past.

Elections vary with respect to the strength of signals that they send. In an environment of imperfect information, politicians try to distinguish idiosyncratic events like a weak nominee from long-term political trends like ideological change. If they make inaccurate inferences about the public and pursue these claims through their legislative agendas, they will be punished at the polls in the future.

For the president, the postelection analysis of the potential for policy change requires two related inferences. The first is the probability that the president can mobilize an electoral coalition around a specific policy change. The second is the ideological distance between the president and Congress. Presidents would like to change the policy agenda to make it more in line with their own preferences, but they do not have an incentive to try to make changes if they believe that they will fail. Thus a president claims a mandate when the election signals strong public support for his agenda or when doing battle with Congress will shift policy outcomes closer to his ideal point. A president does not declare a mandate when he expects that asking for policy changes will make him worse off than the status quo.

Throughout the history of American presidential elections we see three different cases. First, any time politicians believe that the likelihood of mobilizing a majority is greater than 50 percent, the president will declare a mandate and Congress will largely go along. Nobody wants to be on the wrong side of a winning issue. These elections tend to be landslides (large in terms of the magnitude of victory), national in character (the president's party gains and controls Congress), and follow campaigns oriented around sharp differences between the parties on policy issues. Examples of these "popular" mandates would be Franklin Roosevelt in 1932 and Lyndon Johnson in 1964.[6]

Second are "bargained" mandates. In these cases, the president's public backing is weaker, so the decision to declare a mandate depends upon partisan and ideological support in Congress as well as popular support. A president with policy preferences in between those of members of Congress and the status quo has nothing to lose by placing a policy change on the national agenda. He knows that he will encounter opposition, but the outcome will be closer to his own preferences. In 1992, for instance, Bill Clinton won only 43 percent of the popular vote, but Democrats controlled both the House and the Senate. The public opinion polls—and Perot voters—made it clear that jobs and deficit reduction were the major issues that voters cared about. Clinton had every incentive to claim a mandate and push his economic plan.[7]

Finally, there are presidents who do not declare mandates, and policy changes slowly and incrementally, if at all. These presidents win election without a compelling policy story to motivate the election results or a Congress amenable to policy change. They do not declare that voters elected them specifically to enact major policy changes. Examples would be John F. Kennedy, Jimmy Carter, and George H. W. Bush. Since 1828, roughly half of our new presidents have not declared mandates.

The following places the election of 2004 in this context. I argue that Bush falls into the "bargained" mandate group of presidents, though the magnitude of his victory is empirically weaker than presidents who have claimed mandates in the recent past. A Bush advisor noted that in his first term Bush had two insecurities: "there were a large number of people who did not view him as a legitimate president, and there was the specter of his father's loss."[8] After the peculiar circumstances of his first victory, reelection was validating for George W. Bush. Republican gains in Congress would further encourage Bush's mandate claim.

An Election Overview

The 2004 presidential election was bound to be contentious, given its historical place following the election of 2000. Four years earlier, Bush became president in a bitterly disputed election in which Democratic nominee Al Gore won the popular vote and Bush won a bare majority of the Electoral College vote. Many Democrats believed that the 2000 election was stolen, first by the Republican Party in Florida and then by a partisan Supreme Court. Forty percent of the public did not believe that Bush won the election legitimately.[9] For Republicans, the 2004 election would vindicate George W. Bush and put to rest any questions about whether he had the support of the American people. Democrats looked to the 2004 election to confirm that the 2000 electoral process had picked the wrong man.

While it is difficult to defeat a sitting president, several factors gave the Democratic Party hope. First, Bush was not exactly an incumbent running in a time of economic prosperity. Throughout the general election campaign, at least 55 percent of survey respondents said that they were "dissatisfied" with the way things were going in the United States.[10] By mid-August, more respondents claimed that economic conditions were getting worse than getting better; by mid-October fully half of those polled would say that economic conditions were getting worse.[11]

Second, wartime presidents tend to win reelection, but the American public was by no means unified on the war in Iraq. Throughout the campaign, nearly half of those surveyed responded that the war in Iraq was not worth it.[12] Casualties continued to mount as insurgents targeted U.S. troops as well as Iraqi civilians cooperating with the United States. By early September 2004, 1,000 U.S. soldiers had lost their lives in Iraq. Nearly 60 percent of voters characterized the stabilization and reconstruction of Iraq as going "very badly or somewhat badly." [13]

Finally, Bush's overall presidential approval ratings were comparatively low, hovering around 50 percent from the start of 2004 (see Table 6.1). A 50 percent average approval rating in the quarter before the election is modest compared to other incumbent presidents who have gained

Table 6.1

Bush Approval Ratings (percent)

"Do you approve or disapprove of the way George W. Bush is handling his job as president?"

Date	Approve	Disapprove
July 11	47	49
July 21	49	47
August 1	48	49
August 11	51	46
August 25	49	47
September 5	52	46
September 15	52	45
September 26	54	44
October 10	47	49
October 24	51	46
October 31	48	47
November 7	53	44

reelection. Ronald Reagan and Bill Clinton had average approval ratings closer to 55 percent. No president since Harry Truman has been reelected with a job approval rating below 50 percent. Furthermore, according to Gallup polls, perceptions of Bush are the most polarized along party lines for any president. "Never before have so many people of one party held such strongly positive views of a president at the same time that so many of the other party have held such strongly negative views."[14] A full 71 percent of Republicans strongly approved of Bush while 68 percent of Democrats disapproved of him. Polarizing political figures tend to be less successful at winning over moderate voters.

The Republicans, on the other hand, also had reason to be optimistic. First, foreign policy and national security were already major issues in the minds of voters. As in past elections, the Republican nominee was perceived as better able to handle issues of foreign policy and national security (see Table 6.2). The war in Iraq was controversial, but most opposition came from those who already identified strongly with the Democratic Party. To vote for the Democratic candidate, moderate voters would have to decide to abandon their commander in chief in wartime; they would have to reject "staying the course." Change would seem unpredictable and potentially worse; change could be construed as unpatriotic.

Second, Democratic nominee John Kerry was relatively unknown,

Table 6.2

Most Important Problem Facing the Nation (percent)

"What do you think is the most important problem facing this country today?"
(October 11–14, 2004)

War in Iraq/fear of war	23
Economy in general	21
Terrorism	16
Health care	13
Unemployment/jobs	12
Ethics/morals	6
National security	5
Education	5
Federal budget deficit	3

"Which candidate would better handle each of the following issues?"
(October 14-16)

	Kerry	Bush
The economy	51	45
The situation in Iraq	45	51
Terrorism	37	59
Health care	52	43
Budget deficit	53	42
Medicare	54	41
Social Security	52	42
Taxes	45	51

which would allow Republicans to take part in defining his candidacy. It is always more difficult for the challenger to control his image, particularly in the context of negative campaigning. Though the Democrats were perceived to be better at handling domestic political issues such as the economy, health care, and Social Security, Republicans were confident that they could use Kerry's Senate record to define him as a big-government liberal. Finally, Bush may be polarizing, but he knows how to mobilize the party faithful and raise money.

From the start, pollsters and pundits expected the outcome to be close. Whether because of the Iraq war, the closeness of the 2000 outcome, or the polarizing figure of George W. Bush, surveys showed heightened interest in the election. Voters perceived clear differences between the candidates and the political parties. The surge in voter participation and clear differences between the candidates meant that the election outcome would be viewed as informative, a true picture of the American political landscape.

Table 6.3

Support for Kerry and Bush Among Likely Voters (percent)

Date	Kerry	Bush	Nader
May 2–4	47	47	3
June 3–6	49	43	5
July 8–11	50	45	2
July 19–21	47	46	4
July 30–Aug. 1	45	51	2
Aug. 9–11	46	48	3
Aug. 23–25	46	48	4
Sept. 3–5	45	52	1
Sept. 13–15	40	54	3
Sept. 24–26	44	52	3
Oct. 1–3	49	49	1
Oct. 9–10	48	49	1
Oct. 14–16	44	52	1
Oct. 22–24	46	51	1
Oct. 29–31	49	49	1

The Horse Race and Battleground States

Table 6.3 shows the estimated vote shares for Kerry and Bush among likely voters throughout the general election campaign. Though the race was close, Bush retained a slight lead most of the time. Kerry received the smallest postconvention bounce in the polls for any challenger since George McGovern in 1972.[15] The largest margin of support for President Bush occurred in September immediately following the Republican convention. The race then became too close to call in October after Kerry did well in the three televised debates. Ralph Nader was on the ballot in thirty-five states plus the District of Columbia, though Democrats tried to discourage his candidacy by reminding voters that he may have cost Al Gore the election in 2000. As Table 6.3 shows, Nader's support among likely voters dwindled to roughly 1 percent as the election approached.

Throughout the campaign, pollsters and pundits argued that voters were "settled" and "partisan." Like Bush's approval ratings, voters appeared to be highly polarized and intense about their choices. By mid-July, fully 79 percent of surveyed voters reported that their minds were already made up; 64 percent felt that way in July 2000.[16] A Pew Research Center poll reported that 63 percent of voters said that it "really matters" who wins the election, up from only 45 percent in 2000. [17]

Table 6.4

Battleground States

State	Electoral College votes	2000 Election results
Florida	27	Bush
Pennsylvania	21	Gore
Ohio	20	Bush
Michigan	17	Gore
Minnesota	10	Gore
Wisconsin	10	Gore
Colorado	9	Bush
Iowa	7	Gore
Nevada	5	Bush
New Mexico	5	Gore
New Hampshire	4	Bush

Given the closeness of the race, both parties focused on a small number of states that had been closely contested in the 2000 presidential election. By the end of April, before the official end of the Democratic primary season, the campaigns had already spent $90 million dollars on political advertising in 18 battleground states.[18] By October the candidates were spending most of their time and resources in the 11 states listed in Table 6.4. The three states that loomed largest for the candidates were Florida—no surprise given the 2000 election—and Pennsylvania and Ohio. As the campaign wore on, Ohio was singled out as particularly significant because no Republican had ever won the presidency without it.

The Democratic Approach

John Kerry had the delegates to secure his party's nomination by mid-March. The candidacy of Howard Dean had made it clear that a majority of Democrats were passionately opposed to the war in Iraq. It was also clear that partisans disliked Bush so much that many Democrats would vote for "anybody but Bush," and perhaps even stomach a move to the center on the part of the Democratic nominee for the sake of winning. Kerry's choice of Senator John Edwards of North Carolina as his vice presidential running mate was widely viewed as smart. Edwards was Kerry's strongest opponent in the primaries and he appealed to voters in the rural Midwest and West.[19] Kerry reportedly asked Republican Senator John McCain to join a bipartisan ticket, but McCain refused and actively campaigned in support of the Bush-Cheney ticket.

The Democrats wanted to do two things: get domestic issues like the flagging economy back on the public agenda and convince voters that their candidate would be a plausible commander in chief in a dangerous world. Kerry would ask voters to unite to "make America stronger at home and respected in the world." Kerry also asked voters to question the integrity and leadership of President Bush and members of the Bush administration. As he said in his stump speech, "The W stands for wrong." Perhaps because only two sitting senators have ever made the leap from the Senate to the White House (Warren G. Harding and John F. Kennedy), the Kerry campaign made little reference to his time in the Senate. Instead, he was portrayed as a "combat veteran," "former prosecutor," "father," or, in a quest for National Rifle Association votes, "hunter." He made only one brief direct reference to his time in the Senate during his acceptance speech at the Democratic convention.

The Domestic Appeal

On domestic issues, Kerry's positions reflected long-standing Democratic Party positions. He supported abortion rights and federal funding for abortion and abortion counseling; he said that he would appoint only judges who would not overturn *Roe v. Wade.* Kerry opposed the death penalty except for terrorists. He argued against private-school vouchers as a drain on the public education system. With respect to the environment, Kerry argued for tougher vehicle emissions standards and opposed drilling in the Arctic National Wildlife Refuge. He opposed a constitutional amendment banning gay marriage and argued that individual states should decide. He would let gays serve openly in the military. Kerry offered a health plan that would expand health insurance coverage to all children and allow the importation of cheaper prescription drugs from Canada. He opposed giving younger workers the choice of placing their Social Security payroll tax in individual retirement accounts and opposed raising the retirement age or reducing payments.

At their convention in late July, Democrats sounded familiar themes. Former President Bill Clinton criticized Bush's tax cuts and attacked Republicans as the party of "concentrated wealth and power." Vice presidential nominee John Edwards spoke of "two different Americas," one for people who are "set for life," and the other for "most Americans who live from paycheck to paycheck." Both Clinton and former Democratic nominee Al Gore asked versions of Ronald Reagan's oft quoted line,

"Are you better off than you were four years ago?" At the National Convention, rising Democratic star and Illinois Senate candidate Barack Obama sounded a call to unity: "There is not a Black America and a White America and Latino America and Asian America. There's the United States of America." His keynote speech was well received by the delegates.

The War in Iraq and Its Impact on the Election

Polls showed weak support for the war in Iraq, particularly as casualties mounted and troops were stationed in Iraq longer than expected. In addition, members of the Bush administration offered two major reasons for going to war that were undermined by evidence after the end of major combat operations. Administration officials argued that Iraq was developing weapons of mass destruction and that Iraq worked with terrorist organizations such as Al Qaeda. American troops found no evidence of weapons of mass destruction after they invaded Iraq, and there appeared to be no evidence of a direct link between Saddam Hussein and the September 11 terrorist attacks, a conclusion reached in the final report of the September 11 Commission in June 2004.[20] In April 2004, before the report was issued, 50 percent of the public believed that the government's account before the war had been misleading.[21]

In the Senate, Kerry had voted to authorize the use of force; during the campaign, he explained that his decision was based upon faulty information and false assurances from the Bush administration. He had believed its story about weapons of mass destruction and he had believed that Bush would use force as a last resort. "Invading Iraq has created a crisis of historic proportions, and, if we do not change course, there is the prospect of a war with no end in sight. . . . Today President Bush tells us that he would do everything all over again, the same way. . . . Is he really saying that if we knew there were no imminent threat, no weapons of mass destruction, no ties to Al Qaeda, the United States should have invaded Iraq? My answer, resoundingly, is no."[22]

Kerry criticized the Bush administration for fighting a war "without a plan to win the peace." He repeatedly argued that he would seek more countries to share the burden of reconstruction. "We should have strengthened, not scorned, the alliances that won two world wars and the Cold War." [23] Kerry also argued that nuclear proliferation was the most important threat in the world, and that the United States needed to renew alliances and practice diplomacy to meet that threat. The war in Iraq, he argued, simply spawned more hatred and resentment against the United States. A Kerry administration would restore trust and credibility in the world.

Kerry worked to convince voters that he would be a strong and capable commander in chief. Though Kerry had protested the war in Vietnam after his return, he would be no dove in the face of terrorism. "I defended this country as a young man and I will defend it as president. Let there be no mistake: I will never hesitate to use force when it is required. Any attack will be met with a swift and a certain response."[24] He characterized President Bush's behavior as "stubborn incompetence."

Vietnam Remembered

Kerry was viewed as one of the strongest challengers to President Bush because he was a decorated combat veteran who would not be perceived as weak on foreign policy. Moreover, Kerry's combat service in Vietnam would contrast favorably with the domestic National Guard service of the incumbent president. But when Kerry returned from Vietnam, he protested the war. Republicans used Kerry's protest as evidence that he was indecisive and unreliable, and very likely a 1960s "liberal" in terms of his moral values. As it turns out, both campaigns were derailed and damaged by revisiting Vietnam.

In the weeks leading up to the Republican Convention at the end of August, a group of veterans called the Swift Boat Veterans for Truth emerged (see chapters 2 and 4), charging that Kerry lied about the circumstances leading to his three Purple Hearts, Bronze Star, and Silver Star. In paid television and radio advertisements and television appearances, they called Kerry a liar and criticized him for making antiwar statements as a young soldier after his return from Vietnam. The Kerry campaign released a television advertisement accusing the Bush campaign as the force behind the group of veterans questioning Kerry's war record: "Bush smeared John McCain four years ago. Now he's doing it to John Kerry. George Bush: Denounce the smear. Get back to the issues. America deserves better."[25] While the swift boat veterans originally claimed to be independent, their ties to the Republican Party soon emerged.[26] President Bush told reporters that he thought all such ads should be stopped. They were not.[27] Former veterans such as Senator John McCain (R-AZ) also condemned the swift boat advertisements.

President Bush had his own military service questioned. On September 8, right after the Republican Convention, both the "CBS Evening News" and "60 Minutes" broadcast a report that questioned President Bush's service in the National Guard based upon personal files of Bush's squadron commander. The documents suggested that Bush did not meet performance standards and that he received favorable treatment because of his political and family connections. Almost two weeks later, Dan Rather and CBS News admitted that they could not authenticate the documents that formed the basis of their report. The former National Guardsman who gave the network the memos admitted he lied.

By mid-September, the residue of the Vietnam controversies lingered. When asked whether President Bush was being honest in his statements about his National Guard service, 51 percent of respondents believed that he was "mostly telling the truth, but hiding something"; 20 percent of respondents believed that he was mostly lying.[28] Almost 50 percent (49%) of voters believed that Kerry was "mostly telling the truth, but hiding something" about his service in Vietnam; 13 percent believed that he was mostly lying. Kerry's image was definitely hurt by the attacks. Polls also showed that voters felt he spend too much time attacking President Bush and talking about the past, rather than outlining what he would do as president.[29]

Republican Appeal

Republicans had a two-part strategy: portray Kerry as a flip-flopping liberal and emphasize Bush as a strong and decisive leader who delivered results, particularly in foreign policy. They contrasted Vice President Dick Cheney's record with the inexperience of Democratic vice presidential nominee John Edwards, a first-term senator. Whereas the Democrats seldom mentioned President Bush by name at their convention, Republicans readily criticized John Kerry. At the Democratic convention, the most frequently used words were "jobs," "war," and "health care."[30] At the Republican convention, the most frequently used words were "freedom," "war," and "Kerry."[31]

The sign on the office door of Bush's communication director read "It's the hypocrisy, stupid!" a play on the 1992 Clinton campaign mantra "It's the economy, stupid!" The Republican war room pored over Kerry's Senate record and speeches, looking for liberal votes and changes in position. Republican ads would often begin with a stated position by

John Kerry, and then evidence that he had switched positions. They even used Kerry himself making statements like "I actually did vote for the $87 billion [bill funding U.S. troops] before I voted against it." Former New York mayor Rudy Giuliani's convention speech was typical: "Maybe this explains John Edwards's need for two Americas—one where John Kerry can vote for something and another where he can vote against that same thing." Starting in February, when it became clear that Kerry would be the eventual Democratic nominee, Republicans also began attacking Kerry as "out of sync" with most voters and "culturally out of step with the rest of America," an extreme liberal from Massachusetts. As Bush would say on the campaign trail, "There is a mainstream in America and my opponent sits on the far-left bank."

On the issues, the centerpiece of the Republican campaign was the international fight against terrorism. This formed the substance of the vast majority of Republican advertisements, convention speeches, stump speeches, and imagery of George W. Bush. Given public dissatisfaction with the economy, the campaign chose to focus on national security rather than jobs. To the extent that domestic politics entered into the campaign, the Republicans directed attention to social issues like the ban on gay marriage in order to rally social conservatives.

Republicans on Domestic Issues

Bush's domestic policy agenda was almost the polar opposite of the positions outlined by Senator Kerry. Bush opposed abortion, except in cases of rape, incest, or when a woman's life is endangered, and he opposed federal funding for abortion. He supported the death penalty, vouchers for private school tuition, and federal funding for education tied to the results of school testing (as in his 2002 "No Child Left Behind" Act). He rejected the Kyoto Protocol on limiting global warming gases and proposed opening the Arctic National Wildlife refuge to drilling. Bush opposed gay marriage and supported a constitutional amendment defining marriage as the union of a man and a woman. He argued against patients' right to sue federally regulated health plans and proposed capping medical malpractice awards. He signed a law giving the elderly limited prescription drug coverage under Medicare. Finally, he favored changing Social Security to give younger workers the right to set up personal retirement accounts with some of their Social Security payroll tax.

Bush framed his policy agenda using two broad themes. First, he placed himself and John Kerry in the familiar big government–less government framework. "His [Kerry's] politics of tax and spend, of expanding government rather than expanding opportunity, are the politics of the past. We are on the path to the future and we are not turning back."[32] At the convention, Bush stated "I am running with a compassionate conservative philosophy: that government should help people improve their lives, not try to run their lives."[33] Second, Bush talked about his agenda as building an "ownership society," promoting ownership of health care plans, homes, and personal savings accounts using Social Security taxes.

The Republican convention featured centrist speakers like California governor Arnold Schwarzenegger, Arizona senator John McCain, and former New York City mayor Rudy Giuliani. To the extent that they mentioned the economy and jobs, the speakers were upbeat and optimistic. Schwarzenegger, for instance, said "To those critics who are so pessimistic about our economy, I say don't be economic girlie men! The U.S. economy remains the envy of the world." The Republican Party platform was much more conservative than the speakers, denouncing legalized abortion, gay marriage, and other forms of legal recognition for same-sex couples.[34]

Republicans on Foreign Policy

As indicated earlier in this book, Bush's first term was fundamentally altered by the September 11, 2001, terrorist attacks. The first few months of the first term were marked by tepid public support and little policy success. But within days of the attacks on the World Trade Center, Bush's popularity rose to 90 percent, the highest rating received by a president since Gallup started conducting popularity polls in the 1950s. Bush shifted his focus to foreign policy, calling the war on terrorism the purpose of his administration.

Within months after the attacks, he sent U.S. forces to Afghanistan to topple the Taliban regime for harboring terrorists like Osama bin Laden. In his 2002 State of the Union address, he turned his attention elsewhere, charging that states like Iraq, Iran, and North Korea "and their terrorist allies constitute an axis of evil, arming to threaten the peace of the world. By seeking weapons of mass destruction, these regimes pose a grave and growing danger. They could provide these arms to terrorists, giving them the means to match their hatred." When Iraq refused to cooperate with UN weapons inspectors, the U.S. Congress (including Senators Kerry and Edwards) passed a resolution authorizing Bush to use military force if necessary to enforce compliance with UN resolutions concerning weapons inspections. The UN Security Council threatened "serious consequences" if Iraq did not cooperate. Iraq finally allowed weapons inspections to resume.

Despite the return of weapons inspectors, the Bush administration argued that Saddam Hussein was not fully cooperating. President Bush sought a UN resolution authorizing the use of force against Iraq. Several countries and key members of the UN Security Council—including France, Germany, Russia, and China—wanted to give weapons inspections more time and strongly opposed the use of force without UN approval. NATO was similarly divided, with the United States, Britain, and Spain pitted against Germany and France. Bush's threats of war with Iraq were greeted with mass popular protests at home and abroad.

Dissent in the international community and popular protest at home did not deter the Bush administration. When the UN Security Council would not authorize the use of force, the United States, Great Britain, and a small number of allies pursued military action on their own. In March 2003, U.S. and British forces invaded Iraq and forced Saddam Hussein from power. President Bush argued that national security is best served by taking preemptive military action. In the case of Iraq, Bush argued that Saddam Hussein should be deposed before he had the chance to develop and sell weapons of mass destruction to terrorists.

Two months after the invasion, Bush declared the official end to combat operations. At that time, three-quarters of Americans approved of the president's handling of the situation in Iraq. Unfortunately the transition from dictatorship to democracy in Iraq proved more difficult than expected. After the declared end to major combat operations, American soldiers continued to be targeted by insurgents, who used grenade attacks, ambushes, and suicide bombings to fight against the American "occupation" of Iraq. Within six months of Bush's victory speech, American casualties after the end of combat operations exceeded the total number of casualties during the war. Bush's approval ratings began a long decline.

The Bush campaign framed the war in Iraq as part of a larger war against global terrorism. The Republican convention, held in New York City, invoked images of the president's response to the September 11 attacks—the president hugging NYC firemen, holding a bullhorn to shout support above the ruins of the World Trade Center towers. The first night of the convention featured September 11 widows, former Mayor Giuliani, and New York City police commissioner Bernard Kerik (later nominated to replace Tom Ridge as secretary of the Department of Homeland Security, a nomination withdrawn after he was accused of a number of unethical acts). Senator John McCain quoted Franklin Roosevelt, to say that the war against terrorism is this generation's "rendezvous with destiny."

In his stump speeches, Bush told voters "This will be the first election since September 11, 2001. Americans will go to the polls in a time of war and ongoing threat to our country. The enemies who killed thousands of innocent people are still dangerous and determined to strike us again. The outcome of this election will set the direction of the war against terror, and in this war, there is no place for confusion and no substitute for victory."[35] He argued that the United States was safer and better off for getting rid of an "outlaw dictator." As for the United Nations, Bush argued, "The Security Council promised serious consequences for his defiance and the commitments we make must have meaning."[36]

Bush charged that Kerry lacked the resolve to handle the war. "Senator Kerry has turned his back on 'pay any price and bear any burden,' and he has replaced those commitments with 'wait and see' and 'cut and run.'"[37] The Republicans attacked Kerry as reactive and weak. Cheney argued "A good defense is not enough, so we've gone on offense. . . . Senator Kerry seems to object. He's even said that by using our strength we are creating terrorists and placing ourselves in great danger. That is a fundamental misunderstanding of the way the world works. Terrorist attacks are not created by the use of strength. They are a result of the perception of weakness."[38]

Character as a Selling Point

From the start, Republicans emphasized Bush's decisiveness and willingness to take a stand, one of his greatest selling points with the public. Table 6.5 shows the results of two Gallup poll surveys about presidential character, the first taken right after the Democratic convention and the second taken three weeks before the general election. President Bush is clearly perceived to be more decisive and resolute, the candidate who "does not change his positions on issues for political reasons." Senator Kerry's strong points—like previous Democratic nominees Gore and Clinton—are his perceived intelligence and caring about ordinary people.

Table 6.5

Character Traits (percent)

	July/August		October	
	Kerry	Bush	Kerry	Bush
Cares about the needs of people like you	52	4	51	43
Will unite the country and not divide it	52	39	46	44
Is honest and trustworthy	46	44	42	47
Shares your values	48	46	46	49
Expresses himself more clearly	—	—	57	38
Is intelligent	—	—	49	35
Has a clear plan for solving the country's problems	—	—	44	44
Is a strong and decisive leader	42	52	38	57
Can manage the government effectively	39	49	—	—
Stands up for what he believes in	35	52	—	—
Does not change his positions on issues for political reasons	33	54	—	—
Is believable	—	—	40	50

Source: www.gallup.com.

Note: Respondents were asked, "Thinking about the following characteristics and qualities, please say whether you think each one applies more to John Kerry or more to George W. Bush." A small percentage volunteered "both," "neither," or "no opinion." The July/August poll was taken right after the Democratic convention. The October polls were taken two to three weeks before the election. Blanks indicate that the character trait was not repeated.

Kerry never closed the gap between himself and Bush with respect to leadership qualities. If anything, the gap widened as the campaign progressed. In addition, Bush gained ground on those traits where Kerry initially led. For instance, respondents initially perceived Kerry to be more honest and trustworthy, but by October, Bush was perceived to be most trustworthy. In late July, there was a 13-point difference in the percentage of respondents who believed that Kerry was more likely to unite the country rather than divide it. By mid-October, Kerry led by only 2 percent of respondents. It seems that the Republican campaign to contrast Bush's resolve with Kerry's "flip-flopping" on the issues worked.

The Ground War (in America)

The 2004 election may be remembered as the return of the "ground war." Though both campaigns spent generously on television advertising, they also embarked upon an unprecedented effort to get out the vote. Given the polarized nature of the electorate, and fewer swing voters than usual, both sides sought to go door-to-door, and website-to-website, to find supporters and get them to the polls. "We're going to find every Bush voter, we're going to call them, we're going to write them, we're going to knock on their doors, and when the day comes, we're going to physically take them to the polls," said Ralph Reed, a regional coordinator for the Bush-Cheney campaign.[39] After an Electoral College victory stemming from a mere 537 votes in Florida in 2000, both sides seemed to get the message that every vote counts. New campaign finance rules allowed more soft money contributions to flow to get-out-the-vote activities.

Across the country, boards of elections saw a record surge in the number of new voter registrations. In Cleveland, for instance, the Cuyahoga County Board of Elections registered 230,000 new voters, more than double the number of new registrations in 2000 when President Bush won Ohio by little over 165,000 votes.[40] Registration in Tallahassee, Florida, was up over 20 percent. In addition, 23 states offered some form of early voting. About eight other states offered absentee balloting in which voters were free to ask for an absentee ballot and cast it immediately after filling it out. In some counties in Florida, about 15 percent of voters had cast their ballots before Election Day.[41] Both parties braced themselves in anticipation of a close election outcome.

Republicans questioned the record levels of registration in swing states. Democrats argued that Republicans were trying to suppress turnout. Party officials in states like Ohio recruited citizens to serve as monitors on Election Day, to guard against the possibility of fraud on the part of newly registered Democrats. The Democratic Party in Ohio filed a legal suit against the Republican secretary of state attempting to block his rulings on how to handle provisional ballots. In Florida, Democrats filed several lawsuits against Republican officials. In New Mexico, Republicans sued the Democratic secretary of state to require that new voters show identification at the polls.[42]

The McCain-Feingold campaign finance reform law banned soft money contributions to the political parties but allowed unlimited contributions to 527s like Swift Boat Veterans for Truth, MoveOn.org Voter Fund, and America Coming Together. The 527s are allowed to raise unlimited money for any political purpose, as long as there is no coordination with the candidates or political parties. Initially, Democratic-leaning

527s raised the most money, but Republican-oriented groups quickly caught up and outspent the pro-Democratic groups by 3 to 1 in the final weeks of the campaign.[43] The groups may not have been explicitly tied to the political parties, but they ran extremely negative ads against the candidates. The 527s were lauded for voter registration but criticized for negative campaigning.

The Debates in Perspective

By September, Bush's job approval ratings were climbing. In mid-September, Gallup polls showed Bush with a 14-point lead over Kerry among likely voters. Bush was shifting the campaign from a referendum on his administration to a referendum on John Kerry. Senator Kerry brought in some of President Clinton's former aides to help refocus his campaign. But Kerry soon saved himself and his campaign over the course of three televised presidential debates in late September and early October.

The first debate, on foreign policy, was widely perceived as a win for Kerry, even among some Bush supporters. Kerry appeared self-assured and knowledgeable; Bush seemed irritated and uncomfortable, and Bush often appeared defensive. For instance, when Bush stated that the war in Iraq had been launched as a response to the September 11 terrorist attacks, Kerry reminded the president: "Saddam Hussein did not attack us. Osama bin Laden attacked us." The president muttered "Of course I know Osama bin Laden attacked us. I know that." On the Iraq war, Kerry repeated his mantra that "It's one thing to be certain, but you can be certain and be wrong . . . and certainty can sometimes can get you into trouble."[44] Bush attacked Kerry's character, saying, "You cannot lead if you send mixed messages. Mixed messages send the wrong signal to our troops."[45] Moreover, Bush said, "What my opponent wants you to forget is that he voted to authorize the use of force. And now he says it's the wrong war at the wrong time at the wrong place . . . what message does that send our troops? What message does that send our allies? What message does that send the Iraqis?"[46]

Polls after the first debate showed that the public continued to believe in Bush as a man of his word who would make the right decisions to protect the country from another terrorist attack. Overall, however, Kerry's favorability ratings improved and for the first time since late August, the horse race was too close to call. Kerry seemed to have mounted the challenger's hurdle of establishing himself as a plausible commander in chief.

Throughout the second and third debates, Bush attempted to portray Kerry as a big-government liberal. "He's been a senator for 20 years. He voted to increase taxes 98 times."[47] He repeatedly referred to Kerry as a politician without a moral compass. "People love America. Sometimes they don't like the decisions made by America. But I don't think you want a president who tries to become popular and does the wrong thing."[48] Kerry pledged not to raise taxes for families with an income under $200,000, saying, "The president is just trying to scare everybody here with throwing labels around."[49] He tried to shift the focus from character to the poor economy. "This is the first president in seventy-two years to preside over an economy in America that has lost jobs—1.6 million jobs."[50]

In the only vice presidential debate, on October 5, Vice President Cheney was unapologetic about the administration's policy in Iraq. "The world is safer today because Saddam Hussein is in jail, his government's no longer in power, and we did exactly the right thing." Senator Edwards responded, "Mr. Vice President, you are still not being straight with the American people." Like Kerry, Edwards charged that Republicans conflated the threat of Al Qaeda with the threat from Saddam Hussein. Vice President Cheney asserted "You're not credible on Iraq because of the enormous inconsistencies that John Kerry and you have cited time after time during the course of the campaign. Whatever the political pressures at the moment requires, that's where you're at . . . [T]here's no indication at all that John Kerry has the conviction to successfully carry through on the war on terror." [51]

Final Projections

The presidential debates boosted John Kerry enough to make the race competitive in the final weeks of October. As the race came down to the wire, both candidates shifted resources to concentrate on 11 swing states, spending $60 million on advertising in the last week before the election.[52] In television ads and speeches, the Bush campaign focused on the fight against terrorism. The Kerry campaign, on the other hand, promised that Senator Kerry would better manage the war in Iraq and also fight for the middle class, creating jobs and a viable health care system. Television advertisements played on voter fears and anxieties. Kerry ads showed images of soldiers wounded in Iraq, parents of soldiers killed in Iraq, and headlines about continued violence and beheadings. The Bush campaign ran ads with images of terrorists and September 11th, asking, "Would you trust Kerry?"[53]

Late developments in the war on terror did not boost either candidate. One week before the election, the interim government in Iraq warned the United States that nearly 380 tons of powerful explosives were missing from a military installation that was supposed to be secured by U.S. forces.[54] Kerry called the disappearance of the explosives "one of the great blunders of Iraq," another instance where Bush's incompetence put troops at risk. On October 29, the Arabic language network Al Jazeera aired a videotape of Osama bin Laden directly addressing the American people. Mr. bin Laden did not threaten new terrorist attacks but said, "Your security is not in the hands of Kerry or Bush or Al Qaeda . . . any state that does not mess with our security naturally guarantees its own security." Both candidates immediately and similarly responded that the United States would not be "intimidated." When Senator Kerry lamented that Bush had erred in not using American forces to hunt down and kill bin Laden in Afghanistan, Bush accused him of politicizing national security.

As Election Day approached, the candidates, voters, and journalists braced themselves for another potentially long and drawn-out election. Since 2000, over 25 percent of all election jurisdictions changed voting systems.[55] Officials worried about vote fraud, particularly with new electronic voting systems. The Help America Vote Act of 2002 allowed voters whose names could not be found on the voter rolls to cast provisional ballots. These ballots would be counted separately, one by one, after the election. Officials worried that the numbers of new voters, and provisional ballots, might be enough to swing the election in key states. In the final days, both campaigns focused on three swing states—Florida, Ohio, and Pennsylvania. Whoever won two of the three largest swing states would be difficult to beat.

The Outcome

As expected, the election came down to the state of Ohio. President Bush won Florida and Senator Kerry won Pennsylvania. By 1:00 A.M. November 3, roughly half of the news networks gave Ohio to President Bush; half did not. Nobody was willing to call the election, after the embarrassment of prematurely calling the 2000 election. At 2:30 A.M. John Edwards took the stage to announce that Kerry would not concede until all votes were counted in Ohio, including provisional ballots. By 11:00 A.M., however, Kerry called Bush to concede. In his concession speech, Kerry noted that "it is clear that even when all the provisional ballots are counted, which they will be, there won't be enough outstanding votes for us to be able to win Ohio."

In the end, Bush won the race with almost 51 percent of the popular vote to Kerry's 48 percent. Bush won 286 Electoral College votes; Kerry won 252. Bush won the South and West (except California, Washington, and Oregon) while Kerry won the upper Midwest and Northeastern states. Bush lost only one state that he had carried in 2000—New Hampshire—and he gained both Iowa and New Mexico. Bush won among seniors, Catholics, evangelicals, and veterans. He closed the gender gap. Only 43 percent of women had voted for him in 2000; in 2004, 48 percent of women voters cast a ballot for Bush. Republicans retained control over both chambers of the Congress. They gained four seats in the Senate, for a party balance of 55 to 44 in their favor. Republicans also retained control of the House, gaining four seats for a total of 231 seats compared to 200 seats for the Democrats. The only Senate incumbent to lose was the Democratic Party minority leader, Tom Daschle of South Dakota.

One of the biggest stories was the large turnout. Fifty-six percent of the voting-age population turned out to vote (76% of all *registered* voters), the largest turnout since 1968. The conventional wisdom was that higher turnout would benefit the Democrats, since more members of the public identified themselves as members of the Democratic Party. Moreover, the assumption was that more elderly and poor voters would be registered, and these kinds of voters tend to support the Democratic Party. But in 2004, Bush's chief campaign advisor Karl Rove pushed to raise Republican turnout, especially among evangelical Christians. Though more first-time voters voted for Kerry, Republican turnout was crucial for Bush's win.

Interpretations of Victory: A Mandate?

In many ways, the outcome was not a surprise. The race was expected to be close, particularly in a small number of swing states, and turnout was expected to be much higher than usual. All but three states fell into the same column as 2000. Yet journalists, pundits, and voters had readied themselves for another long and drawn out search for a winner. Instead, Bush won a solid and uncontested victory in both the popular vote and the Electoral College. Republicans gained a firm majority in the Senate. For Bush and his supporters, his reelection was validating. After his reelection, one headline read, "President Feels Emboldened, not Accidental, After Victory."[56]

At his first press conference after the election, a reporter asked President Bush if he felt more "free to do any one thing in a second term that perhaps you were politically constrained from doing in the first." Bush replied:

> I feel it is necessary to move an agenda that I told the American people I would move . . . you go out and you make your case. And you tell people this is what I intend to do. And after hundreds of speeches and three debates and interviews and the whole process where you keep basically saying the same thing over and over again that when you win there is a feeling that the people have spoken and embraced your point of view. And that's what I intend to tell the Congress. That I made it clear what I intend to do as the president . . . and the people made it clear what they wanted. Now let's work together. . . .
>
> You asked do I feel free. Let me put it to you this way. I earned capital in the campaign, political capital. And now I intend to spend it. . . . And I'm going to spend it for what I told the people I'd spend it on, which is, you've heard the agenda: Social Security and tax reform, moving this economy forward, education, fighting and winning the war on terror. . . .[57]

Though he does not use the word "mandate," Bush claims that the election provided him with a political opportunity and he links this opportunity to his ability to mobilize voters. Bush's advisors noted the marked increase in voter turnout and the fact that Bush received more votes than any previous president. The political parties were polarized in terms of their issue agendas and the candidates made clear their differences throughout the campaign. Fellow Republicans pointed to polls showing that moral values and the war against terrorism were high priorities for Bush supporters.

Bush did not declare a mandate because of a landslide popular victory. Presidents like Franklin Roosevelt, Lyndon Johnson, and Ronald Reagan each won elections where they garnered at least 90 percent of the Electoral College vote and over 55 percent of the popular vote. Bush's percentage of the popular and Electoral College votes in 2004 is below average for presidents since 1828, particularly for presidents since Franklin Roosevelt.[58] At the same time, Bush now has evidence that he can mobilize a majority of voters. As an incumbent, he knows that those

Table 6.6

Exit Polls: Most Important Issue to Your Vote

	Percent	Percent voting for Bush among those who selected issue as most important	Percent voting for Kerry among those who selected issue as most important
Moral values	22	80	18
Economy/jobs	20	18	80
Terrorism	19	86	14
Iraq	15	26	73
Health care	8	23	77
Taxes	5	57	43
Education	4	26	73

Source: Edison/Mitofsky nationwide survey of voters leaving the polls; voters were asked to choose one of these seven alternatives as most important to their vote for president.

who voted for him know exactly how he governs and what he fights for. Moreover, the parties seem fairly evenly matched in terms of getting votes at the presidential level—hence the close outcomes in 2000 and 2004. Bush may have a slim margin of public support, but most of it appears fairly stable.

In addition, the Republican Party gained seats and further consolidated their control over the House and Senate in 2004. It seems plausible that Bush's claim emerged from his belief in his ability to mobilize voters in combination with his perceived support among Republicans in Congress. He figures that the Republican Congress can compensate for coming up short when he lacks majority support around the country for any of his programs. What does he have to lose by pushing further for his agenda?

What remains a matter of controversy is the substance of his mandate. Bush's immediate response (quoted above) was to claim legitimacy for his entire policy agenda. But headlines proclaimed, "Bush Rides Moral Issues, Terror Fears to Second Term."[59] Did polls provide evidence that Bush won because voters favored his policy positions?

Voters were surely not expressing support for Bush's handling of the war in Iraq. According to polls, a near majority of the public thinks it was a mistake to send troops to Iraq. The country was almost equally divided as to whether Bush or Kerry would do a better job handling the situation in Iraq. As an alternative, some claimed that moral values were the defining issue of the election.[60] Table 6.6 shows the exit poll data on which this claim was based. Some 22 percent of voters said that "moral values" mattered most in their decision, and fully 80 percent of those individuals voted for Bush. But almost as many voters—20 percent—cited the economy as the issue that mattered most and 80 percent of those individuals cast their ballots for Kerry. Voters were asked a closed-ended question, which means that answers were determined in part by the content of the list. On most social issues, the electorate was polarized, not unified, in sending a message to politicians.

The one thing that consistently surfaced in exit polls is that voters said they trusted Bush to keep the country safe from terrorists: 49 percent of voters said they trusted only President Bush to handle terrorism; 31 percent said that they trusted only John Kerry.[61] Of those who said that they trusted only Bush, 97 percent voted for him. Polls showed that some of the narrowing of the gender gap was caused by married women's views about which candidate would keep the country safe. The Republican strategy of focusing on the war against terrorism, as well as Bush's leadership ability, apparently worked.

But fear of terrorism may not hold a coalition together for long. Bush will find that relying on one's party in Congress does not always work. The Republican Party base will attempt to extract all that was promised to them during the election. Unified control means clear accountability if things go wrong. Bill Clinton's mandate in 1992 was followed by major losses for the Democratic Party in the 1994 midterm elections.

The 2004 election is a defining election in the sense that the results reinforce what we have learned from the presidential elections since the late 1980s—the two parties are polarized and very competitive at the presidential level. In 2004 the Democrats had to argue that it would be scarier to stay the course than to change. In the post-9/11 world, running against an incumbent president admired for strong leadership proved to be more difficult than expected.

Notes

1. Transcript of President Bush's News Conference at the White House, *New York Times,* November 5, 2004, A16–17.

2. Richard Ellis and Stephen Kirk, "Presidential Mandates in the Nineteenth Century," *Studies in American Political Development* 9, no. 1(1995): 117–86.

3. See, for example, Robert Dahl, "The Myth of the Presidential Mandate," *Political Science Quarterly* 105 (1990): 355–72; Stanley Kelley, *Interpreting Elections* (Princeton, NJ: Princeton University Press, 1983); Theodore J. Lowi, "Presidential Democracy in America," *Political Science Quarterly* 109 (1994): 401–38; and Wil-

liam Riker, *Liberalism Against Populism* (San Francisco: W.W. Freeman, 1982). For arguments about the role of issues relative to considerations like partisanship and candidate qualities, see James Campbell, *The American Campaign: U.S. Presidential Campaigns and the National Vote* (College Station: Texas A&M University Press, 2000); Warren E. Miller and J. Merrill Shanks, *The New American Voter* (Cambridge, MA: Harvard University Press, 1996); Samuel L. Popkin, *The Reasoning Voter* (Chicago: University of Chicago Press, 1991); and Gerald Pomper, *Voters' Choice: Varieties of American Electoral Behavior* (New York: Dodd, Mead, 1975).

4. Patricia Heidotting Conley, *Presidential Mandates: How Elections Shape the National Agenda* (Chicago: University of Chicago Press, 2001).

5. Richard Fenno, *The U.S. Senate* (Washington, DC: American Enterprise Institute, 1982); Richard Fenno, "Adjusting to the U.S. Senate," in *Congress and Policy Change*, ed. Gerald Wright et al. (New York: Agathon Press, 1986), 123–47; Marjorie Hershey "Campaign Learning, Congressional Behavior, and Policy Change," in Wright et al. *Congress and Policy Change*, 148–72.

6. Other examples include Roosevelt in 1936 and 1940, Eisenhower in 1952, Nixon in 1972, and Reagan in 1980 and 1984.

7. Other bargained mandates include Woodrow Wilson in 1912 and Harry Truman in 1948.

8. Elisabeth Bumiller, "President Feels Emboldened, not Accidental, After Victory," *New York Times*, November 8, 2004, A1.

9. Janet Elder, "Poll Shows Americans Divided over Election," *New York Times*, December 18, 2000, A21. For an account of the political and legal issues surrounding the 2000 presidential election, see Howard Gillman, *The Votes That Counted* (Chicago: University of Chicago Press, 2001); and Cass Sunstein and Richard Epstein, eds., *The Vote: Bush, Gore, and the Supreme Court* (Chicago: University of Chicago Press, 2001).

10. Gallup poll trends reported at www.gallup.com/election2004.

11. Ibid.

12. Ibid.

13. *New York Times*/CBS News poll cited by Richard Stevenson and Janet Elder, "Public Warms to Edwards; Race Still Close," *New York Times*, July 17, 2004, A8.

14. Jeffrey Jones, "Views of Bush Reach New Heights of Polarization," October 21, 2004, Gallup news service, www.gallup.com.

15. Adam Nagourney, "Poll Shows Some Gains for Kerry, but Race Is Tight," *New York Times*, October 3, 2004, A1.

16. Robin Toner, "Voters are Very Settled, Intense, and Partisan, and It's Only July," *New York Times*, July 25, 2004, A1.

17. Cited in ibid.

18. Jim Rutenberg, "Ads Citing War Mix with Reports from the Front Lines," *New York Times*, May 2, 2004, p. 22; Matthew Ericson and Hugh Truslow, "The Great Ad Wars of 2004," *New York Times*, November 1, 2004, A22.

19. David Halbfinger, "Kerry Chooses Edwards, Citing Former Rival's Political Skill," *New York Times*, July 7, 2004, A1.

20. September 11 Commission report.

21. Harris polls reported in Tom Zeller, "The Iraq-Qaeda Link: A Short History," *New York Times*, June 20, 2004, 4.

22. Kerry quoted by Jodi Wilgoren and Elisabeth Bumiller, "In Harshest Critique Yet, Kerry Attacks Bush over War in Iraq," *New York Times,* September 21, 2004, A1.

23. Transcript of Kerry's acceptance speech, *New York Times,* July 30, 2004, P6.

24. Ibid.

25. Adam Nagourney and Jim Rutenberg, "Kerry TV Ad Pins Veteran's Attack Firmly on Bush," *New York Times,* August 23, 2004, A1.

26. Kate Zernike and Jim Rutenberg, "Friendly Fire: The Birth of an Anti-Kerry Ad," *New York Times,* August 20, 2004, A1; Jim Rutenberg and Kate Zernike, "Veterans Group Had G.O.P. Lawyer," *New York Times,* August 25, 2004, A1.

27. Elisabeth Bumiller and Kate Zernike, "President Urges All Outside Groups to Halt All Ads," *New York Times,* August 24, 2004, A1.

28. Adam Nagourney and Janet Elder, "Bush Opens Lead Despite Unease Voiced in Survey," *New York Times,* October 18, 2004, A1.

29. Ibid.

30. Matthew Ericson, "The Words Speakers Use," *New York Times,* September 2, 2004, P4.

31. Ibid.

32. "President Bush's Acceptance Speech to Convention Delegates in New York," *New York Times,* September 3, 2004, P4.

33. Ibid.

34. Robin Toner and David Kirkpatrick, "Social Conservatives Wield Influence on Platform," *New York Times,* August 31, 2004, A1.

35. Bush speech in Wilkes-Barre, Pennsylvania, October 23, 2004; "In His Own Words," *New York Times,* October 23, 2004, A13.

36. Transcript of speech to the United Nations General Assembly, *New York Times,* September 22, 2004, A6.

37. David Sanger, "Iraq Explosives Become Issue in Campaign," *New York Times,* October 26, 2004, A1.

38. Rick Lyman, "Cheney Says Kerry Suffers 'Fundamental Misunderstanding,'" *New York Times,* September 4, 2004, A10.

39. Joyce Purnick, "One-Doorbell-One-Vote Tactic Re-Emerges in Bush-Kerry Race," *New York Times,* April 6, 2004, A1.

40. Kate Zernike and Ford Fessenden, "As Deadlines Hit, Rolls of Voters Show Big Surge," *New York Times,* October 4, 2004, A1.

41. Rick Lyman and William Yardley, "Sharp Increase in Early Voting Alters Campaign," *New York Times,* October 29, 2004, A1.

42. James Dao, "As Election Nears, Parties Begin Another Round of Legal Battles," *New York Times,* November 18, 2004, A1.

43. David Greising, "Republican Leaning 527 Groups Quickly Gained Ground on Rivals," *Chicago Tribune,* November 4, 2004, 6.

44. Transcript of the candidates' first debate in the presidential campaign, *New York Times,* October 1, 2004, A16.

45. Ibid.

46. Ibid.

47. Transcript of the candidates' third presidential debate, *New York Times,* October 14, 2004, A20.

48. Ibid.

49. Transcript of candidates' second presidential debate, *New York Times,* October 9, 2004, A12.

50. Transcript of the candidate's third presidential debate, *New York Times,* October 14, 2004, A20.

51. "Excerpts from the Debate Between the Vice Presidential Candidates in Cleveland," *New York Times,* October 6, 2004, A20.

52. Adam Nagourney and Katharine Q. Seelye, "Bush and Kerry Focus Campaigns on Eleven Key States," *New York Times,* October 24, 2004, 1.

53. Jim Rutenberg, "Scary Ads Take Campaign to Grim New Level," *New York Times,* October 17, 2004, A1.

54. James Glanz et al., "Huge Cache of Explosives Vanished from Site in Iraq," *New York Times,* October 25, 2004, A1.

55. Andrew Romano, "How We'll Pick a President . . . And the Wild Cards Along the Way," *Newsweek,* October 18, 2004, 32.

56. Bumiller, "President Feels Emboldened, not Accidental, After Victory."

57. Transcript of President Bush's News Conference at the White House, *New York Times,* November 5 2004, A16–17.

58. Patricia Conley, "The 2004 Presidential Election: Strategy, Outcome, and Mandate." Paper presented at the annual meeting of the Midwest Political Science Association, April 7–10, 2005.

59. Jeff Zeleny, *Chicago Tribune,* November 4, 2004, 1.

60. Katherine Seelye, "Moral Values Cited as Defining Issue of the Election," *New York Times,* November 4, 2004, 4.

61. Louis Menand, "Permanent Fatal Errors," *The New Yorker,* December 6, 2004, 60.

7

Incumbency, Politics, and Policy

Detour or New Direction?

Jerome M. Mileur

In the final years of his presidency, Bill Clinton spoke often of building a bridge to the twenty-first century. In the 2000 presidential election, American voters, with an assist from the U.S. Supreme Court, chose a different partisan firm, the Republicans, and a new engineer, George W. Bush, for the job. This new party had a different design for the project that took the bridge in a new direction, one that promised to recast the landscape of American politics. In office, mixing compassionate conservatism with neoconservatism, Bush moved to transform the role of the national government both at home and abroad and in doing so framed the central question of the 2004 presidential contest: Was the first term of President Bush a detour or a new direction in the nation's politics?

George W. Bush of course entered the White House in 2001 after one of the more unusual presidential elections in the nation's history. Having lost the popular vote to the Democrat Al Gore by a half-million ballots, he won in the Electoral College by five votes—a victory that came only after the Supreme Court, in a 5–4 decision with justices voting along partisan lines, ended a recount of votes in Florida with the effect that the state's 25 electoral votes went to Bush.[1] The election had left the nation deeply divided between the religious right and other voters, between the big cities and rural areas, between working women and homemakers, gays and straights, union members and nonmembers—divisions that were made sharper by questions of the legitimacy of the Republican victory. Bush inherited a nation at peace, a balanced federal budget with a $5 billion surplus, and a strong economy that had boomed through the 1990s. In his campaign (and later in his inaugural), he put forward an ambitious program that included reform of education, Medicare, and Social Security; a reduction in the role of the national government in the delivery of social services, and greater reliance on the private sector and local government; a reduction in taxes for all Americans; and strengthening the nation's defense capacities including a missile defense system. But the question asked widely was how Bush—a minority president with narrow majorities in both houses of Congress—could and would govern.[2] With good times at home and abroad, many concluded that the prospects for the Bush administration realizing its program were uncertain at best and wondered about what the future held for the president and his party.[3]

On the tenth day of his presidency, Bush announced his faith-based initiative to provide federal funds to religious groups for the delivery of social services. But there was nothing dramatic in the first 100 days of his presidency, which saw withdrawals from international agreements and a number of changes in environmental and workplace rules friendly to business, as well as proposals for education reform and a $1.6 trillion tax cut—both of which were subsequently enacted by the Congress. In his State of the Union Address, Bush had decried an "axis of evil"—Iran, Iraq, and North Korea—declaring that their acquisition and export of weapons of mass destruction would no longer be tolerated, but no immediate actions followed. For the most part, Bush was seen as presiding over a competent, albeit very conservative, administration that was closely controlled and cautious in its actions. After 100 days on the job, he enjoyed a 62 percent approval rating, higher than either his father or Bill Clinton and close to the 67 percent of Ronald Reagan. By late summer, Bush continued to be seen as surrounded by strong people, but questions remained as to whether he would prove a strong leader.[4] Those questions ended on September 11, 2001, with the attacks on the World Trade Center and the Pentagon, when George W. Bush became a wartime leader in a fight against international terrorism.

After September 11, the Bush presidency was dominated by the war on terror. Militarily, it began with a successful assault upon the Taliban regime in Afghanistan, home to the architect of 9/11, Osama bin Laden, and his terrorist organization, Al Qaeda. Bush widened the battle dramatically with the invasion of Iraq, justified as part of the war on terror aimed at removing weapons of mass destruction possessed by the Iraqi regime of Saddam Hussein. Combat successes came quickly in both; but in Iraq the initial "victory" declared by the president was followed by months of occupation with growing American casualties, a determined and violent resistance movement, and shifting justifications for the U.S. action. Terrorism and Iraq framed the 2004 presidential campaign. The administration portrayed them as two parts of a single strategy to defeat terrorism, but Americans tended to see them as separate: a majority approved the president's actions to resist terrorism, while a majority disapproved of the preemptive war in Iraq.

As the election year arrived, the administration also faced a sluggish economy at home, one that had not responded quickly to several large tax cuts and had indeed seen more jobs lost than created during its time in office—the first administration since that of Herbert Hoover in the Great Depression to have a negative record of job growth. Tax cuts and military action in the Middle East had erased the projected $5.6 trillion ten-year budget surplus of 2000, replacing it with a $2.9 trillion deficit. Domestic actions to combat terrorism—the Patriot Act and the Department of Homeland Security—were controversial among Republican conservatives as well as liberal Democrats. In addition, while the administration could point with pride to its education reforms, there were continuing social concerns, on the left, about health care, prescription drugs, and Social Security, and, on the right, about gay marriage, abortion, and moral values. The path of the president to reelection seemed almost as heavily mined as the roadways of Iraq.

The Geography of Presidential Elections

The presidency is the one national office in the hands of the American people, but the election to fill it is not fought as a truly national campaign, as would be the case if the popular vote determined the winner. Instead, as Americans were made so aware in 2000, the winner is determined by vote of the Electoral College, in which each state has a vote equal to the number of senators and representatives it has in Congress. It is almost always the case that the popular vote and the electoral vote go to the same candidate, but there have been exceptions and the 2000 election proved to be one of them.[5] Candidates for president have always understood that campaigns for the office are organized and fought on a state-by-state basis. The political geography of the nation—the partisan predisposition and demographic character of individual states—defines the political playing field for candidates, much as the positioning of troops and armaments have historically defined the battlefield in war.

All strategy in presidential politics begins with geography: the calculus of which states are safe, which are unlikely to be won, and which remain as competitive. The latter become the battlegrounds for the election—battles that are fought in terms of local as well as national issues and demographics. By March 2004, no more than 20 states were considered to be battlegrounds by either the Bush or Kerry campaigns. By late spring the number had shrunk to no more than 17; by early fall it was 14; and by late October fewer than a dozen states were still thought to be in "play."[6] Both of the campaigns concentrated most of their spending on these states, to which they also devoted most of the time of their candidates, their families, and surrogates.

The geography of American politics changed dramatically in the aftermath of the 1960s: The passage of three major civil rights bills by the Democratic administration of Lyndon Johnson led many white voters in the South to abandon their historic allegiance to the Democrats; widespread protests of the war in Vietnam alienated many traditionally Democratic union members and working-class voters from the party; while the counterculture of sex, drugs, and rock and roll and the Supreme Court decision on abortion rights sparked moral concerns about the direction of the nation that gave rise to an active religious right.[7] But it was civil rights and race that, in the 1960s, ignited the movement in presidential politics away from the liberalism of the Democratic Party and toward a new conservatism in the GOP—a movement that began in, but was not confined to, the South.[8] In 1964, Barry Goldwater, who as a senator had voted against the Civil Rights Act of that year, had been the first Republican candidate for president to experiment with a "southern strategy," running as the champion of "states' rights" in an appeal to the traditionally Democratic voters in the South who understood it to mean support for the "southern way of life" with regard to race. Goldwater's bid for the White House was crushed in the massive landslide victory of Johnson, but he did win five of the states in the Deep South—Louisiana, Mississippi, Alabama, Georgia, and South Carolina—and in doing so, drew a new vote to the GOP. Unlike Dwight Eisenhower and Richard Nixon before him, who had run best in the urban South, Goldwater ran strongest in the so-called black belt counties of the rural South.[9]

The movement of white southerners away from the Democratic Party was furthered in 1968 by the third-party candidacy of Alabama Governor George Wallace, who echoed Goldwater's appeal to states' rights. Coming after the second and third civil rights bills had been passed by a Democratic administration in Washington as part of LBJ's Great Society—the Voting Rights Act of 1965 and the Housing Act of 1968—Wallace not only won support across the South but also from suburban working-class white voters in several northern states, who in the 1980s would come to be known as "Reagan Democrats."[10] By 1972 the southern strategy had become a staple of Republican presidential politics and had transformed the electoral map of the nation by adding the states of the Old Confederacy to those in the Great Plains and West to give the GOP what came to be known popularly as a "lock" on the Electoral College. Of the six presidential elections from 1968 to 1972, the Republicans won five.

In 1992 Bill Clinton rearranged the political geography of national politics in America.[11] As Figures 7.1 and 7.2 show, he expanded the geographic base of the Democratic Party significantly by adding three states to it that spanned the continent—New York, Illinois, and California—and which together cast almost 40 percent of the electoral vote needed to win. To this he added most of New England and the Mid-Atlantic states with 82 electoral votes, the Upper Midwest with 44 electoral votes, the other Pacific Coast states with 22 electoral votes, and New Mexico in the Southwest with 5 electoral votes. These states went to Clinton and Al Gore in each of the three presidential contests of 1992, 1996, and 2000, and in 2004, after the reapportionment of House seats following the 2000 Census, had 260 of the 270 electoral votes needed for election. All that was required for victory was to win a state or states with a total of ten electoral votes. Since Clinton's two successful runs for president, finding these ten votes has proven to be a far more daunting task for Democrats than it appears.

The new geography of the 1990s thus changed the turf battle in presidential politics. Strategically, it shifted the party battle to those states north of the Ohio River and along the northern and western banks of the Mississippi River. With the exception of Illinois, these are now the prime battleground states. This was a major strategic change for the Democrats, who through the 1970s and 1980s had been preoccupied with reclaiming at least some of their historic strength in the South. In the 1990s, the party interest in southern states became only that of identifying any targets of opportunity that could provide the ten additional electoral votes needed to win. Florida, with by far the largest number of electoral votes in the South, became the big prize and, in many ways, it seemed a winnable state for the Democrats. But the party could also find the electoral votes it needed in other parts of the country. In part, the story of the 2004 election was the search by Democrats for the additional electoral votes, and the parallel search by the Republicans to frustrate the Democrats and to add states to their column.

Figure 7.1 States Won by the Democrats at Least Twice in the Presidential Elections of 1976, 1980, and 1986

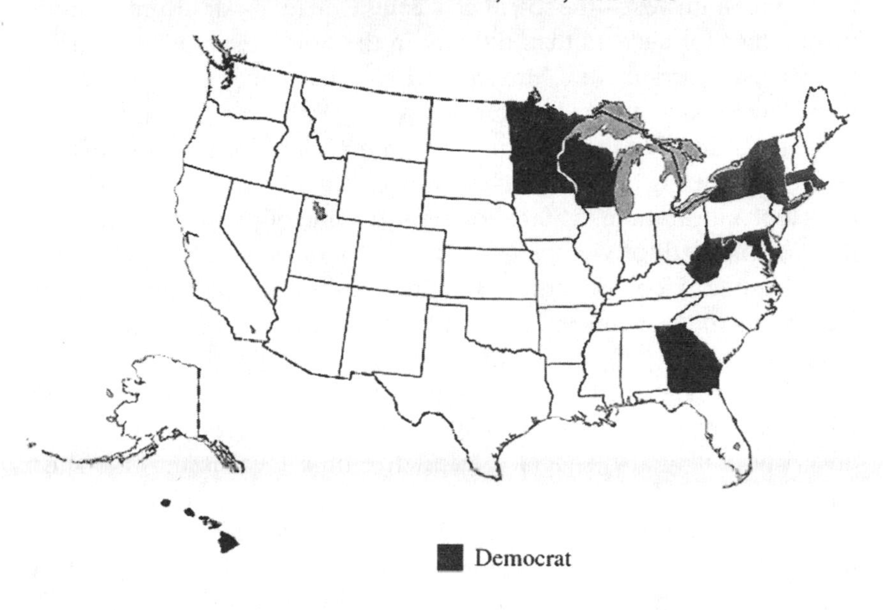

Figure 7.2 States Won by the Democrats at Least Three Times in the Presidential Elections of 1992, 1996, and 2000

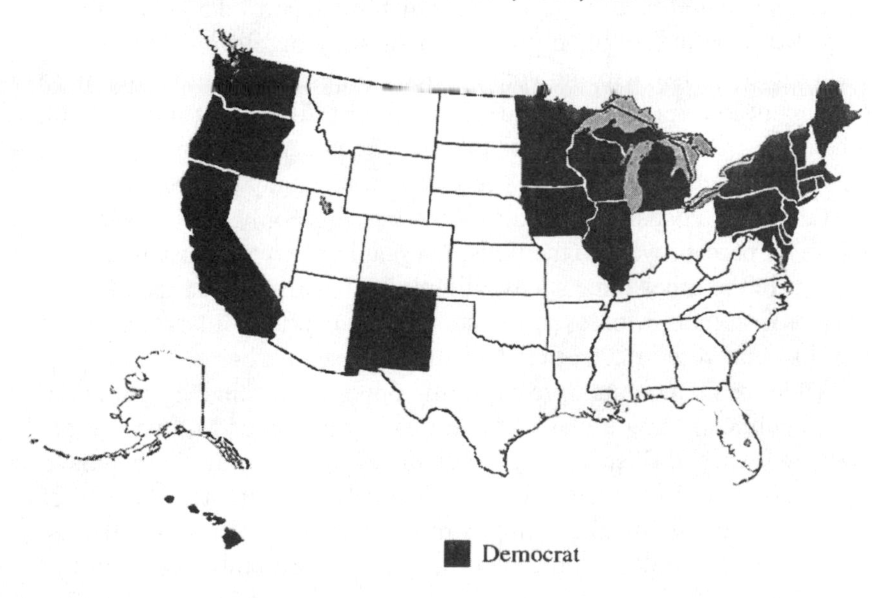

The Democratic strategists saw demographic changes in the states of the desert Southwest—the so-called Cactus Corridor—as affording more opportunity for success than did any in the South, except for Florida. Clinton had carried New Mexico and Nevada twice, while Gore had won New Mexico narrowly but lost Nevada. With the growing Hispanic populations in all of the states in the region, Colorado and even Arizona seemed promising, as well as New Mexico and Nevada, and the Democrats took aim at them in 2004 hoping that some of them would provide the votes needed for victory.

In New Mexico, Governor Bill Richardson led the charge for the Democrats in the Southwest, rallying Hispanics and Native Americans in support of the party, while Senator Pete Domenici did the same for the GOP. In Nevada, the Democrats hoped to capitalize on the large numbers of new residents, especially in the rapidly growing Las Vegas area, where they also sought to capitalize on a local issue—the Bush administration's decision to locate a nuclear waste dump at Yucca Mountain, less than 100 miles from Las Vegas. In Colorado, the Democrats hoped that, by having an Hispanic candidate for the U.S. Senate, they would increase the party vote for president among that population sufficiently to carry the state. Arizona, on the other hand, was always a long shot for them at best.

In the end, the Democrats lost all of these states, coming closest to victory in New Mexico and Nevada, which Bush carried 50–49 percent. They lost Colorado by five points and Arizona by eleven. The Democrats captured the Hispanic vote in each of these states: winning 56 to 60 percent in three of them and taking almost 70 percent in Colorado, where the party's candidate for the U.S. Senate was victorious, but it was not enough to carry John Kerry to victory in any of them. Overall, the turnout of Hispanics was disappointing: high only in New Mexico, where 74 percent went to the polls, but ranging between just 44 and 46 percent in the other three states, slightly higher in Nevada than in Arizona or Colorado. Moreover, President Bush captured a larger share of the Hispanic vote in 2004 than he had four years earlier.

While the Democrats were exploring opportunities in the Southwest, the Republicans saw a clash of cultures in the Upper Midwest, especially in Iowa and Wisconsin and possibly Minnesota, as affording them an opportunity to take states they had lost in 2000. All three states were part of the new political geography drawn in the Clinton years, though their partisan allegiance preceded his tenure. Iowa and Wisconsin had been reliably Democratic since the candidacy of Michael Dukakis in 1988, while Minnesota had long been the most loyal Democratic state in the nation, having given the party candidates its electoral vote in every election after 1972. Moreover, in the three contests from 1988 through 1996, the Democrats had carried these states by comfortable margins, averaging 56 percent of the vote in Minnesota and just under 54 percent in the other two. In 2000, however, Al Gore's margin of victory had dropped significantly in each of them, winning Minnesota by just 2 percent, Iowa by 1 percent, and Wisconsin by less than 1 percent.

The populations of these states are overwhelmingly white and predominantly Protestant, while each has a Catholic population of about 25 percent. The proportion of blacks and Hispanics in them is well below the average for those in the Old North, except for northern New England, as is the number of those who are of other than the Christian faith. Indeed, in 2004, the white vote ranged from a low of 90 percent in Wisconsin to a high of 96 percent in Iowa, while the Protestant and Catholic vote together ranged from 81 percent in Minnesota to 86 percent in Iowa. Christian conservatives, mainly white evangelicals, have long been an important force in Republican Party politics in these states and have been joined, especially in Wisconsin, by growing numbers of conservative Catholics, brought together by the common opposition to abortion, gay marriage, and stem cell research. In Iowa, three-fourths of the registered voters went to the polls, one-third of whom said they were evangelical Christians and voted for Bush by 7–1. Of these conservative Christians in western and northwestern Iowa, political scientist Dennis Goldford observed, "a Massachusetts Democrat is an elitist, someone who looks down on people of faith."[12] With solid backing from the state's Christian Coalition and the Right to Life Committee, Bush carried Iowa, albeit by the narrow margin of 0.89 percentage points—the first time a Republican had carried the Hawkeye State in 20 years. The Democrats won in the other two states in the upper Midwest, by 1 percent of the vote in Wisconsin and just 3 percent in Minnesota.

In the end, the wins and losses in these "opportunity" states did not affect the outcome of the election, nor did they occupy the primary attention of the campaigns. It was instead in the big states of Ohio, Pennsylvania, and Florida that the candidates spent most of their time and much of their money. Jimmy Carter had carried these states for the Democrats in 1976, with his biggest win in Florida by just over 5 percentage points. In 1980, all of them shifted decisively to the Republicans, as

Ronald Reagan carried Pennsylvania with almost 54 percent of the vote, Ohio with almost 55 percent, and Florida with almost 59 percent—a partisan swing of more than 20 percent from the vote four years earlier. In 1984, Reagan won these states even more decisively—Pennsylvania by almost 55 percent, Ohio by almost 59 percent, and Florida by 65 percent. In 1988, George H.W. Bush kept these states in the Republican column, taking Ohio with 55 percent of the vote, Florida with 61 percent, and Pennsylvania narrowly with just over 50 percent.

In 1992, as Bill Clinton was recasting the political map of the nation, two of these states swung to the Democrats, who carried Pennsylvania by 9 percentage points and Ohio by 2, and came close in the third, losing Florida by just 2 points. Four years later, Clinton and the Democrats carried them all by comfortable margins—6 percentage points in Ohio and Florida, 9 points in Pennsylvania. All of them were closely contested in 2000, with the Republicans winning in Ohio by just 4 percentage points, the Democrats in Pennsylvania by 5 points, and Florida going to the Republicans by a few hundred votes. From the outset, both campaigns seemed to agree that these were *the* battleground states in 2004, that the candidate who won two of them would take the election, and that the "opportunity" states were something of a sideshow intended as much as anything to divert the time and money of their opponent from the real arena.

Florida had been the closest and most contentious of these states in 2000, and it drew even more attention in 2004. The state's population had grown by 1 million in four years, with growing numbers of immigrants from Puerto Rico and Latin countries other than Cuba. In addition, a larger share of the Cuban population itself was born in the United States and lacked the intense hostility to Fidel Castro characteristic of older Cubans. These changes provided hope for the Democrats. But Governor Jeb Bush had led a four-year drive to register new voters as Republicans, from which his brother, the president, benefited. A high voter turnout in the Interstate 4 corridor across central Florida and in the Panhandle with a large population of veterans gave the president a solid 5-point victory, 52–47 percent. Bush captured a solid majority of the Hispanic vote, but it was his campaign's success among women, Catholics, and blacks that brought the victory. He won the women's vote by a narrow 50–49 percent, owing largely to concerns about terrorism and greater confidence in the president's ability to deal with it. Responding especially to moral issues, Catholics gave Bush 57 percent of their votes, almost equal to the 59 percent he won among Protestants. In addition, he captured 13 percent of the black vote, which while a relatively small share was appreciably higher than four years earlier.

The Keystone state of Pennsylvania may have seen more visits from the presidential candidates than any other, but while closer than 2000 the Democrats carried it with John Kerry edging President Bush by 2 percentage points, 51–49. The Bush campaign had targeted central Pennsylvania as the area in which the Republican vote could be increased significantly, and they worked it very hard. But high turnout in Philadelphia and its suburbs offset the GOP effort and gave the Democrats their margin of victory. Unlike Florida, Democrats won the women's vote decisively in Pennsylvania 54 percent to 45 percent. They also won 52 percent of the large Catholic vote, which accounted for 35 percent of those who went to the polls. Economic concerns were given as often as moral values as the primary determinant of voter choice, with Kerry taking 82 percent of those for whom the economy was paramount, and Bush 80 percent of those who cited moral values.

It was Ohio that provided the suspense on election night, where a high turnout kept some polling stations open until almost midnight. Both parties had recognized that the election could come down to Ohio, but the Republicans entered the campaign with a two-year organizational head start on the Democrats in compiling and refining voter files and in getting their forces in place on the ground. In March, as Kerry was winning the Democratic primaries that gave him the party nomination, the Bush campaign already had a dozen full-time staff in Ohio and a statewide organization with chairs in each of the state's 88 counties and also its 3,000 precincts. The Democrats had no paid staff and no organization, and would never attain the organizational coherence and capacity of the GOP.[13] But the Democratic constituency, located primarily in the state's big cities, enabled the party to focus its efforts more narrowly and, in combination with the independent efforts of labor unions and so-called 527 groups like America Coming Together, they succeeded in mobilizing a turnout that carried the state's six major cities by majorities that greatly exceeded those of the 2000 Gore campaign in most places.[14]

It was not enough. The Republicans produced a massive turnout of white evangelical voters in the western and southern farm areas of the state and also in the Appalachian area of southeastern Ohio. As in Pennsylvania, the primary reasons given by voters for their choice were concern about the economy and moral values, and again there was a deep division in their vote: 83 percent of the former for Kerry, 85 percent of the latter for Bush. But unlike Pennsylvania, terrorism as an issue weighed more heavily on Ohio voters than did Iraq, and Bush won 90 percent of those in the Buckeye state for whom terrorism was the major concern as opposed to 83 percent in the Keystone state. But as in Florida, the key to the Bush win was women and Catholics. He split the women's vote evenly with Kerry and won 55 percent of the Catholic vote, almost exactly the same as his 56 percent support from the Protestant voters. On the day after the balloting, John Kerry conceded that President Bush had won Ohio and, with it, the election.

And the Meaning of the Election Is . . .

The 2004 election had the "feel" of a big-time contest: a moment of decision that would have decisive and long-lasting consequences for the nation. The intense feelings that voters expressed, favorable and unfavorable, about President Bush, the extraordinary energy expended in the organizational efforts of both parties, the new sources of money that joined with the old to finance a vast advertising war in the battleground states, the prominent figures on both sides who announced their support for the other, all seemed to suggest that something new and electric was moving through the country, that change was afoot, and that America would be somehow different after November 2, 2004. But on election night, as the electronic maps of television news reporters displayed the national results—red states for Bush, blue states for Kerry—there was almost no change from the map of 2000. Only three small states changed sides: Iowa and New Mexico going to the Republicans, New Hampshire to the Democrats, each by 10,000 votes or less. Little, if anything, seemed to have changed.

Adlai Stevenson once quipped that, while others might aspire to comprehend the great complexities, he sought instead to understand the great simplicities. The great simplicities of 2004 election were twofold. The first is that the American electorate—that part of the population that turns out and votes—is about 80 percent white and 85 percent Christian. Win 60 percent of this vote, and you win the election—and to a remarkable degree, this is precisely what President Bush did. He took 58 percent of the white vote, 59 percent of the Protestant vote, 52 percent of the Catholic vote, 80 percent of voters for whom moral values was the issue that mattered most, and 91 percent of those for whom a strong religious faith was the quality that mattered most in a candidate. Since the 1930s, the Republicans have been the party of white America, while from their inception they have been the party of Protestant America, although since the 1970s the party has been transformed from one dominated by socially moderate mainline Protestant churches to one dominated by socially conservative evangelicals and increasing numbers of conservative Catholics.[15]

The second great simplicity was terrorism—the threat and the fear it provoked—for it framed the 2004 election. Iraq may have fanned the fires of anger and opposition to President Bush, and gay marriage may have angered Christian conservatives similarly, but it was voter concerns about terrorism that were in the end key for Bush after a campaign that was relentless, on the one hand, in casting the president as a strong leader with a solid moral core who could be trusted to do what he said and, on the other, in painting John Kerry as an indecisive "flip-flopper" who blew with the prevailing winds of public opinion because he lacked any foundational principles. In 2002, talking about the off-year congressional elections, Karl Rove, the architect of the Bush campaign, proclaimed that the GOP could "go to the country" with the issue of terrorism because voters "trust the Republican Party to do a better job of protecting and strengthening America's military might and thereby protecting America."[16] Rove's strategy for the 2004 presidential campaign proceeded on the same assumption and, by Election Day, it had produced a double-digit lead for Bush as the candidate more trusted by the public to deal with terrorism.

As an issue, terrorism served another purpose for the Bush campaign: it cross-pressured and frequently trumped the unfavorable issues. There had been over 1 million jobs lost during the first three years of the Bush presidency, many of them in northern "rust belt" states like Ohio where the election would likely be won or lost. Economic growth was sluggish, failing to respond to a succession of deep tax cuts; many had lost substantial savings in the stock market decline in the first year of the Bush administration, while others had lost everything in the collapse of Enron and other companies with close ties to the White House. Health care costs continued to rise while the number of people with health insurance declined. Massive tax cuts had widened the gap between rich and poor in America. Voters for whom the economy and jobs were most important—20 percent of the total—gave Kerry 80 percent of their votes, while voters for whom terrorism was the greatest concern—19 percent of the total—gave Bush 86 percent of their votes. The effect of terrorism as an issue was to neutralize that which the economy and job loss had on the outcome of the election.

While a powerful issue in the first presidential election since September 11, terrorism seems unlikely to play the same role in 2008. If there are no further terrorist attacks within the country in the next four years, the issue of terrorism will fade in importance, in addition to which neither of the presidential candidates in that year will have the record of President Bush in waging war against it. If there are additional attacks, the Republicans, solidly in control of the federal government after 2004, will surely be held to answer for the failure to secure the homeland. Terrorism thus does not provide the GOP with an issue upon which to build the reliable partisan majority it has pursued for the past quarter-century. At the same time, with working majorities in both houses of Congress as well as control of the White House, the next four years provide the Republicans with their best opportunity since the 1920s to forge a majority that could restructure the party battle in America for the foreseeable future. Historically, the electoral realignments in which the partisan majority in the nation has changed—the Civil War and New Deal eras—have been the products of successful governance that drew voters to the party in charge. This is the opportunity that the election of 2004 has presented to the Republicans.

All electoral coalitions are fragile. They come with built-in fault lines precisely because they are *coalitions* comprised of different interests that come together at a moment in time to make common cause around a limited set of issues. Some coalitions, like the New Deal Democratic Party of Franklin Roosevelt, are sturdy constructions that organize the party battle for an extended period of time, while others are less hardy and more tenuous in their hold on the electorate. Since the end of the 1970s, both the Republican and Democratic party coalitions have been of the latter variety, much as the party coalitions were at the end of the nineteenth century. The structure of the party battle over the past quarter-century, like that at the end of the previous century, has been remarkably stable and closely contested.[17] The Republicans have won more often than not—five times in seven elections since the 1970s—but excluding the landslide victory of Ronald Reagan in 1984, the GOP has averaged 46.8 percent of the popular vote as compared with 45.6 percent for the Democrats. Clearly, the Republicans have an edge as well as an opportunity.

Republican success since the 1960s was achieved by displacing the economic and class-based electoral cleavage of the liberal New Deal party system and replacing it with one centered in social and cultural issues. The 2004 election attests yet again to the consequences of this reorganization of the contest for the presidency. The familiar election map with its red and blue states is a crude indicator of this change, but Robert David Sullivan has drawn a political map of the nation for *Commonwealth Magazine* that is much more revealing. Instead of following state lines, Sullivan uses voting returns, demographics, and other data to identify ten regions with roughly equal shares of the population.[18] In Sullivan's America, the most Republican region in 2004 was Appalachia, which gave Bush 61.4 percent of its vote. Stretching south from central Pennsylvania across southeast Ohio, West Virginia through eastern Kentucky and Tennessee and western Virginia and North Carolina to the northern reaches of Georgia, Alabama, and Mississippi, plus the northwest tip of South Carolina, this region belonged to the Democrats for well over a century from the 1830s to the 1970s. It is the nation's poorest region, and by almost any standard of economic self-interest ought to be Democratic still. But the social and cultural cleavage effected by the Republicans—the centrality of religious and moral issues in elections—has successfully crosscut the old Democratic cleavage, and now the region delivers its vote as heavily to the GOP as it once did to the Democrats.[19]

Republican support was almost as high—61.3 percent—in the Deep South, in Dixie, a region Sullivan labels "Southern Comfort." Stretching from the west coast of Florida across the southernmost parts of Alabama, Mississippi, and Louisiana into east and central Texas, then north to include eastern Oklahoma, northwestern Arkansas, and southeastern Missouri, this region also had been solidly Democratic from the 1830s into the 1960s, abandoning its ancient allegiance then over racial disagreements with the national party, an issue now largely concealed by the social/cultural cleavage. Sullivan's map shows that traditional support for the GOP remains high in the states of the Great Plains and in the Rocky Mountain north. Democrats dominate in much of the Northeast and coastal Mideast, as well as the big cities of the Midwest. The region of greatest competition, where Bush polled just over 50 percent of the vote, is in the states lying along the upper Mississippi River. Called "Big River" by Sullivan, this region extends from eastern Minnesota and Wisconsin in the north through eastern Iowa, eastern Missouri, most of Illinois, western Kentucky, western Tennessee, and the eastern half of Arkansas. Throughout this region, it was the conservative Christians—evangelical Protestants and conservative Catholics—who tipped the vote to Bush as the champion of traditional moral values. This region also had been part of the Democratic Party base from the time of Franklin Roosevelt to that of Lyndon Johnson and, in the case of the upper Midwest, on into the 1990s. But as social and cultural issues have taken center stage in the nation's politics, this region too has been moving toward the GOP.

Terrorism may have been the issue that returned George W. Bush to the White House, but the partisan coalition that took him there is anchored in the waters of social and cultural conservatism, and therein is both its strength and its weakness. Moral values, unlike economic issues, are not easily divisible. They present zero-sum choices between right and wrong, good and evil, and thus do not lend themselves to political compromise. "Moral values," Joel Achenbach writes, "gnaw at the guts of people who think they know right from wrong and normal from sick."[20] In the immediate aftermath of the election and flush with victory, the religious right—the "ayatollah wing of the Republican party" as liberal columnist Ellen Goodman brands it—is insisting that the GOP make good on its promise to restore America to what they believe it once was and what it should be.[21] Their potential for disruption within the party is evident in their vehement postelection opposition to the choice of Arlen Specter (R-PA) as chair of the Senate Judiciary Committee, organizing a prayerful rally on the steps of the Capitol to protest that the moderate Pennsylvanian was too liberal to be trusted with handling Bush administration nominations for the federal courts.

In a pluralist—indeed, multicultural—nation, the moral strictures of social conservatives will inevitably deepen divisions within the country and could sharpen intramural tensions in the Republican Party as well.[22] Like all successful political parties, the Republicans are a coalition of diverse interests—fiscal conservatives, libertarians, and neoconservatives, as well as social conservatives—that joins the urbane and internationalist outlook of corporate America with the traditional values and localism of rural and small-town America. If President Bush is to capitalize on the political opportunity at hand and bequeath a reliable electoral majority to his party, he will have to negotiate through these differences in a way that simultaneously maintains and expands the current alliance of forces in the Republican coalition.

Conclusion

The Democrats came very close to winning the 2004 presidential election. Instead, they lost not only the White House but also saw Republicans sweep all of the open Senate seats in the South and add seven seats to their majority in the House. They had to look to state legislative races to find any good news. The party is now left to puzzle over what went wrong and what to do about it. Moreover, given the intensity of the anti-Bush sentiment in 2004, Democrats must also wonder whether the narrowness of the outcome might not be an illusion and whether a "normal vote" might have given President Bush an even larger win. Still, it may be, as John Judis and Ruy Teixeira argue, that demography is on the side of the Democrats.[23] Indeed, Robert David Sullivan's map of party strength shows two regions of opportunity for the Democrats. One lies along the border southwest from south and west Texas across New Mexico and Arizona into Southern California, but extending also through New Mexico into parts of Colorado and the southeastern tip of Nevada. John Kerry won this region by ten points, 54.9 to 44.1 percent. But no part of this region encompasses one state, and all of it borders on a region that went to Bush by more than 20 points. The other region is in the South between Appalachia and Dixie, extending from northern Virginia, where John Kerry was strong, south along the Atlantic coast through large parts of North Carolina, South Carolina, and Georgia into northeastern Florida and across the lower parts of Alabama and Mississippi into a large part of northern and central Louisiana. Bush carried this region by less than four points, 51.5 to 47.8 percent, but again no part of this region encompasses an entire state—and it is bordered everywhere by areas that went to the Republican by more than 20 points.

Whatever future prospects Democrats may have in these regions or elsewhere, it is obvious that the nation's immediate future is securely in the hands of the Republican Party. If the 2004 election has charted a new direction for the nation, it is one that will be mapped by a conservative Republican president and a conservative Republican Congress. George W. Bush, who prides himself on being the heir to the Reagan revolution of the 1980s, has given his party and conservatism one thing that Reagan did not: a broader and more *collective* appeal—that of an "ownership society"—which reaches across race, creed, class, gender, ethnicity, and other social divisions in the electorate with the promise of national unity through a fresh and common understanding of what it means to be an

American. At the heart of the Bush reform agenda is the goal of creating a "culture of ownership" that would be less reliant on government. As one GOP campaign ad put it:

> One of the most important parts of a reform agenda is to encourage people to own something. Own their own home, own their own business, own their own health-care plan, or own a piece of their retirement. Because . . . if you own something, you have a vital stake in the future of America.[24]

The idea of an "ownership society" is a potentially powerful appeal—a slogan like the New Deal or the Great Society to which larger numbers of Americans can be drawn into the Republican Party from across the board of American life. Implicit in it are fundamental American values that encompass but move beyond conservative Christianity: the ideal of individualism, the cornerstone of Americanism; the dignity of work, prized as the way to earn what one has; and the America dream itself, a home of one's own and the pride and independence that goes with it. That the policies implemented in the name of an ownership society benefit the rich more than they do middle- and working-class Americans may prove largely irrelevant in a society in which class is not generally seen as important, in which self-interest clearly has a spiritual as well as a material dimension, and in which many vote their aspirations rather than their narrower self-interest. Moreover, the idea of an ownership society fits politically with changes in American life—with what the conservative Grover Norquist has called the "biggest demographic shift in the past thirty years": the increase in the number of Americans who own stocks. Only 20 percent of adult Americans owned stocks when Reagan was elected in 1980, whereas today, Norquist calculates, 60 percent do—and they constitute 70 percent of voting public.[25]

The future of American politics now rests in the hands of the Republican Party. If George W. Bush governs successfully in his second term—if he sells his idea of an ownership society and if it works—the almost certain result will be the completion of a conservative Republican realignment of the nation's politics. The 2004 GOP success in U.S. Senate races in the South is instructive, for it sprang from a strategy predicated on the assumption that these were *national* and not just regional contests—that the choice was not between two candidates but between two national parties.[26] If the next four years are kind to the Republicans, the nation will be given a similar choice in 2008. This will present the Democrats with a powerful challenge. The economic and rights-centered liberalism of the New Deal and Great Society seems unlikely to meet the challenge, nor does the centrist "me-too" moderation of the Democratic Leadership Council. But the greatest challenge for Democrats may be that they must once more think primarily in terms of a party rather than of a candidate, a habit lost in the last three decades in the mists and myths of party reform.

Postscript

On November 2, 2004, George Bush won reelection as president. On the next day, he launched his campaign for an "ownership society," the opening volley being a call to deal with the "crisis" in Social Security. To avert a looming financial shortfall that threatened to bankrupt the program's trust fund, the president urged that younger Americans be permitted to invest part of their Social Security taxes into personal accounts that could earn higher returns and would be their own property. Personal accounts, he asserted, were "an opportunity to help millions of our fellow citizens find security and independence that comes from *owning* something, from *ownership*."[27] In the weeks that followed, Bush repeatedly and urgently pressed his case for personal accounts as key to any viable reform of Social Security and, in his inaugural address, he promised Americans an "ownership society" of which Social Security reform and personal accounts were a critical component. Columnist Peter Canellos of the *Boston Globe* noted that "Bush's decision to push hard for Social Security privatization . . . could be a transformative event that shakes the coalitions of both political parties."[28]

But it was the *Washington Post*'s Albert Crenshaw who, noting that Bush's appeal to "independence, self-reliance and other traditional virtues resonates with much of the public," detailed the implications and significance of the president's promise:

> This shift—from the New Deal to the Ownership Society—is a sea change in the way Americans view the relationship between themselves and the government, and between themselves and the rest of society. Whereas government, unions and other collective organizations were widely seen in the 1930s as placing a safety net under workers and their families, today they are regarded by many people, especially in the "red states," as stifling enterprise and protecting the lazy.

> In contrast to the New Deal, the Ownership Society will have optimal elements, with greater rewards but also far greater risk. While the administration's Social Security plan taps into taxes that workers are already paying, a key element of the Ownership Society is that to take full advantage of it, you must put up a great deal more of your own money—pay to play, if you will. And that principle of pay to play applies in fields ranging from retirement to education to health care.
>
> Many in the upper half may thrive in the Ownership Society. In addition being able to lower their current taxes and provide generously for their own retirement, they will be able to share benefits with their children and grandchildren, perhaps giving them a leg up in their own lives.
>
> In fact, the right to pass on savings to future generations is a thread running through many elements of the Ownership Society. That too is a break with past programs.[29]

The Bush administration quickly organized a campaign to push the president's plan. In early February, Karl Rove, the "architect" of the Bush reelection, told members of Congress at a Republican Party retreat at the Greenbriar resort in White Sulphur Springs, West Virginia, that Social Security was the administration's number 1 domestic priority.[30] Rove followed that with a rousing speech to some 4,000 activists at the annual convention of the Conservative Political Action Committee. Calling the Republicans the party of idealism and reform, Rove called for reform in public policies ranging from the tax code through health care, the legal system, and public education to pension plans, adding that the time to act was now because the president had "put all his chips on the table" in the 2004 election.[31] Rove next met with lobbyists for a group associated with the Business Roundtable who promised to raise $20 million to promote personal accounts, while Treasury Secretary John Snow met with top lobbyists for Fortune 500 companies.[32]

The president also took the campaign for Social Security reform to the American people, crisscrossing the nation, targeting those states with Democratic members of the Senate who were up for reelection in 2006. In early March, the White House announced an ambitious plan for a 60-day, 60-stop tour to promote Social Security and the idea of private accounts.[33] At the same time, House Majority Leader Tom DeLay underscored the extensive and partisan character of the campaign, noting that 70 House Republicans had held more than 250 meetings with constituents and that the House Republican Conference was encouraging all members to meet with their constituents about Social Security reform during their March recess.[34] To support their efforts, members of Congress were given videotapes and PowerPoint presentations to assist in making the president's case, in addition to which White House officials held clinics for members to answer any questions they had about Social Security reform.[35]

In the Capitol itself, President Bush and Vice President Dick Cheney had begun meeting systematically with small groups of congressmen, Democrats as well as Republicans, and by the first of March had between them met with almost 80 members. A "war room" has been set up in the Treasury Department to coordinate the campaign with daily conference calls among the White House, Republican congressional leaders, and Republican national party officials. Meanwhile, the White House was organizing a grassroots campaign modeled on that which had been instrumental in Bush's reelection.[36] The Republican National Committee was also playing a major role planning strategy, issuing daily talking points, and monitoring news report as part of a rapid-response operation.[37] Representative Jim McCrere (R-LA) described the campaign on Capitol Hill and across the nation as "certainly as intensive as anything I've even been involved in."[38]

By the end of March, the campaign had yet to produce the results the White House desired. Some Republican leaders in Congress—principally Representative Bill Thomas of California, Chair of the Ways and Means Committee, and Senators Lindsey Graham of South Carolina and Chuck Hagel of Nebraska—had begun to explore areas of possible compromise on the Bush plan, though almost all of these dealt with fiscal issues. By early March, Democrats had also mounted their own campaign against the Bush initiative. Led by the new Senate Minority Leader Harry Reid of Nevada, who charged that the Republicans really wanted to destroy Social Security, not reform it, and backed by powerful interests like the American Association of Retired Persons and the American Federation of Labor–Congress of Industrial Organizations, the Democrats were urging that voters to "just say 'no'" to reform in general and personal accounts in particular.[39] As public support failed to rally behind the president's initiative, there were rumblings among Republican leaders on the Hill that congressional action on Social Security reform this year was increasingly problematic.[40]

While the public dialogue over Social Security and personal accounts has outwardly gone as might any conventional debate over public policy, discussing the pros and cons of the Bush reform proposal, the sheer scale of administration effort points to issues greater than those being generally discussed. Indeed, Republican conservatives have rejected all suggestions that reform focus narrowly on making the trust fund fiscally viable, because for them the fight involves much more than Social Security itself. David Boaz, executive vice president of the libertarian Cato Institute, calls Social Security "the linchpin of the welfare state," and one of his critics, Henry J. Aaron of the Brookings Institution, alleges that Boaz's goal is nothing less than to "topple the great monument of twentieth-century liberalism."[41]

Indeed, the great appeal of personal accounts for conservatives is that they will replace federal entitlement programs with the free market. Marc Frank, vice president for governmental relations for the Heritage Foundation, makes the point clearly:

> What's at stake here is the future of the social insurance model of entitlement. The Democrats have this avid philosophical attachment to that model—that we all have to be in this together, that everybody pays in, everybody has a stake in this—and the fear is that the moment you allow some people to opt out . . . the juice in the third rail goes with it.[42]

Mike Tanner at the Cato Institute, a lobbyist for private accounts, echoes Frank:

> If the only thing you care about is restoring Social Security to solvency, you can raise taxes and cut benefits enough to make Social Security solvent. But a lot of people, myself included, believe this is not just about solvency. This is about changing the system that allows workers more control over their money and that gives people real wealth. If you give people *ownership* and control of their money, you are indeed limiting government.[43]

For Stephen Moore, president of the Free Enterprise Fund, there is no compromise on this issue. He asserts that for conservative Republicans and organizations like his there are two bottom lines on Social Security reform: no tax increases and the creation of private accounts. Similarly, Representative Tom Feeney (R-FL), a member of the Republican Study Committee, which includes about 100 House conservatives and supports private accounts, calls the fight for personal accounts as part of Social Security reform "a philosophical issue, on top of fixing the fiscal one," and adds that, "If in 75 years retirees are asking, 'Which politician am I most confident will keep his grubby hands off the funds I put in my personal account,' the Republicans will have won, and this will be a freer country."[44] Finally, White House aide Peter H. Wehner puts the fight for personal accounts into political perspective, writing that, "If we succeed in reforming Social Security, it will rank as one of the most significant conservative governing achievements ever."[45]

The contest over Social Security reform may thus be best seen as an epic party battle for control of the future of American government and politics. For conservatives like Franc of the Heritage Foundation, the fight is a straight-up ideological struggle. "If you want to put the stamp of the modern Republican Party, the modern conservative movement, on this reform," he argues, "there has to be a private account to it."[46] For conservatives like former Speaker Newt Gingrich, the logic is more pragmatic but the conclusion the same. Viewing compromises being proposed, he insists, "It would be catastrophic for the Republican Party if we end up as the party of tax increases and benefit cuts."[47] Other Republican conservatives also see the issue in pragmatic but in more immediate partisan terms. Bill Archer, the former House Ways and Means Committee Chair, spoke for them: "We've got a lot of close seats where members won less than 55 percent of the vote. If this plays out badly, it could potentially cost us control of the House."[48] There are as well continuing tensions between social and economic conservatives in the party.[49] But there have been no fatal fractures in the Republican Party coalition, and Representative Mike Fowler of Indiana, a leader among GOP conservatives in the House, offers a cautionary note for those expecting them:

"I have learned to never underestimate the persuasive powers of George W. Bush."[50]

Notes

1. On the 2000 election in general, see James W. Ceaser and Andrew E. Busch, *The Perfect Tie: The True Story of the 2000 Presidential Elections* (Lanham, MD: Rowman & Littlefield, 2001). On the vote in Florida, see David Margolick, Evgenia Peretz, and Michael Shnayerson, "The Path to Florida," *Vanity Fair,* October 2004, 310–22, 355–69.

2. See *National Journal,* December 9, 2000, and *Congressional Quarterly Weekly,* December 16, 2000.

3. See, for example, Alison Mitchell, "High-Stakes Politics: The Race to Rule the Nation," *New York Times,* February 18, 2001, 5; and Daniel Casse, "Bush and the Republican Future," *Commentary,* March 2001, 19–24.

4. See Anne E. Kornblut, "First 100 Days: A Low Profile for Bush," *Boston Sunday Globe,* April 29, 2001, A1, 16–17; Dana Milbank and Ellen Nakashima, "Bush's Team Has the 'Right' Stuff," *Washington Post Weekly–National Edition,* April 2–8, 2001, 11; and Dan Balz and David S. Broder, "Getting Bush in Focus," *Washington Post Weekly Edition,* August 13–19, 2001, 6.

5. The other exceptions are the elections of 1824 in which Andrew Jackson received a plurality of the votes cast, but no one received a majority in the Electoral College, and ultimately John Quincy Adams was chosen by the House of Representatives; 1876 in which Samuel Tilden received a majority of the popular vote but Rutherford Hayes won in a much-disputed vote in the Electoral College; and 1884 in which Grover Cleveland won a plurality in the popular vote but Benjamin Harrison prevailed in the Electoral College.

6. Dan Balz and Jim VandeHei, "Red States, Blue States," *Washington Post National Weekly Edition,* March 22–28, 1004, 13; Kathy Kielty and Susan Page, "17 is the Prime Number Doing the Math of Presidential Politics," *USA Today,* May 25, 2004, 13A–14A; Dan Balz, "A Smaller Battleground?" *Washington Post National Weekly Edition,* September 20–26, 2004, 13; and Adam Nagourney and Katharine Q. Seelye, "Bush and Kerry Turn Focus to 11 States, *New York Times,* October 24, 2004, 1.

7. On the 1960s in general, see Allen J. Matusow, *The Unraveling of America* (New York: Harper & Row, 1984). On the rise of conservatism in the 1960s, see Rich Perlstein, *Before the Storm* (New York: Hill and Wang, 2001).

8. See Earl Black and Merle Black, *The Rise of Southern Republicans* (Cambridge, MA: The Belknap Press of Harvard University Press, 2002).

9. See Bernard Cosman, *Five States for Goldwater* (Birmingham: University of Alabama Press, 1966).

10. See Dan T. Carter, *The Politics of Rage* (New York: Simon & Schuster, 1995).

11. See Jerome M. Mileur, "The General Election Campaign: Strategy and Support," in *America's Choice: The Election of 1992,* ed. William Crotty (Guilford, CT: Dushkin Publishing Group, 1993), 45–60.

12. Dennis Goldford, quoted in Brian Mooney and Raja Mishra, "Religion-based Voters Provided Critical Edge," *Boston Globe.* November 4, 2004, A33.

13. See Judy Keen and Richard Benedetto, "Team Began Planning for Election Soon After 9/11," *USA Today,* November 4, 2004, 5A.

14. See Matt Bai, "Who Lost Ohio?" *New York Times Magazine,* November 21, 2004, 67–74.

15. On the political marriage of conservative Protestants and conservative Catholics, see Laurie Goodstein, "How the Evangelicals and Catholics Joined Forces," *New York Times,* May 30, 2004, 4.

16. Quoted in Keen and Benedetto, "Team Began Planning for Election Soon After 9/11."

17. See Jonathan Knuckey, "The Structure of the Vote in the 2004 Presidential Election," paper presented at the Northeastern Political Science Association Meeting, November 13, 2004, Boston.

18. See Robert David Sullivan, "Beyond Red & Blue 2004 Election Analysis," *Commonwealth Magazine* at www commonwealthmagazine.com; reprinted as "Beyond Red and Blue (Again)" *Boston Sunday Globe,* November 14, 2004, E1.

19. On the cross-cutting effects of social and cultural issues, see Ralph Whitehead, Jr., "A Class Identity Flip-flop for GOP and Democrats," *Boston Sunday Globe,* August 8, 2004, D12.

20. Joel Achenbach, "Whose Values Won the Election?" *Washington Post Weekly –National Edition,* November 8–14, 2004, 10.

21. Ellen Goodman, "The Specter Spectacle," *Boston Globe,* November 18, 2004, A23.

22. An example of these divisions may be found in the November 8, 2004, issue of *The American Conservative* at www.amconmag.com.

23. See John B. Judis and Ruy Teixeira, *The Emerging Democratic Majority* (New York: Scribner, 2002).

24. Quoted in John Cassidy, "Tax Code: Tax Cuts Were Just the Beginning; the President is Signaling a Far More Radical Agenda," *The New Yorker,* September 6, 2004, 70.

25. Ibid., 75.

26. See Kirk Victor, "Road to Realignment," www.nationaljournal.com (June 18, 2004).

27. Quoted in Jim Barnett, "Social Security in for Overhaul," *Las Vegas Sun,* December 12, 2004, 1D. Emphasis added.

28. Peter S. Canellos, "Social Security Focus Will Test GOP's Unity," *The Boston Globe,* February 8, 2005, 3.

29. Albert B. Crenshaw, "Upping the Ante on Retirement," *Washington Post Weekly–National Edition,* January 24–30, 2005, 18–19.

30. See Andrea Stone and Judy Deen, "Parties Take Social Security Debate on Tour," *USA Today,* March 7, 2005, 8A.

31. See Nina J. Easton, "Rove Issues Call for Action to GOP Conservatives," *Boston Globe,* February 18, 2005, A3.

32. See Jim VandeHei and Mike Allen, "Bush Launches a Blitz," *Washington Post Weekly–National Edition*, March 7–13, 2005, 13.

33. This effort had reached its midpoint by the first of April after more than 100 events were held in 76 cities involving more than 20 administration officials during March, including cabinet members as well as the president and vice president. See William M. Welch and Richard Benedetto, "30 day, 100-plus Events, Scoreless," *USA Today,* April 1, 2005, 10A.

34. Stone and Deen, "Parties Take Social Security Debate on Tour."

35. See Mike Allen, "Mobilizing the Opposition," *Washington Post Weekly–National Edition*, February 21–27, 2005, 11.

36. See Judy Keen and Andrea Stone, "White House Courts Lawmakers on Both Sides to Back Overhaul," *USA Today,* March 7, 2005, 1.

37. Stone and Deen, "Parties Take Social Security Debate on Tour."

38. Quoted in ibid. Democrat Ben Nelson of Nebraska, facing reelection in 2006 and a target in the White House campaign, commented, "The White House policy folks work with me, while the White House political operatives work on me." Ibid.

39. See Keen and Stone, "White House Courts Lawmakers on Both Sides to Back Overhaul," and Mike Allen, "Mobilizing the Opposition," *Washington Post Weekly–National Edition*, February 21–27, 2005, 11.

40. Returning from the congressional March break, House Speaker Dennis Hastert (R-IL) said that approval of Social Security reform did not appear realistic this year. See Rick Klein, "GOP Stalwarts Wary on Social Security," *Boston Globe,* April 4, 2005, A2.

41. Both are quoted in Jeffrey H. Birnbaum, "Whose Idea Was It?" *Washington*

Post Weekly–National Edition, February 28–March 6, 2005, 11. This story also details the role of the Cato Institute as the parent of the idea of personal accounts.

42. Quoted in Wes Allison, "Compromise a Tough Sell on Social Security," *St. Petersburg Times,* March 9, 2005,1, 4.

43. Ibid., 4. Emphasis added.

44. Ibid.

45. Quoted in Johathan Weisman, *Washington Post,* February 24, 2005, A01.

46. Ibid.

47. Quoted in Michael Kranish, "Friendly Fire Waged on Social Security," *Boston Globe,* March 24, 2005, A3.

48. Quoted in Bill Nichols and William M. Welch, "Bush Discusses Plans for Social Security," *USA Today,* December 10, 2004, 10A.

49. See Cannellos, "Social Security Focus Will Test GOP's Unity."

50. Quoted in Stone and Deen, "Parties Take Social Security Debate on Tour."

8

The 2004 Congressional Races

John S. Jackson III

The Strategic Setting

In the 2004 elections, the electoral majority the Republicans had enjoyed in the U.S. Congress essentially, and almost continuously, since the 1994 elections, entered its second decade. By that time Republican control had been consolidated and had matured into at least a "semipermanent majority." The dominance of the Republicans in the House has been uninterrupted for ten years. Over the decade between 1995 and 2004, the GOP's House total ranged from a high of 230 in 1995–96 to a low of 221 in 2001–2. At the time of the fall 2004 elections the Republicans had 227 House seats, the Democrats 205, with 1 Independent who usually voted with the Democrats. The magic number was 218 needed to control the majority in the House, so the Republican advantage of 22 seats was a fairly comfortable one going into the November 2004 elections.

In the Senate, before the 2004 elections, the Republican hold on power was somewhat more tenuous, as Senator James Jeffords's rebellion proved when the Vermont senator left the Republican Party in May of 2001, thus taking away their majority from then until December of 2002 when the results of the November elections changed the Senate majority back to Republican again. These results left the Senate at 51 Republicans, 48 Democrats, and 1 Independent, thus giving the Democrats some reasonable hope that they could recapture the Senate in the 2004 elections; however, that ambition was not realized for many reasons that will be explored in this chapter. Those include especially the advantages of incumbency and redistricting. However, one of the major reasons the Republicans continued to do so well and the Democrats did so badly is the fact that the congressional races nationally were dramatically overshadowed by the race for the presidency. To the extent that the two parties developed a nationalizing theme for the congressional races, it was a contest that clearly worked for the Republicans. They had a theme of supporting President Bush and the war on terrorism, the war in Iraq, and traditional moral values. The Democrats had nothing comparable to unify their congressional campaigns.

The congressional races are always conducted against the dominating backdrop of the presidential election if it is the year when they are held together. The race for the presidency gets most of the news coverage and attention, and if there is an incumbent president, his administration and campaign tend to dominate the news and popular interest. The congressional elections, at best, are usually discussed in the context of what they may mean for the ability of the president to govern and to get his programs passed. The aggregate outcome of the congressional races is given the status of a national story; however, it is one played out in the larger context of the race for the White House. Even in the midterm years, the president and his party's prospects for gaining or losing seats usually supply the major story line for whatever the national implications are of the disparate 435 House races and races for approximately one-third of the Senate every two years.

This uneven and distinctly second-class treatment of the story of the congressional races is one indicator of just how much the president and presidential government have come to dominate the American system. Madison's separation of powers and checks and balances system may still be the constitutional norm from the eighteenth century; however, in political terms, the dominance of presidential government early in the twenty-first century is quite far advanced. So it was with the story of the 2004 congressional elections. They were taken at large as a worthy story, if one looks at the national results; however, they were distinctly the leitmotif behind the epic struggle of George W. Bush versus John Kerry.

Nevertheless, the U.S. Congress is still legally and constitutionally an important partner with the president in making public policy, and the question of which party controls Congress is intrinsically important in its own right and is also important to the president's policy aspirations and ability to govern. A brief perusal of Bill Clinton's last six years under divided government amid constant pressure and opposition from the Republican majority in Congress, which ultimately led to his impeachment by the House and trial in the Senate, gives us a view of just how vital the Congress can be in opposing a president from the other party.

Compare that situation with George W. Bush's second half, post-2002 elections, when the coordination and cooperation between the White House and the Republican majority in the House and Senate was particularly close. Even Bush's first half, 2001–2, before the midterm elections, with Republican control of the House and the very close division in the Senate, provided the president with much political cover and significant policy maneuvering room as the Republicans made common cause on many initiatives. Controversial policies such as the president's tax cut plans, funding prescription drugs for senior citizens, the post-9/11 response, the invasion of Afghanistan, and the runup to the invasion of Iraq were all facilitated for the Bush administration by Republican majorities in the Congress. Then when things went wrong, as in the failure to find weapons of mass destruction or in the Abu Ghraib prison scandal, it was very useful in containing the damage and in circumscribing the extent of the congressional investigations to have the various committee majorities in relatively friendly Republican hands.

The contrast of the recent unified government under Bush and the Republicans, versus the divided government under Clinton in the 1995–2000 era, with all the political conflict engendered by the Republican control of the Congress and Democratic control of the White House, is instructive. It shows that one party in control of a unified majority can indeed move much of its agenda through both houses and onto the president's desk with relatively little contribution from the other party. After 2002 the minority Democrats complained vociferously about the way the majority Republicans were excluding them from the law-making process. That complaint was ironic since a decade earlier the Republicans had been raising the same complaint. This bipartisan abhorrence of being in the minority position does illustrate well the relatively ineffectual situation of the party relegated to that status. About the only weapon the out party has in such circumstance are the rules of the U.S. Senate and the threat of a filibuster. That threat is limited to the ability to block action in some issue areas, but it does not provide much prospect of advancing a policy agenda.

The Democrats used that threat of filibuster to obtain some limited concessions and to stop some of the president's initiatives during George W. Bush's first term; however, overall it was only a blunt instrument. Even the threat of a filibuster, especially with respect to delaying votes on federal judges the president wanted to appoint, was circumvented in some cases by the president's use of recess appointments not requiring the approval of the U.S. Senate. In addition, the delaying tactics adopted by the Democrats became a campaign issue, with both the president and Republican congressional candidates citing those tactics as a tool to attack Democratic congressional candidates. So, the out party, the party that is not in control of the White House, is also not in control of many effective parliamentary or political tools to build a party image and record and a unified and coherent case for their congressional candidates. Their only hope is to create or catch a tidal wave of alienation and disgust with the Congress as an institution and/or a massive revulsion against the president, which can then become the rationale for the out party to be swept into office and for the in party to be replaced. Such a popular wave comes along only rarely. A congressional majority-shifting election is composed of a series of around 470 different state and congressional district-level races, but those races must be nationalized effectively for the out party to replace the majority party in the Congress. The party that does not have control of the White House, which is also the minority party in both houses of the U.S. Congress, must make a compelling case in order to become the majority party in either house or to win the White House at the same time as it is winning control of the Congress.

Those elections with such cataclysmic change occur only very rarely. It takes a very special set of circumstances, usually coming in the wake of either deep domestic dislocations in the economy or a foreign and defense policy disaster, as in a war that goes on longer than the American people are willing to tolerate. In the twentieth century, only 1932 and 1952 qualify as elections when both the White House and both houses of the Congress changed party hands. In addition, the partisan shift of 1952 in the Congress was essentially temporary, and it lasted only two years. In the 1994 elections, the tidal wave of political change removed the dominant New Deal–derived Democratic Party from power from both houses of the Congress for the first time in 40 years—that is, for the first time since the 1953–54 interregnum. This dramatic sweep of the congressional party, which had been the majority party for so long, was accomplished only by the brilliant strategy of former Speaker of the House Newt Gingrich in nationalizing that election. Gingrich led the Republicans in almost every congressional race to run not only against their specific Democratic opponent, but also to run against the Clinton administration and the Congress as it existed at that time. It was a watershed election, the ramifications of which were still being felt ten years later in the 2004 congressional contests. However, 1994 was a mid-term election, and thus Democrat Bill Clinton remained in the White House and was reelected in 1996 to again face the opposition party in control of the Congress. That control would remain in Republican hands, with the small exception of the Jeffords-induced aberration in the U.S. Senate, from 2003 through 2004.

The Intersection of Presidential and Congressional Elections

Thus, the questions facing the American voters in the fall of 2004 were two. First was the question of whether to reelect President George W. Bush, or to elect Senator John Kerry. That was most crucially a referendum on George W. Bush's first administration and on his stewardship of the government if we follow the compelling logic of "retrospective voting."[1] To the extent that John Kerry fitted into that equation, it was in the voters' calculus of whether he seemed to have what it took to serve successfully in the demanding role of the president and whether he seemed to be a better long-run choice than four more years of Bush. This is a simple form of what is known as "prospective voting," which is an alternative to the more utilized retrospective voting calculus. This was the complicated calculus of the presidential choice facing the mass voters as they made over 116 million discrete presidential voting decisions, one voter at a time.

Second was the question of whether to reelect a Republican majority in the U.S. House and Senate, or replace that majority with a Democratic majority in one or both houses. That set of decisions taken at the aggregate or national level would determine whether the United States would face unified or divided government over the next two or four years. There is not much empirical evidence that the voters think of divided versus unified government in those exact terms. They make a series of decisions regarding their presidential vote, their vote for the local House member, and for their U.S. Senate candidate, if their state has such an election that year, in mostly separate and seriatim fashion. They utilize a combination of candidate image, party identification, their position on the issues, and personal knowledge to make that decision. To the extent that these separate decisions are unified, they are unified by the simple expedient of party identification and party image providing some consistency for partisans, and particularly for strong partisans.

However, the number of strong partisans has been shrinking, and the number of independents and split-ticket voters has been increasing at least up until recently. The core of most loyal voters for each party is absolutely crucial to their electoral success, and that is why both parties work so assiduously to shore up their base voters first and foremost in the campaign. That core of loyal partisans can even be enough to elect that party's candidate in the safe-seat congressional districts. However, the core for both parties nationally falls well below what is needed to achieve a majority of the popular vote. Thus, partisanship alone does not produce party government among the mass of voters. Voters in congressional elections predominantly choose the candidate they know or have at least heard of, that is, the incumbent regardless of party affiliation, and incumbents usually win, especially in the House races.[2] There is not a lot of evidence of conscious strategic voting designed to achieve a partisan counterweight to the White House, although in the abstract voters will approve the concept. Indeed, when questioned directly about the advantages of divided government, of the checks and balances provided by one party's control of the White House, and a different party's control of the Congress, the great majority of voters will approve the divided government option, at least in the abstract.[3] They do not necessarily act as strategic voters to accomplish that result; however, they generally say they like to have one party available to watch out for the abuses of power that may be perpetuated by the other party.

That potential for checks and balances could have helped Democratic congressional candidates in those districts where it was acceptable to assume that Bush was going to be reelected; however, it was not a theme the Democrats could adopt overall in order to nationalize the election because it would be tantamount to conceding the presidential election. Punishing the Bush administration or the Republicans who controlled the Congress for policy failures, the war in Iraq, or the economy was about the only effective theme that Democratic congressional candidates would have available if they wanted to nationalize the election. This amounted to an incremental change strategy that Democratic congressional candidates had to advocate if they wanted to appeal to the advantages of taking back the House or Senate. This is not a message most congressional candidates want to purvey. Instead, the average Democratic candidate for the House or Senate probably wanted the voters to concentrate on their particular race, their record and image, and on the issue positions they brought to the contest and the service they could render to the state or district much more than they wanted to focus on the larger national picture. In many congressional districts and states where Bush was popular, there was no real advantage to be gained by running in tandem with John Kerry's campaign. Those Democratic congressional candidates who wanted to run with Kerry had to make the harder case for a much more profound change in the direction of the entire government, that is, get rid of the Republicans in Congress and in the White House.

Republicans by contrast generally did not have a great deal to gain by running away from President Bush and his record, even though some of them appeared to get nervous as bad news filtered out of the war in Iraq. Nevertheless the Republicans' major theme, echoed by both the president and most of their candidates for Congress, was "stay the course; the president's plans for the economy, especially the tax cuts, are working their magic and things will turn out alright in Iraq and it was the right thing to do." That is not a terribly inspiring message, but it was fairly simple and about all that was needed as a nationalizing theme for the disparate Republican congressional candidates. It had the advantage of being succinct, relatively easy to explain, and reassuring. It was also reasonably optimistic, at least for the long-run perspective. It is the way most congressional and presidential elections are won.

By contrast, a more radical rejection of the dominant in party for a wholesale housecleaning is very rare in American elections. It requires a Great Depression, a major revulsion against a war such as the ones in Vietnam and Korea, and a singular sense of being fed up with the party in power, usually attendant some scandal or abuse of power, to bring off such a political revolution at the national level. Not surprisingly, very few congressional candidates make the nationally oriented appeal to elect a majority of their party and effect radical change needed in Washington. If they do, it is of the "clean up the mess in Washington" variety. The Newt Gingrich–engineered "Contract with America" in 1994, where the many different House elections were effectively nationalized into one race by a common theme and strategy, was an unusual political occurrence. It was a rare event when over 300 Republican congressional candidates adopted the basic tenets of the contract and effectively ran on a national party platform to which they pledged some form of allegiance. It amounted almost to an American version of the well-known responsible parties model.[4]

The 1994 campaigns remain the one recent successful archetype for congressional election realignment, and their effects are still evident. That is, the Republican congressional candidates that year stood for a systematic set of public policies. It is also an example difficult to emulate and rarely duplicated. It might have been an implicit example for the out-party Democrats in the congressional races of 2004; however, they did not produce an overall strategic plan with a well-articulated public theme. The closest thing the Democrats had to a national theme in 2004 was to decry the loss of jobs and outsourcing of jobs and increases in the number of those without health insurance, which had occurred under the Bush administration. They had no fundamental agreement and coherent message regarding the war in Iraq or on fighting terrorism in general and no reply to the charge that the Democrats lacked moral conviction. In short, the Democrats running for office in the congressional races of 2004 had no Newt Gingrich to lead them, and very little national strategy to guide them. The congressional campaigns thus became a series of localized appeals centered on local issues and personalities, replete with promises to bring home the bacon to the incumbent's or the challenger's constituents.

Such incremental and uncoordinated decision making was not at all likely to result in an overall change in control of the U.S. Senate and even less likely to change majority control of the U.S. House. The conditions were simply not ripe and the American people were not ready for a housecleaning of that magnitude. They were unhappy with many elements of the Iraq war and with the jobless recovery and other economic hardships, such as high gasoline prices; however, they did not uniformly hold either George W. Bush or the Republican majorities in the House and Senate accountable for whatever ills they perceived the nation to suffer from in 2004. None of this was well designed to help the Democratic congressional candidates in their individual electoral contests. They could capitalize on some unease and some feeling of national malaise in some cases; however, it was not of such a magnitude as to threaten to sweep the Democrats into office as a part of a popular national rebellion that could lead to a fundamental congressional realignment.

The Republican congressional candidates in 2004 faced far better strategic conditions at the outset of the campaign season. They had the majority in both bodies and they only needed to maintain that control. Protection of the status quo in American politics is usually much easier than advocacy of significant change. The Republican candidates, especially the incumbents, wanted a series of discrete races where they made their appeal based on their own personal record of service to the constituency and ability to get good things done in Washington. To the extent that they wanted any focus on the national picture, it was to reassure the voters that the nation and the president were on the right track. They could point to an improving national economy and the end of the economic recession as proof that the president's economic policies (i.e., the tax cuts), which almost always they had also supported, were indeed working. The Republican Party had come to stand for one thing above all else on the domestic front and that was tax reduction. If the tax cuts also brought the added benefit of an economic recovery, as they could claim, then that was all the better for campaign purposes. Clinton was blamed for the 2001 recession and the bursting of the dot-com bubble, and the escalating deficit was blamed on the 9/11 terrorist attacks anyway.

In foreign policy, the war in Afghanistan was quick and entailed limited casualties, and the victory over the Taliban who ruled there seemed quite decisive. The war in Afghanistan was followed by the invasion of Iraq, and the first battle for Iraq resulted in a quick and easy victory when Baghdad fell, so the war in Iraq was initially popular with well over a majority of the American people. There was a substantial minority who were opposed to the invasion and the war from the start; however, the widespread conviction that the war was a mistake came much later. It was, of course, the aftermath in Iraq, the hard slog of "nation building" and the constant drip of bad news out of the insurgency attacks on coalition forces, as well as the specter of constant and continuing battle casualties long after the war was supposed to be over and the "mission accomplished" (in the unfortunate phrase from the aircraft carrier off the California coast where the president landed in a flight suit in May of 2003), that cast a pall over the Bush administration's case for intervention in Iraq. As the casualties count grew and chaos and anarchy seemed to reign in many cities in Iraq, the president's overall job approval ratings and the ratings of how he was handling the war in Iraq began to decline precipitously.

Those poll numbers made Bush's chances for reelection appear to be somewhat precarious. On the other hand, none of the problems generated by the war in Iraq was really held against the members of the Congress. They had taken such a low-key role in the planning and execution of the war in Iraq that the average voter would rarely think of holding a member of the Congress accountable for anything that was going wrong there. The last time the Congress declared war was 1941. In spite of the fact that they had to vote the funds for the war, it was the president's decision and his war, and most members of the Congress found that situation to be very advantageous. They had largely ceded the war-making powers to the president, and the Congress neither sought nor received much accountability for how the decision to go to war was made and for the conduct of the war. Congressional scholar Norman Ornstein summarized this bipartisan lack of congressional interest in accountability over Iraq in the following terms: "The Democrats who ran the Senate in 2001–2002 did not exactly distinguish themselves with penetrating oversight on Iraq and defense. But the lack of any strong sense of independent legislative authority, and the pervasive sense of Congress as a subsidiary body to the presidency, is much stronger in this Republican Congress than I have seen it in three and a half decades, and unusual in American history."[5]

Of course when the prisoner abuses of the Abu Ghraib scandal erupted there were hearings in the House and Senate and the Senate was especially aggressive in launching an investigation of what went wrong. However, that series of hearings did not become a long-running investigation and the whole story lacked the staying power to become a defining issue in the fall general election season. The recriminations over who had done what in the decision to go to war, and the questions about whether it was a wise or justified decision and what the long-term costs were likely to be did not break out for extended public debate until the spring of 2004, long after most congressional candidates had filed for office. It was not until August of 2004 that the public opinion polls showed a 50:50 split in the nation over whether President Bush had made a fundamental mistake in invading Iraq.[6] By then, most House and Senate candidates had been recruited and their campaigns planned long before. Neither the Iraq story nor the war on terrorism became the foundation for fundamental debate at the congressional district level or the basis for a unified Democratic framing of the issues, which could have resulted in nationalizing the individual races.

The Republicans also had control of the White House with decent prospects of maintaining that control. While President George W. Bush was not overwhelmingly popular nationally, his polling numbers were within the parameters, or at least at the margins, of an incumbent who had a good chance at a second term. Initially the president's job approval ratings hovered around the 50 percent range, and the head-to-head trial heats with various Democratic contenders showed him to be competitive during the primary season when the Democrats were trying to select a candidate. One of the claims that propelled the Kerry candidacy to victory in the Democratic primary season was the assertion that he was the candidate most likely to beat Bush in the general election. The polls generally validated this claim by the time Kerry achieved the nomination on March 2, 2004. The polls showed Kerry to be approximately even with Bush in the head-to-head horse race or occasionally leading Bush; however, his lead over Bush was never very large, and it was often within the margin of error of the poll.

Another indicator of how much trouble an incumbent may be in is the so-called right track–wrong track question. Generally an incumbent with 50 percent or more "right track" responses is not likely to be in trouble on reelection, while one in the low 40 percent "right track" response range is likely to be very vulnerable. The rankings on this amorphous indicator were often exactly at the 50 percent mark, or in the mid-to-high 40s. While this was not terribly positive news for Bush, it was still manageable, although as the indicator sank into the mid-40s during the spring on a steady drumbeat of bad news out of Iraq, the race appeared to be more and more competitive. Those who focused on the "wrong track" data could point to the losses by Jimmy Carter and the first George Bush as examples of presidential candidates who lost when the wrong track data declined below the 40 percent range. Those who supported the president could maintain that terrorism and his handling of it rendered all those earlier precedents inoperable.[7] The public opinion polls made the race for the presidency seem very competitive; however, the polls provided little guidance to the congressional candidates on how to frame their campaigns.

Part of the issue of how vulnerable an incumbent appears to be at the outset of the nominations season is indicated by the number and stature of opposition candidates who choose to run. The fact that the Democrats had only a handful of candidates, and no particularly well-known national names in the 1992 primary season, supported the early belief that George H.W. Bush was a very strong contender for reelection and it also helped Bill Clinton's effort to attain the Democratic nomination.

In 2004, during the early "invisible primary" season, ten Democrats announced for their party's nomination. This indicated that many viable candidates believed the incumbent president to be vulnerable in 2004. Some of those candidates were fairly well known and people of acknowledged national standing. Senator Joseph Lieberman, for example, had been the vice presidential candidate with Al Gore in 2000. Representative Richard Gephardt had run for president in 1988 and had been Speaker of the House and Democratic majority and minority leader in the House. John Kerry and Bob Graham were respected, if lesser known, members of the U.S. Senate. This Democratic Party lineup promised a spirited fight for the presidential nomination.

On the Republican side, the lack of any intraparty competition for the nomination was, in itself, a very good sign for the president. In addition, Bush had won 30 states to Gore's 20 states in 2000, even though he lost the popular vote. The 30 states Bush won had gained seven electoral votes in the decennial reapportionment and the Gore states had lost seven votes. Bush had won far more congressional districts than Gore had carried in 2000. This put far more Democratic congressional candidates in contests where Bush had won the state or the congressional district in 2000 than Republican congressional candidates who faced a record of a Gore victory in 2000. Also, the national polls tended to indicate a very close division in the nation with regard to the voters' aggregate preferences for which party they would like to see win the Congress in the fall. As of mid-August 2004, that question elicited a 50:50 toss-up response from the national sample.[8] Either party could take comfort from that result.

Money is always an important factor, and the potential for winning the money race tended to favor the Republicans in 2004. Bush's campaign set a primary season campaign finance goal of $200 million in a contest where he had no opponent. The Republican National Committee and the Republican "capitol hill committees" promised to raise and spend whatever it took to protect their majority, and their past performance made that pledge quite creditable. Money would be no object for the Republicans in most of the 2004 races. All of this would have been a part of the strategic context in which candidate recruitment took place in the summer and fall of 2003 and the early spring of 2004. These indicators provided a fairly positive strategic environment for those Republican Party officials attempting to recruit quality candidates. The overall assessment of most campaign experts was that the Republicans had a good candidate recruitment season. They did not get all the high-quality candidates they sought out; however, they had a formidable lineup as the congressional campaign began.

Given their none-too-promising strategic lineup, it is perhaps somewhat surprising that the Democrats also had a relatively good candidate recruitment season. They managed to recruit a number of high-profile and experienced candidates to run for the open Senate seats and for some of the open House seats. Current or former governors and sitting or former members of the House or other statewide officeholders make ideal candidates for the U.S Senate, and the Democrats were able to entice a number of candidates into the Senate races who had those credentials. Their lineup for the House was not as impressive; however, they did have a significant number of well-regarded candidates, those with political experience, and fund-raising ability, for at least some of the marginal seats that the Democrats wanted to challenge. Overall, the Democrats did not begin the congressional campaign in as positive a strategic position as the Republicans did; however, they had expectations of being competitive.

The Democrats have almost always fared better on domestic issues than on those of foreign policy. They felt that the state of the economy under Bush, especially the "jobless recovery," would work to their advantage. Everywhere there were signs of economic distress among workers and particularly among the unemployed and underemployed. In addition, the cost of gasoline seemed to escalate in the spring and summer of 2004 and that fueled some serious discontent in the nation. The discussion of moving jobs "offshore," meaning to lower-wage nations overseas, became much more intense. Health care costs and the 45 million people without health insurance were thought to be a source of some potential support for the Democrats, and the matter of the high costs of prescription drugs and the importation of drugs from Canada were used by Democratic candidates who promised to take positive action on the health care problems of the nation. This nest of domestic policy issues and discontent with the status quo came about as close as the Democrats got to articulating a coherent national issues-oriented campaign.

In addition, there was always the war in Iraq and the occupation of Iraq looming in the background. The longer it dragged on, and the more the insurgency intensified against the American occupation, and the more the Iraqi population seemed to resent and hate the American soldiers there, the more vulnerable the Bush administration could prove to be on Iraq. Most important, the longer the war dragged on, and the more casualties suffered by American soldiers and civilian contractors alike, the more there was a chance that public opinion would turn against Iraq and the administration that had led the nation in intervention there. If the Republican members of the Congress had taken a more prominent role in the advocacy of the war, and had given more than rhetorical support for their president and for the nation's troops in the field, they might have been vulnerable. But the Congress had rather successfully shielded itself from such criticism and accountability by effectively ceding its war-making powers to the president. The congressional elections of 2004 did not get presented to the American people as a referendum on Iraq, much less as a referendum on the Republican Party's advocacy for the Iraq invasion. If it had, there might have been more incumbent members of Congress vulnerable as the fighting continued and intensified. As it was, most of the incumbents were considered to be safe at the start of the campaign season, and they remained safe throughout the campaign.

The vast majority of the congressional district races were decided effectively by the redistricting process that took place in the wake of the 2000 census. That process massively favored the incumbents. Even in open seats, the ability to draw a partisan map is now so sophisticated that it is quite possible to ensure a victory for the party that has the power to draw the state's congressional district map. This very substantially reduced the amount of total competition available in the congressional districts. It also reduced the likelihood that the majority party in the House and Senate is going to be replaced by the minority. The authoritative *Roll Call* newspaper published for members of the Congress and their staff estimated that at the most 25 to 30 House seats were "truly contested" in 2004.[9] The incumbents and the districts with a distinctly partisan cast were more Republican than Democratic after the redistricting process ran its course. In American congressional elections, incumbents generally win, and 2004 proved to be no exception to that widely understood rule.

Congressional Quarterly Ratings of the Races

At the outset of the campaign *Congressional Quarterly* (CQ) provided its usual service of handicapping every House and Senate race across the nation. Near the end of 2003, after many but not nearly all the candidates had been selected, CQ provided the projections found in Table 8.1 for the Senate and House races.[10] These projections are an important part of the early strategic environment with implications for candidate recruitment and fund-raising alike.

Table 8.1

CQ Initial Balance-of-Power Projections for 2004

	House		Senate	
	D	R	D	R
Present	205	229	48	51
Safe	176	197	8	7
Favored	11	21	6	4
Leans	9	16	1	4
Projected	196	234	44	51

Source: Congressional Quarterly, Politics Daily, December 4, 2003.

Since it takes only 218 to constitute a majority in the House and 51 (or 50 plus the vice president) to constitute a majority in the Senate, the Republicans entered the campaign season with a clear strategic advantage. All they needed to do was to hold the seats that were considered safe and favored and they would have the 218 majority needed in the House. In the Senate the calculations were a bit more complicated but essentially the same conditions prevailed, that is, virtually any combination of the Republicans winning the safe and favored and leans Republican seats, plus the initial three-vote advantage (not counting Jeffords the Independent) they held after the 2002 elections would give them working control of the Senate. CQ ranked the projected Senate margin at 51 to 44 going into the start of the general election season in recognition of the Republicans' initial advantages. Both parties set out to re cruit the strongest slate of candidates they could possibly field. The national conditions and the prospects for President Bush to carry the states, especially in the South and Southwest, where most of the open House seats were located, probably favored the Republicans.[11]

On the Senate side, in the initial candidate recruitment wars, the biggest surprise probably was Republican senator Ben Nighthorse Campbell of Colorado, who declined to stand for reelection. He had some staff scandal problems and decided to leave the Senate. This set off a scramble in both parties. The Democrats recruited a very strong candidate, Ken Salazar, the attorney general of the state. The Republicans initially had a strong field that included a sitting member of the House and the Coors Beer executive, Peter Coors. Coors won the primary, thus setting up a close contest in Colorado. This is typical of the jockeying for position that takes place, especially when a Senate seat comes open late and unexpectedly. This development shifted Colorado from a sure bet for the Republican to a leans-Republican and later to a competitive race. It turned out to be one of only two pickups of a Republican seat for the Democrats.

Probably the Democrats' greatest opportunity for a takeover of a Republican seat was in Illinois. There a young African American state senator, Barack Obama, won a hotly contested Democratic primary in March. When he was tapped by the Kerry campaign to give the keynote address at the Democratic National Convention in Boston, he became almost overnight a rising star on the national political stage. The Republicans were trying to defend an open seat that had been held by a one-term senator, Peter Fitzgerald. At the end of a difficult primary, the Republican nominee was a telegenic former investment banker turned private school teacher, Jack Ryan. His campaign was, however, quickly derailed by a building scandal over the records of his divorce and child custody fight with his former wife, television actress Jerri Ryan. When the unflattering papers were made public, Ryan dropped out of the race. After six weeks of floundering, the Illinois State Central Committee of the Republican Party chose radio commentator and former two-time candidate for the presidency Alan Keyes. Keyes, who then had to move from his home in Maryland to Illinois, never did seem able to get his campaign on track. Obama ultimately cruised to an easy victory in Illinois.

In Oklahoma when long-time Senator Don Nickles retired, a number of strong Republicans lined up to try to take his place. Dr. Tom Coburn, who had been a member of the House and was an arch conservative, won the very competitive Republican primary. Since he was a member of the most conservative wing of the Republican Party, some Democrats believed he could be beaten by their candidate, Representative Brad Carson, who was a moderate and who was a member of the Cherokee Nation in a state with a large Native American population. Nevertheless, since Republicans dominated the state of Oklahoma and since it had voted overwhelmingly for Bush in 2000, CQ left this one in the Republican-favored column. Alaska featured a Republican incumbent, Senator Lisa Murkowski, who had been appointed to the Senate by her father, Frank Murkowski, who had been elected governor in 2002. This bit of nepotism apparently did not go down well with the public in Alaska. When the Democrats nominated a popular former governor, Tony Knowles, this Senate seat in a solidly Republican state suddenly looked competitive.

So, overall, the four open seats formerly held by Republicans all offered the Democrats some hope for gains in the Senate. This calculation has to include, however, the fact that the Democrats were also trying to defend five open seats, formerly held by Democratic senators in the South. Only in Arkansas was there an incumbent Southern Democrat, Senator Blanche Lincoln, who was not locked in a highly competitive race. The races in Florida, Georgia, South Carolina, North Carolina, and Louisiana were all in states where President Bush was expected to do well and which he had won in 2000. In addition, the South as a whole was trending Republican among its white voters, so the probability of the Democrats holding onto all the southern Senate seats was remote. If they lost all five closely contested seats in the South, the Democrats could win all four of the Republican-held and competitive open seats outside the South and still finish with a net deficit of one. This demanding calculus also included the Democrats holding onto their contested seats in South Dakota where the Senate minority leader, Tom Daschle, was being pressed hard by John Thune; in Wisconsin, where incumbent Russ Feingold was challenged; and in Washington State, where incumbent Patty Murray seemed somewhat safer. Nevertheless, the total picture in the Senate did not look too promising for the Democrats, although their chances of a takeover there were greater than in the House.

In the House, the Democrats' challenge to taking over a majority looked even more forbidding after an unusual legislative session in the spring of 2004 in Texas. The biggest changes in the initial House lineup occurred in Texas. There, a coup of sorts, reportedly masterminded by House Majority Leader Tom DeLay, got the original 2000 state redistricting plan thrown out and a new one adopted. The original plan had resulted in 17 Democrats and 15 Republicans from Texas in the U.S. House. There was a tradition, but not a formal rule, that states would redistrict themselves only once after the census every ten years. DeLay and his supporters argued that Texas Republicans far outnumbered the Democrats in the state. The Republicans took control of both houses of the Texas state legislature on the heels of the 2002 elections, and won the governorship with Rick Perry who had been George W. Bush's lieutenant governor. Perry had taken the governor's office upon Bush's election to the White House in 2000. Perry's election to the governorship in 2002, plus GOP gains in the state legislature, gave them control of both branches after 2002. This opened the opportunity for a new redistricting map in 2003–4, and DeLay took advantage of the opportunity. After many political and court battles, the Republicans won and the Democrats lost. The Republicans developed a highly partisan new map that gave them potential control of five additional House seats from Texas alone. Several incumbent Democratic congressmen were pitted against Republican incumbents or were given new districts with almost no potential for victory. The Texas equation alone significantly altered the prospects for a Republican victory in the House in the fall.[12] The Democrats needed a net pickup of 12 additional seats to reach the majority in the House and that seemed highly unlikely on Election Day.

At the end of the recruitment season, in mid-September of 2004, CQ had a revised projection of the potential line up for the general elections.[13] By then CQ was projecting an overall total of 197 Democrats in the House compared to 232 Republicans. This projection consisted of 190 safe Republican seats, 28 where the Republicans were favored and 14 leaning Republican, and 174 safe for the Democrats, 13 favored for the Democrats and 10 leaning Democratic. In short, the Democrats could win all their favored and leaning races and still be 21 seats short of regaining the majority according to the CQ estimates. The impact of the Texas remap plus other recent developments was evident.

On the Senate side, CQ was projecting a clear Republican advantage of 49 to 44 with 1 Independent. This projection included eight safe seats for the Republicans, three where they were favored and two leaning Republican versus eleven safe for the Democrats, two where Democrats were favored and two leaning Democrat. There were six races rated as "no clear favorite" and thus holding the potential balance of power in the Senate. This revised result showed that the Senate would once again be the more competitive of the two bodies, with at least some possibility for an upset by the Democrats in the Senate, although that outcome was a long shot at best. The Democrats had to win all the "safe," "favored," and "leans" races plus all the "no clear favorite" to even score a 50:50 tie (with Senator Jeffords's vote added), according to the CQ projections at a point where all the candidates had been recruited for the fall. If that were to be the case, the vice president would presumably vote to break the tie.

There was almost no chance from the outset that the Republicans were going to lose control of the House in 2004. They had controlled the majority in the House since their upset victory in 1994, and they had continued that control for ten years. If they prevailed in 2004, this would be five consecutive election cycles where they had been able to maintain the majority originally established in 1994. This was not nearly the record of an enduring or almost "permanent majority" that observers formerly attributed to the Democrats in their 40-year run as masters of the House of Representatives; however, it was beginning to resemble at least a "semipermanent" majority.

What has changed about American politics to take us from a longtime dominant Democratic majority in the House and most of the time in the Senate to a Republican-dominant era in the House and to a lesser extent in the Senate? Probably the most significant change was the realignment of the white South, and its influence was particularly marked in 2004. In addition, the strong showing by President Bush in 2004 undoubtedly contributed somewhat to the success of Republican congressional candidates. The value of incumbency, superior finances in many races, and the pull of President Bush on the party's base in many southern and western states proved to be a powerful combination for Republican congressional candidates.

The Results

In the end, the congressional elections of 2004 were a resounding victory for the Republicans and pretty much a disaster for the Democrats. The Republicans won the House handily as expected. At the end they had a total of 231 seats outright with 2 to be decided later in Louisiana.[14] The Democrats were projected to be at 201 at the end. The Democrats lost four of their five challenged incumbents in Texas under DeLay's second-round redistricting plan. The Democrats' share of the House dropped to a pre–New Deal level and they appeared to be relegated to being the minority party in the House for the foreseeable future. A very conservative House of Representatives was set to become even more conservative after the 2004 elections.

On the Senate side the results were perhaps even more dramatic because in some respects they were more unpredictable due to the relatively larger percentage of competitive seats in the Senate. The Republicans swept eight of the nine most competitive Senate races. The only really competitive race the Democrats won was the Ken Salazar victory over Peter Coors in Colorado. That victory and Barack Obama's victory in Illinois over Alan Keyes in a seat formerly held by Republican Peter Fitzgerald were the only bright spots for the Democrats in an otherwise dismal night for them. Perhaps the hardest blow to take was the loss of their Senate minority leader, Tom Daschle, who lost to former Representative John Thune in South Dakota. He was the only Senate incumbent to lose, and it was the first electoral loss for a Senate leader since Scott Lucas of Illinois lost to Everett Dirksen in 1952. Daschle's 18-year Senate career came to an end and the Senate Democrats were suddenly without a leader. In fact, the entire national Democratic Party suddenly seemed virtually leaderless and rudderless. They were immediately plunged into a period of stock-taking and soul-searching about what went wrong and what could be done to fix it.

For the most important consideration, the power of incumbency worked to the Republicans' clear advantage, as was noted earlier. In the House it is almost impossible to beat an incumbent. In 2002 in the House, a total of only eight incumbents lost their seats. Of those, four lost to other incumbents who had been thrown into the same district by the redistricting process. This advantage to the incumbents did not change in 2004 as only two incumbent Republicans lost and five incumbent Democrats (four from Texas) lost in the House.

In addition, the Republicans have a natural advantage in fund-raising given their constituency base. Those who have the discretionary income to give campaign donations as individuals favor the Republican Party. Raising the individual donation limit from $1,000 to $2,000 per election clearly helped augment the already significant advantage the Republicans had here. On interest groups, too, the PACs that give campaign contributions favor incumbents, and this helped the Republicans in 2004.

The redistricting process favored the Republicans even without the intervention of Tom DeLay in Texas. The Texas case provided the Republicans with their biggest single state bonanza of additional new seats in 2004. After the reapportionment of seats following the 2000 census, it was clear that the so-called red states—that is, those who had voted for Bush in 2000, most of whom routinely voted for Republican presidential candidates—had gained a total of seven seats in the House. Thus the Electoral College totals, as well as prospects for partisan control of the House, had shifted somewhat in a pro-Republican direction because of population movement. Overall, the reapportionment and redistricting process had left the Republicans with a sizable advantage over the Democrats. It was an advantage not likely to be overcome without a major nationalizing campaign by the Democrats, and a major mass revulsion against the party in power. Such a campaign requires a lot of planning and just the right electoral and economic conditions with a well-designed message to kick out a significant number of incumbent rascals from the beginning. This was highly unlikely to be the scenario in 2004. The Democrats seemed incapable of putting together a national campaign with a compelling rationale for getting rid of the Republicans and taking advantage of whatever voter anger and alienation existed out there in the hinterland, even though there was palpable voter unease reflected in the polls. The Democrats seemed completely incapable of devising a national message and campaign appeal remotely on the order of the Republican campaign conceived by Newt Gingrich in 1994. If Congress was not really in charge of either the war in Iraq or the economy, then it was not going to be held accountable at the ballot box. Without such a major nationalizing effort, the Democratic candidates were relegated to a series of local, within-district contests, with their own logic and momentum. None of that was ever likely to produce a new Democratic majority in the U.S. House. While the Senate was closer, and the nationalizing influences perhaps a bit clearer, there too, the Democrats' prospects for taking back the Senate in 2004 appeared to be none too bright as the general election season began. While nine Democrats fought tenaciously for competitive seats in the general election, only Salazar of Colorado prevailed narrowly and Obama of Illinois won easily in what ordinarily should have been a very competitive race.

As a national party, the Democrats were in their worst condition since Franklin Roosevelt assembled the New Deal Coalition in 1932. While the presidential election was close, the Bush victory was nevertheless rather thorough and complete. Bush won 31 states, and the dramatic red swath in the nation's heartland emphasized just how completely Bush dominated the geographical majority. Kerry carried 19 states plus the District of Colombia. Bush's 286 electoral votes, compared to 252 for Kerry, was a closer margin; however, Kerry's blue states clustered in the Northeast, the upper Midwest, and the West Coast. The Democratic Party had receded to these limited regional geographical bases. These largely urban states could provide the foundation for future electoral fights; however, they were significantly short of a majority.

The news at the individual voter level of analysis was brighter for the Republicans than it had been for half a century. The Republicans were equal to or ahead of the Democrats in party identification, although both trailed the Independents.[15] The Republicans were especially advantaged among those who considered moral issues to be crucial in making their voting decisions. This, coupled with Bush's advantage in the war on terrorism, clearly helped the president and his Republican allies in the Congress.

To the extent that there was a national or unified campaign by the national parties, that unified effort favored the Republicans. Those individual Republican Senate and House candidates who were locked in the competitive races did not hesitate to link themselves to President Bush. They wanted to identify with his image, his war on terrorism, and his stance on such issues as the proposed constitutional amendment to outlaw same-sex marriage. Even Senator Daschle in South Dakota featured himself and President Bush embracing at the 9/11 memorial services.

Conversely, those Democratic House and Senate candidates in the most competitive races were almost all in the South, Southwest, and West, where Senator Kerry was not expected to fare well. Thus, they did not feature Senator Kerry in their advertising. The Republicans in those states, by contrast, tried to attach their opponent to Senator Kerry, Senator Edward Kennedy, and Senator Hillary Rodham Clinton as often as possible. The label and image of being a "liberal" in modern American politics continues to be much more negative than positive in many parts of twenty-first-century America, and it continues to be a major deficit for the Democrats.

In the American electoral process, the moderate middle, which used to be heavily populated by Southern and Midwestern Democrats and Northeastern and Midwestern Republicans, is largely disappearing or being relegated to a very marginal position in both parties. The Republicans who won in the Senate and in the House were mostly from the South, Southwest, and West. In an earlier era many of them would have been regarded as ideological extremists because of their beliefs and issue positions. Today they are well within the mainstream of the modern Republican Party and they form the backbone of the Republicans' congressional majorities. The new Senate, especially, promises to be significantly more conservative than the old one. Congressional Republicans have become very conservative or conservative, with the few moderates relegated to a marginal status. The Democrats, too, have become more ideologically and geographically homogenous. Their base is in liberal districts and urban America and in states with big cities. They are losing the battle for achieving even a basic hearing from many Americans in the political debate. The parties have become distinctly polarized.

Ironically, American political scientists have been talking about "responsible parties" for well over 50 years now.[16] It may well be that we have moved a long distance toward achieving a uniquely American variant on the "responsible parties" model.[17] Certainly the ideological and geographical realignment of the American parties seems more advanced after the 2004 results. If so, the Democrats are the clear losers and the Republicans are the clear winners from that realignment so far. Whether the American public will ultimately be comfortable with this brand of highly polarized politics and policies remains a more open question. The answer to that question will go far toward determining the future of American politics well into the twenty-first century.

Notes

1. Morris P. Fiorina, *Retrospective Voting in American National Elections* (New Haven, CT: Yale University Press, 1981).

2. Gary C. Jacobson, *The Politics of Congressional Elections,* 5th ed. (New York: Longman, 2001), chapter 3; Paul S. Herrnson, *Congressional Elections,* 3rd ed. (Washington, DC: CQ Press, 2002), chapter 9.

3. Morris P. Fiorina, *Divided Government* (New York: Macmillan, 1992), chapter 5.

4. On the current status of the responsible parties model, see John C. Green and Paul S. Herrnson, eds., *Responsible Partisanship: The Evolution of the American Political Parties Since 1950* (Lawrence: The University Press of Kansas, 2002).

5. Norman Ornstein, "Abu Graib Hearings Put Dismissal of Congress on Display," *Roll Call,* May 12, 2004, 6.

6. *The Gallup Poll,* August 18, 2004.

7. Dan Balz, "Bad Signs for Bush in History, Numbers," *Washington Post,* May 14, 2004, 1; Joseph Carroll, "Does Mid-40% Satisfaction Level Mean Bush Ouster?" *The Gallup Poll,* August 24, 2004; John Harwood, "Bush Holds Slight Edge, But Faces Hurdles with Undecided Voters," *Wall Street Journal,* August 27, 2004, 1.

8. *The Gallup Poll,* August 18, 2004.

9. *Roll Call,* May 5, 2004, 4.

10. *Congressional Quarterly, Politics Daily,* December 4, 2003.

11. *Congressional Quarterly, Politics Daily,* May 19, 2004.

12. Jonathan Kaplan, "GOP Hope Is Six Seat Gain in November," *Roll Call,* September 7, 2004, 1.

13. *Congressional Quarterly, Politics Daily,* September 14, 2004.

14. *Congressional Quarterly, Politics Daily,* November 3, 2004.

15. Peter Hart and Robert Tetter, "Pre-Democratic Convention Poll," NBC News/ *Wall Street Journal,* July 2004.

16. American Political Science Association, *Toward a More Responsible Two-Party System. A Report of the Committee on Political Parties of the American Political Science Association* (New York: Rinehardt, 1950).

17. Green and Herrnson, eds., *Responsible Partisanship.*

Part III

Conclusions

9

Holy Owned Subsidiary

Globalization, Religion, and Politics in the 2004 Election

Thomas Ferguson

> It is easier for a camel to go through the eye of a needle than for a rich man to enter into the kingdom of God.
> *Mark 10:25*

Coming to grips with the 2004 election is no easy task. In part, this is because too much is going on in the background. The stunning events of September 11, 2001, the bursting of the stock market bubble, and the thunderous split with "old Europe" over Iraq and American "unilateralism," not to mention the run-up in world oil prices, the emergence of India and China as major economic powers, and the slowly building dollar crisis have left almost everyone slightly breathless. That the election perhaps set a new record for the gap between mass and elite perceptions does not help: Vast numbers of Democrats clearly voted for their man out of the conviction that not only was he not George Bush but that he was not John Kerry either—that he simply could not mean what he kept saying about staying the course in Iraq.

But the most profound barrier to understanding the election may well be "cultural"—and the reference here is not to the overblown dichotomy between "blue states" and "red states" or the fact that most Democrats, in or out of Massachusetts, are unlikely ever to start their reflections on public policy by asking "What would Jesus do?" The problem is more fundamental, involving a near complete dissociation between reality and the images of American politics that permeate all levels of American society, including the social sciences.

By now it should be obvious, for example, that some kind of functional system links Fox News, many cable channel public affairs programs, and assorted radio talk show personalities to many major businesses, right-wing foundations, and the top of the Republican Party. It ought to be equally manifest that American politics is money-driven politics—full stop. And that the headlong rush to invade Iraq, with its far-reaching consequences for America and the world, was not dictated by public opinion—though the decision to invade certainly did shape subsequent opinion, less, perhaps, through the customary "rally round the flag" effects, than through the deliberate campaign of disinformation designed to spread the false claim that Saddam Hussein was somehow behind 9/11.[1]

Yet conventional political analysts rarely acknowledge these elemental features of the current political landscape. Instead, many increasingly retreat into fantasy. Not long after the GOP's "golden horde" swept George W. Bush to power in 2000, for example, three MIT scholars brought out a paper denying that money was so important in American politics. In the midst of the most extreme "right turn" in public policy since the early Reagan years, the authors asserted that most individuals who donate to political campaigns should not be suspected of some tinge of self-interest. Instead, they claimed, "campaign contributing is a form of consumption, or in the language of politics, participation." Never mind that their analysis contained serious errors of fact and logic—it was immediately picked up by the National Bureau of Economic Research and then hurried into print at the *Journal of Economic Perspectives.* Soon Princeton economist Alan Krueger was touting its claims in the *New York Times,* while George Will was admonishing justices of the Supreme Court to read it before ruling on the McCain-Feingold campaign finance reform cases.[2]

Similarly, works portraying the American "macro polity" as a wondrous servomechanism, in which elections guarantee fidelity to public opinion, are now extolled as models of social science method. During the campaign, the chronic tendency to see public opinion as driving public policy produced vignettes that bordered on the absurd: In the weeks before the election, for example, the Chicago Council on Foreign Relations released a large-scale study of public opinion on foreign policy. As many commentators noticed, the contrast it implicitly drew between the Bush-Cheney foreign policy and what the populace wanted was glaring. But by then the whole question was "academic" in the most poignant sense.[3]

Election Day itself brought the crowning irony. For decades, the notion of a dramatic party "realignment" that could fundamentally reshape

American politics in lasting fashion had functioned as a widely shared organizing concept among historians, political scientists, journalists, and even many politicians. By 2004, however, the very idea of such "realignments" had become passé. Inside the ivory tower—if definitely not in the White House—realignment theory was now the butt of jokes and ridicule, with leading political scientists openly demanding that the whole concept be abandoned.[4]

But as the votes were tallied—at least most of them[5]—it became obvious that the 2004 election displayed many of the hallmarks of a classic "realigning" election. A single major party won control of the presidency and both houses of Congress, after an extraordinarily intense campaign in which sharp issue differences—at least at the mass level—were evident. With voter registration in many states soaring at rates last seen in the halcyon days of the New Deal, voter turnout rose by an astounding 5 percentage points—the equivalent, in politics, of a glacier suddenly sliding a couple of miles. The winning party also broadened its support in most areas of the country.[6]

In politics, as in the rest of world history, the owl of Minerva takes flight only at dusk. Only time alone will tell if, as Jie Chen and I suggested almost a year before the balloting, the 2004 election becomes an integral part of a realignment process.[7] Still, the election is clearly fraught with weighty implications for both the United States and the world. Efforts to understand what really happened and why are therefore well worth undertaking.

Alas, a full analysis involves inquiries too broad for this chapter. For reasons of time and, above all, space, it is necessary to lay aside many of the largest questions, or answer them summarily. In the mid-1990s, for example, advocates of globalization were trumpeting a "New World Order" in which countries where McDonald's flourished supposedly never bombed each other. Less than a decade later, the theory is hamburger: The country with more McDonald's stands than any other invaded a country that had not attacked it and was claiming the right to attack anybody it suspected of hostile intentions.[8]

What, precisely, explains this turnabout? The obvious response—that while Iraq had no McDonald's, it did have oil—initially appears to beg almost as many questions as it answers: The jump from Dick Cheney easing the entry of American oil companies into Kazakhstan as a member of that country's Oil Advisory Board in the 1990s to his championing the entry of American oil companies into Iraq at the point of a gun a few years later qualifies as an historical leap from quantity to quality if ever there were one.[9]

The same reasons of time and space require that, for once, I set aside most consideration of who paid for the election and why. This is not because the question is not the central fact to understand about any election, but because the postelection discussion in the United States has raised a fresh set of issues that promise to cloud public reflection for a long time to come. These have to be dealt with first, if anyone is to see anything clearly.

That set of issues concerns not money changers, but the temple. Put simply, how important was religion in the Republican sweep? Can it really be true that conservative "values" swamped the influence of the economy and flawed foreign policies in American politics? If so, then what are the implications for the future of American politics?

How Exceptional Is American "Exceptionalism"?

It is instructive to begin the analysis by posing these questions in a comparative perspective. The resurgence of religion around the world in the last several decades has been widely noted. Let us bracket the vexing question of whether the free market fundamentalism that seized Anglo-American policymakers and elites during the late 1970s and then diffused around the world under the tutelage of the U.S. Treasury and International Monetary Fund (IMF) belongs here or not.[10] It is apparent that political conflicts with obvious religious bases have mushroomed in many parts of the globe. In many, though far from all, countries, religion has also made a notable comeback as a mode of popular understanding. Sympathetic interest even among elites has been growing, while a whole school of social scientists, of which Robert Barro and Rachel McCleary are perhaps the best known, now promotes a "market" analysis of religion and insists on the importance of the phenomenon for understanding economic growth.[11]

The irony is, of course, that as Yahweh, Allah, and Jesus loom ever larger in the consciousness of many cultures, their legendary rival, the Golden Calf, has been born again. In the form of the Merrill Lynch bull, it now thunders triumphantly through the kingdoms of this world. The globalization of financial markets, and of many, though far from all, other markets, is perhaps the outstanding theme of contemporary social analysis.[12] Not only in the advanced countries, but in much of what used to be styled the "Third World," consumption, with its newly resonant associations of "freedom" and "choice," has become, virtually, sacred. In Tokyo, New York, Paris, Mexico City, or Shanghai, the mall or its local cognate functions as a kind of church, increasingly open even on the Sabbath. If the lively anticipations of some sects whose members stoutly supported the reelection of George W. Bush are ever realized and Moses suddenly returns to this earth, he will have no trouble figuring out the whereabouts of the idols most in need of smashing.

Is it possible that globalization and this resurgence of religion are somehow linked? If so, then cross-national evidence about the strength of religious convictions might throw light on the U.S. case where, as many have noted, religious feeling has long been uniquely strong and persistent.

The answer is indeed interesting.

In December 2002, the Pew Research Center for the People and the Press released the results of a 44-nation survey of religious attitudes. One of its questions asked respondents to assess how "important religion is in your life" and offered them four choices: "very important, somewhat important, not too important, or not important at all."

The differences between countries were extraordinary. Like many previous surveys, the Pew analysts ended up deeply impressed by the singularity of the United States. They reported that "Religion is much more important to Americans than to people living in other wealthy nations. Six in ten (59%) people in the U.S. say religion plays a *very* important role in their lives. This is roughly twice the percentage of self-avowed religious people in Canada (30%) and an even higher proportion when compared to Japan or Western Europe. Americans' views are closer to people in developing nations than to the publics of developed nations."[13]

The survey amplified this last remark by a pictorial rendition of the time-honored "secularization hypothesis," according to which rising incomes lead to long-term declines in religious feeling. An accompanying figure plotted the percentage of the population with strong religious feelings against per capita income. The result was familiar, if now occasionally disputed, in the literature on religion and society: A straight line ran diagonally down from left to right, showing the clearly negative relation between these two characteristics. Far out on the axis for income, a single data point glowed high above the regression line like the evening star: the United States, the great outlier, both very rich and exceedingly religious.

The Pew study's survey data can be analyzed further. Taking the percentage of the population of different countries that rated religion "very important" as what needed explanation, this analysis combed through variables that promised to close up, or shed light on, the gap between the United States and the rest of the advanced world in a properly specified statistical model.[14] It may help to explain that most of what passes for the sociology of religion is insufficiently historical. Richard Henry Tawney's version of the famous thesis of Max Weber, linking Protestantism to the growth of capitalism, seems quite plausible. Something like the process he described appears to be occurring today on a much smaller scale in parts of Latin America and even the Chinese diaspora.[15] At the same time, after 400 years, Catholicism and many other religions, including many in the East that prior to the Asian "miracle" were often instanced to explain slow growth, have clearly adjusted. Certainly, the record of postwar growth in Italy and some other Catholic countries, not to mention the history of relations between the Vatican and any number of people and institutions whose strategies betrayed doubts that the meek really stood to inherit the earth, such as the Banco Ambrosiano, J. Peter Grace, or even Francis Cardinal Spellman, suggests that much has changed since Pope Pius IX famously denounced the idea of progress in his 1864 *Syllabus of Errors*.

While countries are the basic unit of analysis in this study, they all occupy definite stretches of geography. Since the countries in the Pew sample are scattered around the world, it did not make sense to estimate formal spatial models; instead the sample is checked to see if controls for continent or Catholicism or Protestantism mattered. Also, the data are examined to see whether painful existential facts such as short life spans, poor health, illiteracy, or the treatment of women perhaps influenced outcomes. The variable of greatest interest is that which has, in recent years, received scant consideration in this context: economic inequality. After weighing alternatives, the University of Texas Inequality Project's Estimated Household Inequality Index is best for these analytic purposes. The spirit of Weber, common sense, and claims in the current literature all suggested that two-way causality between religion and the level of economic growth (GDP per capita) was a distinct possibility.[16]

Appendix 9.1 displays the results of the analysis. They indicate that the secularization hypothesis, which has been widely questioned in recent years, remains intact—rising GDP per capita does still correlate with lower interest in religion. But it is also easy to see why. In an age of headlong globalization and rising inequality, many researchers now have trouble picking up the trend: Inequality appears to push in exactly the other direction, sharply increasing the population's readiness to embrace religion. It also appears that, as Barro and McCleary suggested, postcommunist countries exhibit unusually low levels of religious feeling. Religious feeling in underdeveloped Latin America, though high by world standards, also appears to be somewhat less than one might expect, other things being equal. Some variables considered important by proponents of the religious "market" hypothesis are not significant (see Appendix 9.1 on pages 202–3).[17]

While the United States remains something of an outlier, these findings have important implications for the long debate about American exceptionalism. They raise the possibility that Tocqueville, in his celebrated reflections on the prevalence of religion in America, perhaps missed the point: visiting at the height of the 1830s "market revolution," as American economic inequality rose to unprecedented levels (by comparison with the colonial experience, not European standards), he failed to perceive how all the public talk about religion disguised the advance of the Golden Calf.[18] Now that 1989 is history, we can perhaps contemplate with more equanimity the possibility that Karl Marx's famous remark about Locke supplanting Habakkuk is closer to the mark.[19] And we could perhaps even consider whether the opium of the people still, in fact, may not be opium at all.

But these are questions for another day; this chapter has to hold its focus on the 2004 election. And here the analysis' results point to a striking possibility. It is no secret that inequality in America has increased enormously since the 1960s. Could the 2004 election perhaps reflect the workings of a closed loop, in which Republican (and conservative Democratic) economic policies first help run inequality up, thus fanning the strength of religious feeling, and thereby strengthening conservative forces in both parties, but especially within the GOP? Could globalization thus be directly driving the realignment of American mass politics? (It is apparent that globalization indirectly drives political realignments through the impact of merger waves on investor blocs; see Ferguson and Chen, 2004.) Such questions suggest that the first priority in analyzing the 2004 election is to produce a nuanced, quantitative answer to the now famous question about how in recent years religion has so often seemed to trump economics—"What's the matter with Kansas"?[20]

Not in Kansas Anymore?

Because several competing modes of analysis are widely employed in tackling problems such as this, it is worth pausing for a moment to consider which might be the best given the data available. Ever since the advent of mass social surveys, most social scientists have usually answered such questions by reference to national-level opinion polls. In recent years, however, many have also taken states as a unit of analysis and evaluated various models of why outcomes differ at that level.

In part, this newer tendency reflects the practical problems facing major party campaign strategists who talk to the press. Given the closeness of recent presidential elections, they have had to focus sharply on the best ways to gain majorities in the Electoral College. But it also reflects the availability of data that promise at last to offer some usable, if not necessarily perfect, answers to questions that both analysts and many citizens are increasingly asking.

In decades past, the dominance of the nightly evening news programs of the three major national television networks made it easy to assume a universal, almost homogenous, popular understanding of campaigns and elections. With many regional differences in exit poll results, it seemed only natural for someone interested in political business cycles to employ national average data to analyze the economy's effect on voting. Despite clear warnings, most analysts did not bother to check which newspapers that respondents in national polls actually read to see if it made any difference.[21] In the face of even clearer warnings, analysts typically neglected the influence of state-level "regimes" on voting turnout or union strength (where Taft-Hartley's famous provision 14b made states crucial actors).[22]

Save in some studies of southern politics and congressional races, questions about macro-level filters and variables that might influence mass politics in particular areas received short shrift. (The practice also made the South look odder than it probably was.)

Since the 1980s, however, the assumption of a single national political culture has become increasingly tenuous. Especially once the lawsuits contesting the Federal Communications Commission's (FCC's) landmark rejection during the Reagan years of the "Fairness Doctrine" were lost, it became obvious that regulatory changes, new technologies, and the growth of corporate supergiants were revolutionizing the broadcast industry. Increasingly indiscernible from the rest of the often fabulously profitable "entertainment industry," Fox, many cable channels, talk radio, Clear Channel Communications, and the Internet together have shattered the dominance of the major networks. Evidence also suggests that large segments of the population, especially younger people, have almost stopped listening to establishment media. The newer media have, accordingly, led the way in exploring much wider possibilities for mixing entertainment, commercials, and other diversions into political "news." The older networks have, sometimes grudgingly, at times gleefully, followed.[23]

As testified to by the poll evidence that three-quarters of the president's supporters in the 2004 election believed that Saddam Hussein was involved with 9/11, or the eerie unanimity that prevailed on the airwaves as the government cranked up public opinion before the invasion of Iraq, this does not preclude remarkable demonstrations of cooperation between Big Brother and the Holding Companies when all the chips are down.[24] But at less cosmic levels, the net effect is probably to reinforce a tendency toward segmentation and local "political climates." Newspapers and local broadcast stations matter, especially when the latter make their choice of national programs such as Rush Limbaugh's talk radio show.

Studies of the 2000 presidential campaign also indicate that in the midst of all this fragmentation, the fabulous growth of expenditures during presidential campaigns on ads was transforming the *major parties themselves,* and especially the Republican Party (which in recent years had outspent the Democrats by substantial margins) into culturally unifying forces in at least battleground states where they concentrated most of their spending.[25]

For this chapter, despite the airy quality of most discussions of "red states" and "blue states," the method of concentrating on states offers something useful. In the absence of data required for true "multilevel" models that would integrate data about individuals with macro-level determinants, it makes perfect sense to supplement the results of national polls and more conventional approaches with analyses of state-level data. This is particularly the case in presidential elections, where the Electoral College makes states real units of intentional action by parties and financiers. As long as one remembers the yellow flags waving in the background when one considers different forms of analysis (aggregate data and cross-level analysis) and the results that can come from these, there should be no insuperable difficulty.[26]

Explaining the 2004 Election

How best then to explain election outcomes? However popular, simply contrasting red states versus blue states is not an attractive option. Heterogeneity within states is substantial and should not be neglected; in addition, analytic considerations make it opportune to work with a continuous data approach rather than emphasizing sharp dichotomies in election returns. This can be done by focusing on the total presidential vote that Bush received as the outcome to be explained. Put another way, diehard advocates of blue state–red state contrasts can think of this as representing varying hues of "purple."

How to proceed after that is almost, but not quite, straightforward. One searches out factors that help explain the outcome. There is, however, a catch. The states all occupy definite patches of space. Some are neighbors; some are not. It is now well known that data of this sort commonly display what is known as spatial autocorrelation. In plain English, this means that Maine, Massachusetts, and Connecticut are likely to look more like each other than Texas. The implication for electoral analysis is that the trio of data points might yield less information than if the three entities really were independent in a statistical sense.[27]

Such electoral analysis is tricky. But the result is worth the effort. Appendix 9.2 displays the final spatial regression equation. Four variables appear to account for the outcomes in various states.[28] The first concerns the answer to what might be termed the "Golden Calf" question and has been a very powerful predictor of support for incumbents or challengers in elections past: "Compared to four years ago is your family's financial situation better today, worse today, or about the same?" In the 48 separate state polls canvassed to obtain this number, the overwhelming percentages of those who answered "better today" invariably cast their vote for the president. Differences between Mormon Utah (89% for Bush, 10% for Kerry), battleground Ohio (87% for Bush, 13% for Kerry), heavily evangelical Tennessee (87% for Bush, 12% for Kerry), and a presumptive den of iniquity such as California (76% for Bush, 22% for Kerry) are not large. Voters doing better economically favored Bush by lopsided margins. Among those who answered "worse," the choice was Kerry (see Appendix 9.2 on pages 203–4).

Prior to the election, several accounts suggested that the economies of blue and red states differed substantially. It is interesting to note the sizable variations among the states in the overall percentages of voters answering "better." This probably taps the real variation in state economic conditions. It probably does not reflect much of an impulse by voters to bring their view of their pocketbooks in line with their presidential preferences—most state polls carried a separate question about how the voter viewed the condition of the economy.[29]

By themselves, these results indicate the hollowness of claims that values determined the presidential election, unless by values one also means "money." They make it perfectly plain that the Bush campaign had good reason to time the receipt of the refund checks from the tax cuts and otherwise crank up its "political business cycle." The findings also undermine claims, such as that put forward by Democratic National Committee chair Terry McAuliffe as he stepped down after the election, that by itself 9/11 doomed the Democrats. (As a further test of such claims, I checked to see if responses to questions on terrorism in the state polls improved the final calculations as to outcome; they did not.[30])

Perhaps the most valuable service of these results, though, is to help zero in on where conservative "values" and religion mattered. Nationally, voters who said their families' finances had improved made up 32 percent of the total electorate. Voters who described their families' finances as worse comprised 29 percent of those who voted. Given the strong link between these numbers and the final vote, it is obvious where "values" probably mattered most: among the 39 percent of voters who said their financial state was "about the same."[31]

This brings us at last to the answer to the mystery of what's the matter with Kansas (and every other state). Forget all the blood and soil nonsense about the mystical nature of the "South" or postelection noises about the "white fertility rate." (Neither adds anything to the evaluation.[32]) Instead, consider the following: First, evangelical Protestant church membership (taken to include Mormons) across states is strongly predictive of a higher Bush vote.[33] This shows clearly in the results. Despite hard work by Republicans and many Catholic bishops during the campaign, adding Catholics does not improve the explanation. (A glance at the national polls shows why: Catholics were much more likely to vote for Kerry than were white Protestants.[34])

But another powerful economic factor also appears to be at work—one that puts the electoral meaning of religion in 2004 in a new light. Whatever the views about the effects of globalization on income distribution in the world as a whole, there is no doubt that the net effect of the economic policies that accompanied globalization in America has been to increase inequality steeply.[35] This is obvious if one calculates the change in income inequality among the states between, for example, 1969 and 1999. Income inequality increases in every state—no surprises there. But states differ sharply in the *rates* at which inequality has increased. States that witnessed lesser changes in inequality, such as Kansas (the eighth lowest), were far more likely to vote for Bush in 2004. In sharp contrast, states such as Massachusetts, California, New York, or Connecticut, which topped all others in their increases in income inequality, went almost monolithically for Kerry.

Republican campaign rhetoric customarily portrays the liberalism of these states as the product of aloof elites. There might be something to this, since in 2004, as in other recent elections, investment bankers and telecommunications companies are overrepresented among the party's large donors.[36] But the election results suggest that at the mass level, in states with large increases in inequality, the shrinking middle classes may turn against Republican policies. In any event, the GOP lost virtually all of these states.

One final factor also helps predict a high Bush vote. As Walter Dean Burnham has long emphasized, voter turnout varies sharply across states. Recent scholarly work underscores his admonition that participation has important effects on policy.[37] In 2004, state voting turnouts appear to have had significant effects on the outcome. As Burnham has observed, turnouts have generally been declining for decades in the United States as a whole. In certain parts of the Northeast and Midwest, off-year election turnouts frequently bear a strong resemblance to those of the Federalist era, when property suffrage restrictions limited voting. Given recent evidence that 1968 marked the end of the New Deal system, one can calculate the size of the decline in participation between 1968 and 2000 and then test to see if it affected outcomes.[38] The result is simple. The greater the decline in turnout over the course of what could be referred to (perhaps prematurely) as the last party system, the better Bush did in the 2004 realignment.

Conclusion: Limits to Republican Hegemony?

Viewed from a global perspective, the outcome of the 2004 election looks less "exceptional." Given the high levels of income inequality in American society, it is not surprising that religion plays a major role in public life. A country with a distribution of income that increasingly resembles that of a developing country is going to have politics akin to one.

The influence of conservative religious values arises out of definite social and economic conditions. In the boom years of the 1990s, secularization increased and traditional religion declined: The percentage of Americans identifying with some religion dropped from 90 percent to 81 percent, while the percentage of those attached to any form of Christianity fell from 86 percent to 77 percent. The percentage of those declining to answer questions about religious preference (not the hallmark of profound commitment), also doubled to just over 5 percent.[39] As even a casual acquaintance with the outpouring of popular literature idolizing (the term is carefully chosen) CEOs as cultural heroes will confirm, the good times ran rampant.

Save for a few years near the end of the boom, however, income inequality, not to mention the broader measure of wealth inequality, rocketed upward. By 1999, the compensation of top executives was 419 times that of hourly production workers, up from a ratio of approximately 25 to 1 in the late 1960s.[40] In an earlier work critical of "median voter" explanations of politics, the historical experience of democracies is clear: Political parties dominated by elites cannot campaign on making the rich richer.[41] They invariably change the subject—to "freedom," arguments about who really "deserves" help, race, religion, patriotism, marriage, gun control—anything that looks plausible at the time. From this imperative arises a whole venomous discourse that fills American political commentary.

It is a commonplace that it is not we who possess values, but they which possess us. It is unrealistic to think that the Republican Party and conservative Democrats who have bought control of the "opposing" party make people religious, save in the sense that their policies promote this in the long run. But if elites keep insisting that "there is no alternative," as Wal-Mart transforms heartland downtowns into ghost towns, jobs flow overseas, imports pour in, and much of industrial and agricultural America withers away under conditions of long-term exchange-rate overvaluation and chronically insufficient effective demand, then it should come as no surprise if large numbers of people begin longing for saviors not of this world.[42]

The account of the 2004 election put forward here, however, suggests some definite limits to this process. The election provided a dramatic test of the investment theory of political parties. John Kerry and virtually the whole of the Democratic establishment opposed the antiwar candidacy of Howard Dean. Though there is not the space here to develop the point, this is hardly surprising, given that top executives from major defense and aerospace firms such as Raytheon and Loral were early Kerry contributors. Some major financiers, such as George Soros, however, were sufficiently disturbed by the Bush administration's policies that they contributed to Dean's campaign.

But when the party did its best to stop Dean, his campaign collapsed (in part due to a set of TV ads paid for by Democratic Party contributors reluctant to identify themselves but with close ties to the Democratic leadership) and the strongly anti-Bush financiers rallied behind Kerry. Soros, insurance executive Peter Lewis, and a comparative handful of other donors made huge contributions to so-called 527 organizations.[43]

These were fund-raising entities not formally connected to any major party or campaign and exempt from the fund-raising limits imposed by the new McCain-Feingold campaign finance law. It was not difficult to see that some of these, such as the Democratic Governors' Association or the Democratic Attorneys General Association, flourished only a very short "arm's length" away from party officials. Most of these, like the leaders of the business-oriented New Democratic Network, had for years been paying lip service to the idea of registering new voters and trying to raise turnout. But virtually nothing had happened; the talk of new voter registration had always stayed mostly talk. A number of party leaders helped sabotage various initiatives designed to sign up large numbers of new voters. The Democratic Party mounted get-out-the (existing)-vote drives. It did not stage massive efforts to register new voters. It is a crucial distinction.

During the campaign, a substantial number of businesses made donations to 527 organizations. While most gave substantially more to Republican-oriented 527s (and many donated only to these), a fair number of large firms also contributed at least some money to Democratic-oriented 527s, but only of a certain type.

A close look at the data shows a remarkable pattern. Through approximately the end of October,[44] virtually *all* of the money donated to Democratic-oriented 527s by the biggest businesses in the United States went exclusively to the conservative, establishment, "official party" 527s like those discussed or to the New Democratic Network.

In sharp contrast, donors such as Soros or Lewis made occasional contributions to these organizations. But far more of their money went to more venturesome 527s, such as MoveOn.org or the Media Fund. In effect, a second party was coming to life inside the moribund shell of the official Democratic Party. This second party depended on Soros and other anti-Bush financiers, who would not support a Ralph Nader or a Dennis Kucinich, but who favored policies well to the left of the Democratic establishment, including Kerry himself. When the organizers of this "second party" turned up in the battleground states, they did not begin by checking in with the local Democratic county chair to see if it was O.K. to register new voters. They just did it—in at least one case broadcast over National Public Radio during the campaign, venturing out to Skid Row to sign up potential voters.

It was clearly this second party within the party that made the election as close as it was. The gigantic Republican countermobilization, which included the organization of GOP-oriented 527s and major efforts to mobilize likely conservative voters on a carefully targeted basis, narrowly pulled the president through. The relatively close margin, however, has an interesting implication.

At the time Senator John McCain finally came out for the reelection of President Bush, the two men appear to have reached an agreement to try to more severely regulate 527s. If the Republicans succeed in regulating 527s out of existence, or even seriously curtailing them, then the next presidential election is likely see a sharp fall in the *Democratic* percentage of the total vote.[45]

But if they do not, then American politics might soon resemble the famous parable of the frog. If a frog is dropped into boiling water, then it quickly jumps out. If, however, the water temperature rises only gradually to the boiling point, then the frog waits and gets cooked. The change in the income inequality in this chapter's analysis of state presidential voting may function analogously. States where income inequality rose sharply virtually all went Democratic. In states with less extreme swings, talk about values was potent, as the GOP intended. In the event the "ownership society" President Bush promises for his second term actually delivers, the status quo could maintain itself or even improve. But the current account deficit is now almost out of control. Federal deficits are expanding beyond the dreams of the most ardent Keynesians. The president is heralding the partial privatization of Social Security, which is guaranteed to produce what it has elsewhere—enormous sums diverted in fees to financial houses and growing ranks of the elderly poor.[46] With vast cuts in domestic spending in the offing, the United States is hemorrhaging blood and treasure in its forlorn effort to "democratize" the Middle East and stabilize the Caucasus, while the major powers in those regions raise the price of oil and Russia revives.[47] In turn, global anti-American sentiment is mushrooming.

It would be going too far to say that the handwriting is on the wall, but one scarcely needs to be an evangelical to see faint signs of the Last Days. It is possible, as some despondent Democrats all but said after the election, that the frog is already parboiled. And anyone aware of what the rapid growth of large numbers of "nonimmunized" citizens has meant in past periods of political convulsion might worry about the many younger Americans who have tuned out of politics and history.[48] But wait a while. All over America—even in Kansas—the real heat is only now coming on.

Appendix 9.1

Two-Stage Least-Squares Instrumental Variables Regression Equation Predicting Percentage of Population Ranking Religion "Very Important"

1st Stage (Instrument for GDPPC2001 is LATINDX)

GDPPC2001 = 15284.61 – 305.5815 INEQUAL + 5.8278 LATAM –9434.293 POSTSOV + 24707.29 LATINDX

Number of obs = 37
F(4, 32) = 17.34
Prob > F = 0.0000
R-squared = 0.6843
Adj R-squared = 0.6448

2nd Stage

RELIGIONP = 38.4335 -.0027GDPPC2001 + 1.1344 INEQUAL - 14.3285 LATAM

–38.4335 POSTSOV

All terms in 2nd stage equation except two are significant at .00 level; INEQUAL is significant at (.148); the constant is not significant. Calculation is for heteroscedasticity-robust standard errors.

Number of obs = 37
F(4, 32) = 55.19
Prob > F = 0.0000
R-squared = 0.8263
Variable Definitions and Sources:

RELIGIONP = Percentage of those saying religion is "very important" in their lives, from Pew Project (2002, 1-3).
INEQUAL = Gross Household Income Inequality, University of Texas Inequality Project EHII2.3 (Dec. 04) – Gini index, expressed as percentage .
POSTSOV = Dummy variable, former communist regime = 1, Otherwise 0.
LATINDX = Instrumental variable for GDPPC – Latitude, from Sachs dataset, physfact.dta; www2.cid.harvard.edu/ciddata/Geog/physfact.csv
Transformed after Hall & Jones (1999, 83-116) p. 101.
GDPPC = GDP per capita 2001, from Maddison (2004). This study took great care to adjust its GDP figures for problems of international comparison.
LATAM = Dummy variable, Latin American country = 1, otherwise 0.

Appendix 9.2

Spatial Regression Predicting Bush Votes Across States

Spatial Regression (Conditional Autoregression)
BUSH = 18.07 + .92 FINPOSBETT + .27 CHTURNOUT + -87.57 CHGINI9969 + 3.06 NATLOGEVGM
All the coefficients are significant at .00 level.
Moran Test for Spatial Autocorrelation of Residuals is not significant:
Correlation = 3.701e-4
Normal p-value (2-sided) = .81

Variable Definitions and Sources:

BUSH = Percentage of total state presidential vote cast for President Bush.

FINPOSBETT = Percentage describing family financial position as better, separate state Election Day polls conducted for TV networks and AP by Edison Media Research/Mitofsky International, as posted on Web site, *Washington Post.*

CHTURNOUT = Change in voter turnout, 1968 – 2000; voter turnout figures from Walter Dean Burnham; larger number implies turnout decline is bigger.

CHGINI9969 = Change in Gini coefficient (expressed as a decimal) for income inequality in state, 1969 to 1999; data from U.S. Bureau of Census; a larger number implies greater inequality.

NATLOGEVGM = Natural Log of Percentage of Population who are Evangelicals or Mormons, from Jones (2002).

Notes

I would like to acknowledge the substantial debts incurred while working on this chapter. Jie Chen was of enormous assistance in thinking through statistical issues and practice. I profited from many discussions with Walter Dean Burnham and Robert Johnson. I should also like to thank Gerald O'Driscoll, Alain Parguez, Walker Todd, and one former central bank governor, who probably wants to stay in the background, for stimulating exchanges. Burnham also helped greatly on several data questions. Daniel Feenberg, James K. Galbraith, W.C. Heath, Nancy McArdle, Karen Norberg, and M.S. Waters all gave very helpful advice in places. I am also very grateful to Kent Cooper, whose Political Money Line is invaluable for scholars interested in money and politics, for vital assistance.

A fuller discussion and analysis of the points raised in the "Notes" can be obtained from the author or the editor.

1. On the media, perhaps the best general treatment is Brock (2004), but see also the excellent discussion in Barker (2002). Compare Frank (2004). For the money-driven character of the U.S. political system, see, for example, Ferguson (1995).

The last Gallup poll, conducted before just before the president's ultimatum to Iraq in advance of the order to attack, showed 50 percent of Americans opposed the United States proceeding without submitting a new resolution to the United Nations; only 47 percent of respondents supported the policy the White House actually pursued. After the president spoke, of course, the familiar "rally round the flag" dynamic took hold. Polls at the time indicate that the public anticipated a "splendid little war." See *Gallup Poll Tuesday Briefing,* March 17, 2003, 19–20, and March 18, 2003, 21–22. For a detailed discussion of Iraq's irrelevance to 9/11, see Clarke (2004), but also United States (2004, 97). For a blunt warning of what might well go wrong delivered months before the attack, see Thomas Ferguson and Robert A. Johnson, "Oil Economics Lubricates Push for War," *Los Angeles Times,* October 13,

2002, M3. As was widely noted, Vice President Cheney repeatedly attempted to link 9/11 and Saddam Hussein during the campaign. See, for example, James Gerstenzang, "Cheney Presses Hussein-Qaeda Link," *Boston Globe online,* October 3, 2004, available at www.boston.com.

2. See Ansolabehere et al. (2003, 105–30); Alan Krueger, "Lobbying by Businesses Overwhelms Their Campaign Contributions," *New York Times,* September 19, 2002, C2; George Will, "Campaign Donations an Issue of Participation, Not Corruption," *Chicago Sun Times,* December 29, 2002, 38.

3. Erikson et al. (2002); for the Chicago Council on Foreign Relations study, which quite undermined any "macro polity" view, see, for example, Farah Stockman, *Boston Globe,* "Many at Odds With Bush Foreign Policy, Survey Indicates Majority Disagree on War, Treaties," September 29, 2004, www.boston.com.

4. Mayhew (2002); see the discussion in Ferguson and Chen (2004).

5. The irregularities were large enough to stimulate an investigation by the General Accounting Office; this chapter simply cannot enter the controversies here.

6. For the surge in voter registration, see Kate Zernike and Ford Fessenden, "As Deadline Hit, Rolls of Voters Show Big Surge," *New York Times,* October 4, 2004, A1. Note that non-"battleground" states did not necessarily share in this surge; the lesson is surely that mobilization efforts are required for turnout to rise even in high-stimulus elections.

7. Ferguson and Chen (2004). The paper was first presented at the Southern Political Science Annual Meeting in January 2004 and subsequently at a Sociology Department colloquium at New York University in March.

8. Thomas Friedman of the *New York Times* popularized the "'Golden Arches' theory of international peace" and then had to defend it after the U.S. intervention over Kosovo. Compare the various editions of Friedman (2000). A series of studies examined how often democracies fight wars against each other. It turned out that the statistical issues are relatively complex; more so than can be discussed here.

9. For Cheney and Kazakhstan, see Greg Rohloff, "Cheney's Experience Pays Off as a CEO," *Amarillo Business Journal,* June 13, 1998; the reference comes from the *Journal*'s web issue, http://businessjournal.net/stories/061398/ABJ pays.html. Cheney was also active in Azerbaijan; see David Ottaway and Dan Morgan, "Caspian Oil Draws Crowd of Ex-Washington Heavyweights," *Austin American-Statesman,* July 13, 1997, J6.

10. See Stiglitz (2003).

11. Barro and McCleary (2003, 760–81); Barro and McCleary (2004, 1–60). Whether the revival of religion should be treated as a purely cultural trend is highly doubtful. Typically, where religion comes high on a national agenda, obvious political forces are at work. See the discussion in Mamdani (2004, chapter 1).

12. The literature is too enormous to be mentioned; Held et al. (1999) is a comprehensive effort to measure the phenomenon.

13. See Pew (2002, 1–3). My reference comes from the copy on the Project's website, http://people-press.org/reports/pdf/167.pdf.

14. Included in the sample are all the countries in the Pew survey for which usable data exist. In the end, the sample comprised 37 countries.

15. Note, however, that empirical work on the United States suggests that conservative religion actually hinders economic growth. See the very interesting study of Heath et al. (1995, 129–42), which raises major problems for analyses of the

"market" school. As they point out, conservative religious beliefs can have serious costs for economic growth, too. It is hard to believe, for example, that in the past business discrimination against Catholics and Jews did not have serious economic costs. See the discussion in Ferguson (1999, 777–98). The "market" school needs to address these questions.

16. The idea of an instrumental variable regression is to find something that tracks the variable one is really interested in, but that cannot be correlated with the error in the regression equation. The instrument for GDP per capita is latitude; however improbable this may seem to readers who have not followed debates over economic growth in history, the variable is now widely used in this way. See the discussion in Hall and Jones (1999, 83–116). The data sources for the variables used in the final regression are listed in Appendix 9.1.

17. This includes Barro and McCleary's Herfindahl index of religious pluralism ("competition") and their indicators for the presence of state religion and the state regulation of religion.

18. See the graph comparing the advance of inequality and voting turnout during the Jacksonian Revolution in Ferguson (1995, 51).

19. The passage is from the opening of Marx's *Eighteenth Brumaire of Louis Napoleon.*

20. See Frank (2004). His title, as he notes, echoes a famous question of William Allen White about populism a century earlier. A lucid compendium of statistics on inequality can be found in Phillips (2002).

21. See Robinson (1974, 587–94).

22. For the former, the reference, of course, is to Walter Dean Burnham's work. See, for example, Burnham (1970). Ferguson and Chen (2004), using spatial regression techniques, show that outside the South the huge decline in U.S. voter turnout after 1896 that Burnham extensively discussed was in fact strongly correlated with the advance of industrialism.

23. The literature is enormous, if very uneven. See, however, Litman (2001, 171–98) and Mindich (2005). This literature tends to bypass questions such as those addressed in Brock (2004).

24. See, for Iraq, the data presented in "The Separate Realities of Bush and Kerry Supporters," Program on International Policy Attitudes, University of Maryland, October 21, 2004. This study received wide publicity; the text is also available on the program's website, www.pipa.org/OnlineReports/Pres_Election_04/Report10_21_04.pdf. The striking degree of misinformation shown here is a strong piece of evidence that if Kerry and the Democrats had taken a more openly critical stance on foreign policy, a fair number of voters could have been won.

25. Johnston et al. (2004); see especially their "Introduction." This study presents strong evidence that Bush got as close as he did to Gore in the popular vote thanks to the substantially larger war chest that he had for TV ads in the closing days of the campaign.

26. The multilevel modeling approach is outlined in Raudenbush and Bryk (2002). Such an approach can be useful when more than one level of data is relevant to predicting responses.

27. The standard test for this is a Moran test. Its results indicated the presence of substantial spatial autocorrelation. It is therefore necessary to employ spatial regression techniques. One cannot make the case by means of ordinary least-squares

regression, the stock in trade of political scientists and journalists. The regression results refer to the 48 contiguous states; they do not include Alaska and Hawaii.

28. A single index for the explanatory power of spatial regressions on the model of the R-squared for ordinary least squares does not exist, because of the way these estimates are calculated. But a linear version of the equation has an R-squared of .82.

29. I think this is true even though certain aspects of the economy perhaps conduced slightly more than usual to confusion. The sharp rise in housing values in some parts of the country as a consequence of the Federal Reserve's easy money policy, for example, may have raised the net worth of voters whose salaries lagged. One may doubt if most voters can clearly sort out wealth and income effects in their financial circumstances.

30. See Adam Nagourney, "Democratic Leader Analyzes Bush Victory," *New York Times,* December 11, 2004, A16. I also checked whether a variable indicating battleground state status or the presence of a referendum on marriage affected the estimates; neither did.

31. *New York Times,* November 7, 2004, C2.

32. The latter has been promoted by David Brooks, "The New Red Diaper Babies," *New York Times,* December 7, 2004, A27; but especially by Steve Sailer, "The Baby Gap: Explaining Red and Blue," in *The American Conservative,* December 20, 2004, www.amconmag.com/2004_12_06/cover.html. The argument can be subjected to multivariate testing. Sailer's website, www.isteve.com/babygap, reproduces Census Bureau data on fertility rates. I tested his variable; neither white fertility rates nor a dummy for southern states add anything to the equation's explanatory power. The argument does seem to have a political aspect: the implication is that Democrats are really antifamily.

33. This point is extremely important. In the 1990s, the term "fundamentalism" was widely felt to be unhelpful by many evangelicals. Social scientists also introduced new terminology; there was a political dimension to some of this in that "fundamentalism" often rang old alarm bells. Published estimates of evangelicals among the states in the 2004 election commonly left out Mormons. The theological case for separating Mormons from evangelicals is strong, but not when analyzing American politics. The two need to be totaled. Given what the church data predict, there is no point in getting lost in arguments over whether the notion of "values" in the main Election Day poll was misleading or not. See the discussion in the *New York Times,* November 6, 2004, A11.

34. See the poll presented in the *New York Times,* November 7, 2004, C7. Catholics were virtually at the national average in choosing between Kerry and Bush. For reasons of space, we pass over the often interesting contacts between the Bush administration and the Vatican in this period.

35. The following is based on Census Bureau data on state Gini coefficients for the distribution of income in the years 1969–99 as the measures.

36. Compare the tables for 1996 in Ferguson (2001) and for earlier elections in Ferguson (1995).

37. See Lindert (2004, chapter 7); and Burnham (1970).

38. See Ferguson and Chen (2004), which confirmed earlier results of Aldrich and Niemi. As suggested earlier, I tested a large number of alternative specifications, including many involving demographic variables of different types. None improved results, including those for various minority groups.

39. These data come from the summary of the results of the 2001 American Religious Identification Survey, a large-scale study conducted by researchers working under the auspices of the City University of New York. This closely tracked an earlier National Survey of Religious Identification, whence the 1990 data come. See the longer presentation on the website of the CUNY Graduate Center of the City University of New York: www.gc.cuny.edu/studies/key_findings.htm.

40. See my review of Phillips (2002) in the *Washington Post Book World,* May 19, 2002, 7.

41. See Ferguson (1995, "Appendix: Deduced and Abandoned, Rational Expectations, the Investment Theory of Political Parties, and the Myth of the Median Voter," pp. 377–419).

42. For an econometric analysis of a contrasting case, when aggregate demand stimulus and exchange rate flexibility worked powerfully to reduce inequality during the New Deal, see Ferguson and Galbraith (1999, 205–57). This can be contrasted with the rhetoric concentrating mostly on "education" from both Democrats and Republicans during the recent campaign. This is not to deny that education matters, but so do exchange rates and aggregate demand.

43. For the anti-Dean TV ads, see the excellent discussion by Charles Lewis, "Who Mugged Howard Dean in Iowa?" *Counterpuch,* March 6–7 2004, www.counterpunch.org/lewis03062004.html. Robert Torricelli, late of the Senate, contributed; so did fund-raisers associated with Kerry, Gephardt, and Clark. Soros spelled out his case against the president in Soros (2004).

44. The cutoff point of my survey. Note that the discussion is about final sources of money; in particular locales, the different groups sometimes collaborated on particular projects. The whole business often resembles the interbank market for funds.

45. See Ferguson and Chen (2004).

46. See Paul Krugman, "Buying into Failure," *New York Times,* December 17, 2004, A35.

47. Certain telltale signs as the new administration begins suggest that the goal of democratization is being watered down or abandoned. It cannot be stressed too strongly that for over a decade, American policy in both the Middle East and the Caucasus has been premised on a weak Russia. Oil at over $40 a barrel, however, undermines that premise.

48. "Nonimmunized" comes from Burnham's analysis of the Weimar Republic. See Burnham (1972, 1–30).

References

Achen, Christopher, and W. Phillips Shively. 1995. *Cross-Level Inference.* Chicago: University of Chicago Press.

Aldrich, John H., and Richard G. Niemi. 1990. "The Sixth American Party System: The 1960's Realignment and the Candidate-Centered Parties." Durham, NC: Duke University Program in Political Economy.

Ansolabehere Stephen, John de Figueiredo, and James Snyder. 2003. "Why Is There So Little Money in U.S. Politics?" *Journal of Economic Perspectives* 17: 105–30

Barker, David C. 2002. *Rushed to Judgment.* New York: Columbia University Press.

Barro, Robert J., and Rachel McCleary. 2003. "Religion and Economic Growth." *American Sociological Review:* 760–81.
———. 2004. *Which Countries Have State Religions?* Cambridge, MA: National Bureau of Economic Research.
Brock, David. 2004. *The Republican Noise Machine.* New York: Crown.
Burnham, Walter Dean. 1970. *Critical Elections and the Mainsprings of American Politics.* New York: Norton.
———. 1972. "Political Immunization and Political Confessionalism: The United States and Weimar Germany." *Journal of Interdisciplinary History* 3: 1–30
Clarke, Richard. 2004. *Against All Enemies.* New York: Free Press.
Erikson, Robert, Michael MacKuen, and James Stimson. 2002. *The Macro Polity.* Cambridge: Cambridge University Press.
Ferguson, Thomas. 1992. "Money and Politics." In *Handbooks to the Modern World—The United States,* ed. G. Hodgson, vol. 2, 1060–84. New York: Facts on File.
———. 1995. *Golden Rule: The Investment Theory of Party Competition and the Logic of Money-Driven Political Systems.* Chicago: University of Chicago Press.
———. 1999. "Big Business Leadership and Discrimination: An Alternative Econometric Test." *Industrial and Corporate Change* 8: 777–98.
———. 2001. "Blowing Smoke: Impeachment, the Clinton Presidency, and the Political Economy." In *The State of Democracy in America,* ed. W Crotty, 195–254. Washington, DC: Georgetown University Press.
Ferguson, Thomas, and Jie Chen. 2004. "Investor Blocs and Party Realignments in American History: A Box-Jenkins Approach." Paper presented at the Annual Meeting of the Southern Political Science Association, New Orleans, 2004.
Ferguson, Thomas, and James K. Galbraith. 1999. "The American Wage Structure 1920–1947." In *Research in Economic History,* vol. 9, ed. A. J. Field, 205–57. Greenwich, CT: JAI Press.
Frank, Thomas. 2004. *What's the Matter with Kansas?* New York: Metropolitan.
Friedman, Thomas. 2000. *The Lexus and the Olive Tree.* Expanded ed. New York: Anchor.
Gallup Poll Tuesday Briefing. 2003. *Public Support for Iraq Invasion Inches Upward.* Princeton, NJ: Gallup International.
———. 2003. *Public Approves of Bush Ultimatum by More Than 2–1 Margin.* Princeton, NJ: Gallup International.
Hall, Robert E., and Charles I. Jones. 1999. "Why Do Some Countries Produce So Much More Output per Worker than Others?" *Quarterly Journal of Economics* 114: 83–116.
Heath, W.C., M.S. Waters, and J.K. Watson. 1995. "Religion and Economic Welfare: An Empirical Analysis of State Per Capita Income." *Journal of Economic Behavior & Organization* 27: 129–42.
Held, David, Anthony McGrew, David Goldblatt, and Jonathan Perraton. 1999. *Global Transformations.* Stanford: Stanford University Press.
Ivins, William M. 1887. *Machine Politics and Money and Elections in New York City.* New York: Harper.
Johnston, Richard, Michael Hagen, and Kathleen Hall Jamieson. 2004. *The 2000 Presidential Election and the Foundations of Party Politics.* Cambridge: Cambridge University Press.

Jones, Dale E. et al. 2002. *Religious Congregations and Membership in the United States 2000.* Nashville, TN: Glenmary Research Center.

Kelley, Stanley. 1983. *Interpreting Elections.* Princeton, NJ: Princeton University.

Lindert, Peter. 2004. *Growing Public: Social Spending and Economic Growth Since the Eighteenth Century.* Cambridge: Cambridge University Press.

Litman, Barry R. 2001. "Motion Picture Entertainment." In *The Structure of American Industry,* ed. W Adams and J. Brock, 171–98. Upper Saddle River, NJ: Prentice Hall.

Maddison, Angus. 2004. *The World Economy—Historical Statistics.* Paris: OECD.

Mamdani, Mahmood. 2004. *Good Muslim, Bad Muslim.* New York: Pantheon.

Mayhew, David. 2002. *Electoral Realignments: A Critique of an American Genre.* New Haven, CT: Yale University Press.

Mindich, David. 2005. *Tuned Out.* New York: Oxford University Press.

Pew Project on Global Attitudes. 2002. *Among Wealthy Nations the U.S. Stands Alone in Its Embrace of Religion.* Washington, DC: The Pew Research Center for the People and the Press.

Phillips, Kevin. 2002. *Wealth and Democracy: A Political History of the American Rich.* New York: Broadway Books.

Raudenbush, Stephen, and Anthony Bryk. 2002. *Hierarchical Linear Models.* London: Sage.

Robinson, John P. 1974. "The Press as King-Maker: What Surveys from [the] Last Five Campaigns Show." *Journalism Quarterly* 51: 587–94.

Soros, George. 2004. *The Bubble of American Supremacy: The Costs of Bush's War in Iraq.* New York: Public Affairs.

Stiglitz, Joseph. 2003. *Globalization and Its Discontents.* New York: Norton.

United States, National Commission on Terrorist Attacks Against the United States. 2004. *The 9/11 Report.* New York: St. Martin's.

10
The Armageddon Election

John Kenneth White

It was a tough, competitive election. As was the case four years earlier, this presidential race was characterized by vitriolic rhetoric that further polarized an already alienated and exhausted public. One opponent dubbed the incumbent president's tenure as "one continued tempest of malignant passions," adding, "As president, he has never opened his lips or lifted his pen without threatening and scolding."[1] The president's defenders responded that "everything must give way to the great object of excluding" the challenger from the White House.[2] On election night, the contest was decided by a handful of votes in a single state. And the winner . . . *Thomas Jefferson.*

There are many parallels between the George W. Bush–John Kerry race of 2004 and the partisan fervor that roiled the John Adams–Thomas Jefferson contest of 1800. For starters, the Adams-Jefferson fight was a continuation of a bitter rivalry that began in 1796. That election was the first open-seat race for the presidency after George Washington's abdication. Adams, the standard-bearer for the Federalist Party, and Jefferson, the nominee of the Democratic Party, fought to a 71–68 near-tie in the Electoral College—much as George W. Bush and Al Gore did in 2000.[3] In each case, the Electoral College split reflected a profound geographical division. Adams's strength lay in his native New England (the blue states of their day), while Jefferson's strength was in the South (the red states of their time). What cinched the 1796 election for Adams was his New York State win—the 1796 version of Florida. But Adams's victory hardly cooled voter passions. Political writer and ardent Democrat James Callender expressed the bitterness felt by many of Jefferson's partisans toward the new president:

> The historian will search for those *occult* causes that induced her to exalt an individual [Adams] who has neither that innocence of sensibil-

> ity which incites it to love, nor that omnipotence of intellect which commands us to admire. He will ask why the United States degrades themselves to the choice of a wretch whose soul came blasted from the hand of nature, of a wretch that has neither the science of a magistrate, the politeness of a courier, not the courage of a man?[4]

As was the case following George W. Bush's election (or, as Democrats like to say, "selection") in 2000, the passions that inflamed John Adams's victory in 1796 had not cooled. Between 1796 and 1800, the two parties conducted the first of their many "permanent campaigns."[5] With Adams ensconced in the White House, Jefferson secured the backing of New York's Democratic senator Aaron Burr, and he arranged to have Burr become his vice president by creating a tie in the already-creaky Electoral College.[6] This marriage of convenience was cemented by their mutual opposition to the Federalist-backed Alien and Sedition Acts—controversial laws whose criticisms are echoed in today's debates surrounding the Patriot Act. The 1798 Sedition Act made it a misdemeanor to publish false or malicious information, and provided that anyone convicted of conspiring to hinder the operations of the federal government would be subjected to heavy fines and possible imprisonment. In fact, James Callender spent nine months in jail for writing so passionately and negatively about the president.[7] The Alien Acts, which also became law in 1798, made it easier to deport political adversaries who were not citizens.

Jefferson and his Democratic Party followers came to believe that Adams and his Federalist Party were endangering the same civil liberties that the American Revolution had been fought to acquire. Adams's partisans responded that the elevation of a culturally alien Jefferson—whom they denounced as an atheist and a miscegenationist—would lead the country into a civil and cultural war. Members of the Federalist caucus decided to back Adams and Charles Cotesworth Pinckney for president and vice president as "the only thing that can possibly save us from the fangs of *Jefferson.*"[8] Alexander Hamilton warned that Jefferson was "an *atheist* in religion and a *fanatic in politics.*"[9] The *Gazette of the United States* echoed Hamilton's warning with the headline, "God—and a Religious President; or . . . Jefferson and No God!!!"[10]

Given such inflammatory rhetoric, it is not surprising that the reprise of the Adams-Jefferson contest in 1800 was both close and controversial. In three states (Massachusetts, Pennsylvania, and New Hampshire), the popular vote was discarded and the electors—all Federalists—were appointed by the Federalist-controlled state legislatures.[11] In Rhode Island, the popular vote was instituted for the first time, while Virginia shifted its electoral vote count to a winner-take-all system in order to maximize support for Jefferson. But as was the case in 1796, the election hinged on a single state: New York. In May 1800, Abigail Adams—described by historian Joseph Ellis as "the designated vote counter on the Adams team"—predicted that "New York will be the balance in the scaile [*sic*]."[12] Unlike 1796, Jefferson and Burr came away with New York's 12 votes, thanks to Burr's canvass of the state. It need not have turned out this way. A switch of just 250 votes in New York City would have swung the election to Adams. Historian David McCullough has noted the rich irony that "Jefferson, the apostle of agrarian America who loathed cities, owed his ultimate political triumph to New York."[13] While the Democrats' plan to have Jefferson and Burr combine to defeat Adams and Pinckney worked, it resulted in an Electoral College deadlock between Jefferson and Burr. The Federalist-controlled House, dominated by Hamilton, had to settle the matter. Adams, now on the sidelines, enjoyed Jefferson's predicament: "The very man—the very two men—of all the world that he was most jealous of are now placed above him," declared Adams. For their part, Jefferson's partisans warned that any winner other than Jefferson would mean that "ten thousand republican *swords will instantly leap from their scabbards* in defense of the violated rights of the people!!!"[14]

Eventually, the House chose Jefferson after a several inconclusive ballots and one all-night session. But Jefferson's victory did not ease the partisan divisions. Not wishing to appear for Jefferson's inaugural, Adams exited the White House at 4 o'clock in the morning, hours before his successor was to be sworn in.[15] Reflecting on his defeat, Adams told fellow Federalist Elbridge Gerry, "How mighty is the spirit of party."[16] Years later, Jefferson agreed that partisanship had created a rift between the two founding brothers. In a letter to Adams he wrote:

> [In 1800] the line of division was again drawn, we broke into two parties, each wishing to give a different direction to the government; the one to strengthen the most popular branch, the other the more permanent branches, and to extend their performance. . . . [A]s we had been longer than most in the public theatre, and our names were more familiar to our countrymen, the party which considered you as thinking with them placed

> your name at the head: the other for the same reason selected mine. . . . We suffered ourselves, as you so well expressed it, to be the passive subjects of public discussion. And these discussions, whether relating to men, measures, or opinions, were conducted by the parties with an animosity, a bitterness, and an indecency, which has never been exceeded.[17]

In many ways, the 2004 George W. Bush–John Kerry race was characterized by the same degree of intense partisanship. In 1800, the seeds for the 1804 Hamilton-Burr duel were sown during that bitter campaign. In 2004, Georgia Democratic U.S. senator Zell Miller passionately defended George W. Bush in his keynote speech at the Republican National Convention, accusing Bush's rival, John Kerry, of wanting to "outsource our national security" and leave the U.S. military armed only with "spitballs."[18] Yet when Miller was challenged to defend his accusations by television commentator Christopher Matthews, he became incensed and said he wished "we lived in the day when you could challenge a person to a duel."[19] Miller was not the only passionate Bush defender. In Florida, an 18-year-old Marine recruit was arrested for threatening to stab his girlfriend because she planned to vote for Kerry. According to the victim, her boyfriend threatened her, saying "You'll never live to see the election." Sheriff's deputies eventually subdued the Marine with a Taser gun.[20]

Democrats were equally zealous. Prior to the Iowa caucuses, 50 percent of likely participants said they disliked George W. Bush *as a person.* In New Hampshire, the results were nearly identical: 47 percent (a plurality) said they disliked Bush personally.[21] One young Bush voter mourned that her die-hard Democratic family was aghast at her decision, lamenting that after the election, "I'm going to need a new family."[22] A Kerry supporter in Southern California upon hearing the election result said, "I can't decide whether to cry or punch somebody in the face."[23] In my own Maryland cul-de-sac, signs touting either Bush or Kerry appeared on the front lawns of several townhouses. Four years earlier, there had been no such partisan paraphernalia. And the tensions among neighbors was very real, as some stopped speaking to one another while others stayed close to their own partisan side of the street.

This partisanship also produced an unprecedented level of public suspicion about the election outcome. When asked if 2004 were to produce another disputed result similar to that of *Bush v. Gore* in 2000, only *7 percent* of Kerry-Edwards supporters were willing to back another court-decided Bush presidency, whereas 29 percent of Bush-Cheney voters said they would support a President Kerry if he were similarly chosen.[24] As the campaign progressed, the mutual distrust deepened. According to a CBS News/*New York Times* poll taken on the eve of the election, 79 percent of African Americans said that there was a "deliberate attempt" in some states to prevent them from voting.[25] Even after the result was clear, one poll found an extraordinary 23 percent who said Bush had won the 2004 contest either on a technicality or had stolen the election.[26] The Internet blogosphere was rife with theories about miscounted ballots and other wrongdoings.

These deep partisan divisions produced a series of gaps (see Table 10.1). According to the 2004 exit poll, there is a *marriage gap.* Married voters preferred Bush by 15 points; those who were not married backed Kerry by 18 points. There is a *God gap.* White evangelicals who said they had a "born-again" experience gave Bush a 57-point margin over Kerry; those who have not had a "born-again" experience gave Kerry a 13-point edge. This "God gap" extends to church attendance rates whatever the denominational background of the respondent. For example, among those who went to their local church weekly, Bush beat Kerry by 22 points. But among those who never went to church, Kerry bested Bush by 26 points. There also remains a *gender gap.* Men preferred Bush over Kerry by 11 points; women backed Kerry by 3 points. There is a *racial gap.* Whites voted for Bush by 17 points; African Americans gave Kerry an overwhelming 77-point advantage. Latinos also voted for Kerry over Bush by 9 points; Asians, 12 points. There is an *education gap.* High school graduates gave Bush a 5-point lead, while those who had completed some postgraduate study preferred Kerry by 11 points. There was a *gun gap.* Among gun owners, Bush had a 27-point lead; non–gun owners backed Kerry by 14 points. Finally, there was a *sex gap.* Heterosexuals gave Bush a 7-point lead; gays, lesbians, and bisexuals overwhelmingly backed Kerry by 54 points. And as was the case in both of the Adams-Jefferson contests, there is a *regional gap.* The red states—those that supported Bush in 2004—gave him 57 percent of their vote to Kerry's 43 percent. But the blue states—those that sided with Kerry—gave the Democratic nominee 54 percent of the vote to Bush's 43 percent.[27]

But like the Adams-Jefferson contests, the most important gap in the 2004 Bush-Kerry race is the partisan one. Among Republicans, Bush beat Kerry by an astounding *87 points.* Even among Democrats—historically

Table 10.1

A Nation of Gaps, 2004 (in percentages)

Type of gap	Bush	Kerry	Difference
Marriage gap			
Married	57	42	+15
Not married	40	58	–18
God gap			
White evangelical born-again	78	21	+57
Neither white evangelical nor born-again	43	56	–13
Attend church weekly	61	39	+22
Attend church occasionally	47	53	–6
Never attend church	36	62	–26
Gender gap			
Male	55	44	+11
Female	48	51	–3
Racial gap			
White	58	41	+17
African American	11	88	–77
Latino	44	53	–9
Asian	44	56	–12
Other	40	54	–14
Education gap			
No high school	49	50	–1
High school graduate	52	47	+5
Some college	54	46	+8
College graduate	52	46	+6
Postgraduate	44	55	–11
Gun gap			
Gun owner in household	63	36	+27
No gun owner in household	43	57	–14
Sex gap			
Gay, lesbian, bisexual	23	77	–54
Not gay, lesbian, or bisexual	53	46	+7
Regional gap*			
Red states	57	43	+14
Blue states	43	54	–11
Party gap			
Democratic	11	89	–78
Republican	93	6	+87
Independent	48	49	–1

Source: Edison Media Research and Mitofsky International exit poll, November 2, 2004.

*Based upon the actual popular vote of the red states (Bush) and blue states (Kerry).

notorious for their intraparty fracases—Kerry had a *78-point* lead (see Table 10.1). To speak of either a "George W. Bush Democrat," or a "John Kerry Republican" is to describe an endangered species. Of course, there were some notable figures who crossed party lines. The aforementioned

Zell Miller backed Bush. Ed Koch, the former Democratic mayor of New York City, also backed Bush. Ronald P. Reagan, the son of the late president, supported Kerry. Another Republican presidential offspring, John Eisenhower (son of Dwight), also backed Kerry. Senator Lincoln Chafee, a Rhode Island Republican, refused to endorse Bush and wrote in the name of Bush's father, George H.W. Bush. Each had his reasons. For Miller, defense was the primary issue. For Koch, it was Bush's response to the September 11, 2001, terrorist attacks. For Reagan, it was Bush's failure to support broad-based, government-funded stem cell research. For Eisenhower, it was Bush's unilateralism in foreign affairs. For Chafee, it was Bush's environmental record. Still, these high-profile party-crossovers were rare.

Indeed, the elevated degree of partisanship in 2004 is quite unlike previous election contests. Perhaps the most outstanding example is 1988, the year George H.W. Bush won the presidency. In that election, Bush received 53 percent of the vote—a figure that almost rivals the 51 percent of the popular vote given to his son, George W. Bush, 16 years later. But the *scope* of George H.W. Bush's 1988 win was considerably different. The forty-first president received 426 electoral votes and won 40 states—a resounding national victory—while his Democratic challenger, Massachusetts governor Michael S. Dukakis, won 111 electoral votes and 10 states along with the District of Columbia.[28] That year, nearly one in five Democrats defected from Dukakis to back the elder Bush.[29]

Such cross-party pollination was hardly new. In 1964, millions of moderate Republicans deserted the Grand Old Party to back Lyndon B. Johnson in his race against Barry Goldwater. Eight years later, one-third of Democrats bolted their party to back Richard M. Nixon when he ran against George S. McGovern.[30] And in 1980 and 1984, one in four Democrats sided with Ronald Reagan.[31] Indeed, much was made of the so-called Reagan Democrats, who shared Reagan's disdain of government and liked his cultural conservatism.

What is clear about this year's outcome is that *partisanship* determined the outcome. As previously mentioned, both parties suffered few defectors at the polls. And each raised huge sums of money: The Republicans raised $744,429,782 during the 2003–4 election cycle. The Democrats did nearly as well, collecting $618,146,523.[32] Many of these contributions were raised on the Internet. And both major parties mobilized their voters in ways that involved an intensification of resources on a scale that has heretofore never been matched. Something new has happened, and it represents a dramatic shift from the ways Americans have historically picked their presidents.

Historical Eras in Presidential Selection

The Civic-Minded Presidency, 1789–1797

Throughout American history, there have been four different types of presidents. The first was that envisioned by the Founding Fathers: *the civic-minded chief executive.* The often-criticized and much-maligned Electoral College was created by the framers to ensure the selection of high-minded presidents whose character would be above reproach. Writing in the *Federalist Papers,* Alexander Hamilton maintained that the Electoral College would ensure the "constant probability" that the presidency would be "filled by characters pre-eminent for ability and virtue." Like his contemporaries, Hamilton decried political parties as engaged in "the little arts of popularity," and added that "the true test of government is its aptitude and tendency to produce a good administration"—which the nonpartisan Electoral College would ensure.[33] James Madison agreed, writing that any chance of achieving such an admirable government rested on "breaking and controlling the violence of factions"—that is, parties.[34]

But the Framers' conception of a civic-minded presidency was limited to one occupant: George Washington. Washington embodied their idealistic aspirations: a man whose character was above reproach, and whose call for national unification in pursuit of the common good was respected and admired by all. To that end, Washington created a unity government with two of the country's leading political rivals—Thomas Jefferson and Alexander Hamilton—occupying prominent posts in his cabinet. But Washington's grand coalition eventually collapsed when both Secretary of State Jefferson and Treasury Secretary Hamilton departed, their personal and partisan rivalries having intensified. Only Washington's persona was able to suspend the partisanship that quickly came to characterize presidential politics. In 1792, as was the case four years earlier, Washington received a unanimous vote in the Electoral College—the only president ever to achieve such a distinction.[35] But even as Washington won overwhelming personal favor, political controversies and a heated partisanship caused him to seriously reconsider seeking a second term. In a speech drafted but never given in 1792, Washington derided the emerging partisan split and pleaded for unity:

"We are all children of the same country. . . . [O]ur interest, however diversified in local and smaller matters, is the same in all the great and essential concerns of the nation."[36] Four years later, Washington renounced the presidency in his Farewell Address: "[The spirit of party] agitates the community with ill-founded jealousies and false alarms; kindles the animosity of one part against another; ferments occasional riot and insurrection. It opens the door to foreign influence and corruption, which finds a facilitated access to the government through the channels of party passions."[37]

Washington's complaints about excessive partisanship have been echoed across the centuries—most recently by third-party candidates Ross Perot and Jesse Ventura in the 1990s, and consumer activist and erstwhile presidential candidate Ralph Nader in 2000 and 2004.[38] But the reincarnation of the civic-minded presidency—though desired by many critics of the two-party system—has never happened.[39]

The Partisan Presidency, 1828–1936

George Washington's failure to institutionalize a civic-minded presidency resulted in the institution of the thing he dreaded most: *the partisan presidency.* Its beginnings were apparent in the role partisanship played in the Adams-Jefferson contest of 1796, and the nascent party organizations that aided Jefferson's election in 1800. Eventually, partisanship became entrenched when Democrat Andrew Jackson fought back to win the presidency in 1828—this after another Electoral College misfire in 1824 that resulted in the election of another presidential son, John Quincy Adams.[40] Jackson's vice president, Martin van Buren, who himself won the presidency in 1836, celebrated the rise of partisan politics:

> [P]olitical parties are inseparable from free governments. . . . Doubtless excesses frequently attend them and produce many evils, but not so many as are prevented by the maintenance of their organization and vigilance. The disposition to abuse power, so deeply planted in the human heart, can by no other means be more effectually checked; and it has always therefore struck me as more honorable and manly and more in harmony with the character of our People and of our Institutions to deal with the subject of Political Parties in a sincerer and wiser spirit—to recognize their necessity, to give them the credit they deserve, and to devote ourselves to improve and to elevate the principles and objects of our own and to support it ingeniously and faithfully.[41]

The partisan presidency was sustained by a patronage system that rewarded the party faithful with government jobs. Even those who denounced the spoils system used it once they attained power. For example, when Whig Zachary Taylor assumed the presidency in 1849, he received a letter from fellow party member Abraham Lincoln, who wrote that the postmaster in the city of Springfield, Illinois, should be replaced. As Lincoln wrote: "J.R. Diller, the present incumbent, I cannot say has failed in the proper discharge of any of the duties of the office. He, however, has been an active partizan in opposition to us . . . [and] he has been a member of the Democratic State Central Committee."[42]

The patronage system was dealt an initial blow with the enactment of a civil service law following the 1881 assassination of James Garfield by a disappointed office-seeker. It later received a death knell from Franklin D. Roosevelt's New Deal, when many government jobs were folded into the civil service. Still, the era of partisan politics had a long reign, from Andrew Jackson's victory in 1828 to Franklin D. Roosevelt's reelection triumph in 1936. These were partisan presidents chosen by voters who saw political parties as necessary instruments for instituting change. This system was celebrated by Democrats and Republicans alike. Democrat Woodrow Wilson, who was elected to the presidency in 1912, campaigned on a platform that included a lower tariff, reform of the banking system, and greater federal regulation of the workplace (including limitations on child labor). Wilson heralded his victory as more than a personal triumph: "There has been a change of government. . . . No one can mistake the purpose for which the Nation now seeks to use the Democratic Party."[43] Later, Wilson celebrated the "zest of parties [that] has held us together, [and] has made it possible for us to form and to carry out national programs."[44] Wilson's 1912 rival, Republican William Howard Taft, also glorified the two-party system: "In a proper system of party government, the members of each party must agree on certain main doctrines in respect to governmental policy and yield their views on the important ones, in order that they may have united action, and in order that these main and controlling doctrines, when the party is successful at the election and controls the Government, may furnish the guide for governmental action."[45]

From Jacksonian Democracy to Woodrow Wilson's New Freedoms and Franklin D. Roosevelt's New Deal, presidents did not implement their own agendas so much as to ratify a program that had been promulgated in their party platforms. That ended with the onset of World War II and the Cold War, which created the plebiscitary presidency.

The Plebiscitary Presidency, 1940–1988

World War II and the Cold War drastically altered the public's conception of the presidency. In 1940, as the war clouds gathered, Franklin D. Roosevelt brought two prominent Republicans into his cabinet: Henry Stimson, who became secretary of war, and Frank Knox, who served as navy secretary.[46] This was a marked departure from Roosevelt's 1936 denunciation of the GOP as being controlled by "economic royalists."[47] Roosevelt declared that the overseas crisis (World War II began in 1939) created unique conditions that caused him to jettison his retirement plans and seek an unprecedented third term. In 1940 and 1944, FDR won reelection wearing his commander-in-chief hat, not his partisan one.

The euphoria surrounding the end of World War II might have been accompanied by an eventual return to partisan "normalcy" had it not been for the Cold War. This four-decade-plus struggle with the Soviet Union and its communist ideology consumed much of America's psychological and physical energies.[48] As more Americans became attuned to the communist threat, there emerged a powerful feeling that partisanship must cease. "Politics ends at the water's edge" became a common refrain. In 1956, then–Undersecretary of Labor Arthur Larsen penned a book titled *A Republican Looks at His Party.* In it, Larsen wrote that an "Authentic American Center" was needed to combat the communist challenge. "Principles that we have always taken for granted as the air we breathe are now flatly denounced and denied over a large part of the world—the principles, for example, of the preeminence and the freedom and the sovereignty of the individual person."[49] Accepting renomination in 1956, Dwight Eisenhower echoed his cabinet secretary's desire for conformity by recasting the Republican Party away from partisanship and transforming it into a "one-interest party":

> The Republican Party is again the rallying point of Americans of all callings, races, and incomes. They see in its broad, forward-moving, straight-down-the road, fighting program the best promise for their own steady progress toward a bright future. Some opponents have tried to call this a "one-interest party." Indeed, it is a one-interest party; and that one interest is the interest of every man, woman, and child in America! And most surely, as long as the Republican Party continues to be this kind of

> one-interest party—a one-universal interest party—it will continue to be the Party of the Future.[50]

As the Cold War progressed, the presidency became the embodiment of American nationalism. In 1960, Theodore H. White spoke reverently of "a hush, an entirely personal hush" that surrounded the president when it came to making the life-or-death issues that the Cold War imposed. That silence, he noted, was "deepest in the Oval Office of the West Wing of the White House, where the president, however many his advisers, must sit alone."[51]

In this environment, presidential elections became entirely personal affairs. Political analyst Samuel Lubell termed these contests "total elections"—ones where presidents exercised nearly complete control of foreign policy and the economy in a manner designed to control the outcome: "[W]e have been plunged deep into an era of presidential management of our society."[52] According to political scientist Theodore J. Lowi, these plebiscitary presidents were solo artists: "A candidate for president must be above party. A candidate for president must, in the language of the theater, be a 'single.'"[53] With the near-complete absence of party, these Cold War–era plebiscitary presidents often won by landslide margins. As Table 10.2 shows, of the top ten presidential landslides in American history, *five* occurred during the Cold War era.

The Return of the Partisan Era, 1992–Present

Bill Clinton's election signaled a return to the partisan politics of the past. In 1992, Americans were disenchanted with George H.W. Bush, eyeing him as a Cold War president without a Cold War to prosecute. Bush admirably handled the post–Cold War transition, and he assembled a large coalition of countries that waged a successful war to oust Iraq's Saddam Hussein from Kuwait. But having accomplished these missions, Americans were restless. And they were concerned about the economic costs that a post–Cold war economy was extracting from them. Bill Clinton felt their pain, and he promised to guide the nation into a new global future. As the first "baby boomer" to become president, Clinton's election signaled a generational shift, as the veterans of World War II ceded the presidency to the baby boomers.[54]

But Bill Clinton's "baby-boomer presidency" exacerbated an ongoing

Table 10.2

The Top Ten Presidential Landslides in American History

Year	Principal candidates	Winner's percentage of the total vote cast	Winner's margin (in percentage) over the main challenger
1964	Johnson, Goldwater	61.1	22.6
1972	Nixon, McGovern	60.8	23.2
1936	F. Roosevelt, Landon	60.8	24.3
1920	Harding, Cox	60.3	26.2
1984	Reagan, Mondale	59.2	18.4
1928	Hoover, Smith	58.2	17.4
1932	F. Roosevelt, Hoover	57.4	17.8
1956	Eisenhower, Stevenson	57.4	15.4
1904	T. Roosevelt, Parker	56.4	18.8
1952	Eisenhower, Stevenson	55.1	10.7

Source: Partially derived from Everett Carll Ladd, Jr., with Charles D. Hadley, *Transformations of the American Party System* (New York: W. W. Norton, 1975), 279.

Note: Underline indicates a Cold War–era landslide victory.

cultural war. In 1992, Patrick J. Buchanan told the Republican National Convention that the duo of Clinton & Clinton (a reference to Bill Clinton and his wife, Hillary) would engender a profound cultural change:

> The agenda Clinton & Clinton would impose on America—abortion on demand, a litmus test for the Supreme Court, homosexual rights, discrimination against religious schools, women in combat—that's change all right. But it is not the change America wants. . . . It is not the change we can tolerate in a nation that we still call God's country.[55]

As the culture war intensified during the Clinton years, so, too, did the partisanship. Bill Clinton became infamous for his "war rooms," a tactic designed to issue an immediate response to any Republican attack. Republicans also perfected their war games. The result was a vitriolic partisanship that animated voters and elites on both sides. As neoconservatism's intellectual founder Irving Kristol wrote: "There is no 'after the Cold War' for me. So far from having ended, my cold war has increased in intensity, as sector after sector of American life has been ruthlessly corrupted by the liberal ethos."[56]

Further intensifying the partisanship was a shift in electoral behavior. Southern Democrats—long alienated from the Democratic presidential party, thanks to its support of civil rights—deserted the Democrats in droves. As they did, the "Dixiecrat"—that cross-breed between conservative and nominal Democrat—has nearly gone to way of the extinct dodo bird. (Zell Miller is the last of this ancient breed.) Likewise, Yankee Republicans, who savored balanced budgets and railed against government intrusion into their private lives, became alienated by a Republican Party that was so animated by the culture wars that it formed alliances with Christian evangelicals who wanted government to impose their moral codes on private behavior.[57] This caused Vermont Republican Jim Jeffords to leave the GOP in 2001, and has given rise to speculation that he might soon be followed by Rhode Island's Lincoln Chafee. Thanks to this increased polarization, no southern conservative Democrat can realistically expect to win that party's presidential nomination, and no northern moderate (i.e., a social liberal, economic conservative) has much hope of winning the top slot on a Republican ticket.

The result is a form of political entrapment in which the presidency becomes a partisan office once more. As a consequence, presidents are presented with few opportunities to expand their bases of support. Bill Clinton won 43 percent of the popular vote in 1992, and got only 6 percent more in 1996. Because nearly all of Clinton's gains came from *within his own party,* he was unable to capture a majority of the electorate against a weak and inept opponent in Bob Dole. In 2000, Al Gore won 48 percent of the popular vote—a loss of 1 percentage point from Clinton's 1996 score—and this, despite Clinton's impeachment following the Monica Lewinsky affair.

In 2000, George W. Bush suffered a similar fate. He received 48 percent of the popular vote (and fewer votes than Gore). But nearly all of Bush's gains came from Republican-leaners who had favored Ross Perot. In 2004, Bush was able to eke out a popular vote majority. But viewed from another perspective, his 51 percent of the popular vote represented only a 3-point gain from four years before. And this relatively small increase came in spite of the September 11, 2001, terrorist attacks and the loss of nearly 3,000 lives on American soil! Likewise, John Kerry did not add in percentage terms to Al Gore's 2000 popular vote, as each man received 48 percent. *In sum, the era of landslides is over.*

George W. Bush: The (un)Likable Partisan

On September 12, 2001, Americans gave every indication that they were perfectly willing to return to a plebiscitary presidency in the wake of the most horrific attacks on American soil since Pearl Harbor six decades before. In the early days of the new war, George W. Bush rose above the partisanship that became entrenched during the Clinton years to give two very effective public addresses: one at the National Cathedral, the other before a joint session of Congress. The result was near-unanimity in support of the president and his leadership. Three weeks after the attacks, Bush's approval rating rose to an astronomical 90 percent in the Gallup poll—a score that exceeded the all-time record of 89 percent posted by Bush's father during the Persian Gulf War.[58] Bush's strong persona resonated with the public long after the events of September 11, 2001, were seared into the public's memory. A *Los Angeles Times* poll conducted in February 2003 found 71 percent characterizing Bush as a "strong and decisive leader." The same poll showed that more than three-quarters said they liked Bush as a person, and 50 percent described themselves as either "hopeful" or "happy" that he was president.[59]

As the country rallied behind Bush, it also unified in seeking to defeat Osama bin Laden and his Al Qaeda terrorist organization. As a portion of Islamic fundamentalism mutated into a new form of international terrorism, it initially seemed as though the return of a Cold War–like, above-the-partisan-fray commander in chief was inevitable. The Clinton era—replete with all of its partisan attacks and counterattacks—seemed like a distant memory.

With the presumptive return of the plebiscitary presidency came a harkening back to the era of "total elections." George W. Bush achieved a smashing midterm victory in 2002, when political advisor Karl Rove made a strategic decision to "run on the war."[60] The result was a victory that gave the Republicans more seats in the House and saw the party retake control of the Senate.[61] Voters tossed aside their doubts and indecision of 2000. This time, Americans cast "belated ballots" that affirmed Bush's wartime leadership.

Americans came to like George W. Bush.[62] But with the passage of time, the partisan divisions have returned with a vengeance. The increased signs of partisanship came in 2003, when a growing number of Democrats believed that Bush lied about the existence of weapons of mass destruction in Iraq and needlessly took the United States into a war against that country. Although each successive "victory" produced a bump in the polls for Bush, both the rise in support and its duration became smaller each time. For example, according to a Zogby International poll taken just after Saddam Hussein's capture, Bush's job approval rating went from 49 percent to 53 percent—an increase of just 4 points.[63] This kind of political sclerosis could be attributed to the overwhelming support Bush received during his first term from Republicans, while Democrats—especially following the 2002 midterm elections—became passionately angry at Bush, believing him to be dishonest. Former vice president Al Gore captured the feelings of the Democratic base: "Robust debate in a democracy will almost always involve occasional rhetorical excesses and leaps of faith. . . . But there is a big difference between that and a systematic effort to manipulate facts in service to a totalistic ideology that is felt to be more important than the mandates of basic honesty. Unfortunately, I think it is no longer possible to avoid the conclusion that what the country is dealing with in the Bush presidency is the latter."[64]

Many agreed with Gore's charge. As Democratic primary and caucus voters left their polling places, it was clear that while they had their differences, they were united in their antipathy toward Bush. In state after state, Democrats said they were either "angry" or "dissatisfied" with the Bush administration (see Table 10.3). These feelings carried over into the fall campaign. On Election Day itself, the entire country was split: 49 percent said they were "angry" or "dissatisfied" with the Bush administration; 48 percent said they were "satisfied" or "enthusiastic" about it. Not surprisingly, the Bush antagonists broke overwhelmingly for Kerry, while the enthused Bush supporters backed their man.[65]

From E Pluribus Duo to E Pluribus Unum?

The partisan vitriol is likely to increase during the coming years. In many respects, the United States is moving toward an election system that has much in common with a parliamentary one. Never before has the opposition party settled on its presidential candidate so early (Democrats chose John Kerry in March). Gone are the days when the presidential campaign began with Labor Day rallies in Detroit's Cadillac Square and the public began to focus on the candidates following the World Series. This year, 78 percent told the exit pollsters that they had made up their minds about the Bush-Kerry race months before they went to the polls.[66] Moreover, the partisan divide extended to all levels of government. According to a postelection survey conducted by Zogby International, partisanship ruled the day in races for Congress and the state houses. In the Senate races, 90 percent of Democrats supported their

Table 10.3

Attitudes of Democratic Primary Voters Toward the Bush Administration (in percentages)

State	Angry	Dissatisfied	Satisfied	Enthusiastic
Arizona	46	37	13	3
California	49	35	11	4
Connecticut	58	32	8	1
Delaware	51	37	10	1
Florida	49	38	9	2
Georgia	32	43	13	8
Louisiana	33	41	16	8
Maryland	45	40	9	4
Massachusetts	51	35	9	3
Maryland	45	40	9	3
Mississippi	35	50	20	5
Missouri	39	42	13	4
New Hampshire	46	37	14	2
New York	57	31	8	2
Ohio	44	39	12	2
Oklahoma	33	43	17	5
Rhode Island	57	32	7	2
South Carolina	35	49	11	2
Tennessee	39	45	11	3
Texas	42	38	14	5
Vermont	65	26	6	2
Virginia	44	42	8	4
Wisconsin	44	38	12	5

Source: Edison Media Research and Mitofsky International exit polls.

party's nominees; only 9 percent backed the Republican candidate. Republicans went just as solidly for their party's choices: 86 percent backed the GOP Senate candidate; only 12 percent voted Democratic. In the House races, the picture was much the same: 91 percent of Democrats supported their party's congressional candidates; only 9 percent voted Republican. Republicans presented a mirror image: 84 percent supported the GOP House candidate; 14 percent defected to the Democrats. In the governors' races, 90 percent of Democrats voted for their party's nominees; only 7 percent sided with the Republican candidate. Republicans were just as united: 84 percent voted for their party's gubernatorial candidates; just 13 percent backed the Democratic nominee.[67]

Can the divisions be healed? History provides a guide. This chapter began by describing the roiling partisanship that characterized the presidential elections of 1796 and 1800. Yet the 1800 result, although controversial, did produce a political revolution, as Thomas Jefferson later explained: "The Revolution of 1800 was as real a revolution in the principles of our government as that of 1776 was in its forms."[68] In this case, the revolution was the acceptance by the outgoing party of its defeat and the peaceful assumption of the machinery of government by its rivals.

Thomas Jefferson did not gloat in his victory. In his Inaugural Address, he famously intoned, "We are all republicans; we are all federalists."[69] Four years later, partisanship virtually disappeared. Jefferson enlightened the country with a grand vision of exploration (the Lewis and Clark expedition was the modern-day equivalent of traveling to Mars) and destiny (Jefferson's unilateral decision without immediate congressional assent to purchase the Louisiana Territory from the French). Like the infamous party boss George Washington Plunkitt of Tammany Hall fame, Jefferson saw his opportunities and took 'em. The result was the collapse of the Federalist Party. In 1804, the Federalists nominated a token candidate for the presidency who received only 14 electoral votes. By 1820, the party disappeared altogether. Assessing Jefferson's first term, John Randolph wrote: "Never was there an administration more brilliant than that of Mr. Jefferson up to this period. Taxes repealed; the public debt amply provided for . . . sinecures abolished; Louisiana acquired; public confidence unbounded."[70] The so-called Era of Good Feelings began and it lasted through James Monroe's election as president in 1820.

Like the American public following the raucous elections of 1796 and 1800, American voters say they want a change of spirit. At the end of a long campaign, both George W. Bush and John Kerry seemed to recognize this. Speaking to his supporters the day after the election, Bush declared: "We have one country, one Constitution, and one future that binds us. And when we come together and work together, there is no limit to the greatness of America."[71] Kerry agreed: "We are required now to work together for the good of our country. In the days ahead, we must find common cause. . . . America is in need of unity and longing for a larger measure of compassion."[72] In making their pleas for unity, Bush and Kerry echoed Jefferson's long-ago call for national unity.

But can Bush succeed? His 2004 victory was unthinkable to many Democratic partisans. Likewise, the prospect of a Kerry presidency was anathema to Bush supporters. Thus, the phrase used to title this chapter: "the Armageddon election." With so much at stake, no wonder it was said over and over again that the 2004 election was "the most important of our lifetimes." Most Americans agreed: 67 percent told ABC News and the *Washington Post* in September that the outcome of the Bush-Kerry race was "one of the single most important elections of [their] lifetime"; only 15 percent belittled the contest as unimportant.[73]

During his first term, George W. Bush squandered two chances to bring the country together. The first was one of his own making. Introducing himself to voters in 2000, Bush frequently described himself as a "compassionate conservative." The very phrase suggested that he wanted a more compassionate, tolerant, and even activist government. In his 2001 Inaugural Address, Bush pledged the nation (and his administration) to a great goal: "When we see that wounded traveler on the road to Jericho, we will not pass to the other side." Yet in that very same speech, Bush acknowledged the partisan divide: "Sometimes our differences run so deep, it seems we share a continent, but not a country."[74]

Compassionate conservatism could have been more than a literary device. It could have been a legacy to a twenty-first-century Republican Party governing at a time of enormous demographic and social change. True, President Bush established the White House Office of Faith-Based Initiatives. But Republicans never took compassionate conservatism seriously. No one at the Republican-oriented think tanks, for example, saw much merit in devoting attention to the notion of compassionate conservatism as a governing philosophy. Republican members of Congress never organized themselves into a caucus of "compassionate conservatives." Indeed, the Republican faithful made their position clear, saying in effect: "We will cede the poetry of politics to moderate-minded spokespersons. But we will never cede the prose." Thus Republican conventions have featured the moderate voices of Arizona senator John McCain, former New York City mayor Rudolph Giuliani, New York State governor George Pataki, and California governor Arnold Schwartzenegger. But the prose contained within the GOP platform remains decidedly less compassionate and more conservative.

The other opportunity Bush had to stitch the country together came after the September 11, 2001, terrorist attacks. Bush could have followed Franklin D. Roosevelt's example and brought prominent Democrats into his inner circle. Certainly, they were willing. Al Gore, who had reluctantly ceded the presidency to Bush only a few months earlier, told an audience of partisan Iowa Democrats, "Regardless of party, regardless of ideology, there are no divisions in this country where our response to terrorism is concerned."[75] The most picturesque bipartisan moment came when Senate Majority Leader Tom Daschle hugged Bush following his congressional speech. Democrats implored their followers to support Bush in this new war on terror, even as they remained on the sidelines. But that changed in 2002, when Bush decided to cast any Democratic resistance to his war plans—including his desire to make war against Iraq—as unpatriotic. The most egregious example of Bush's political overreach occurred when Republicans ran television advertisements against Georgia senator Max Cleland, comparing him to Osama bin Laden and Saddam Hussein, all because Cleland wanted labor protections written into the new Homeland Security Department. Cleland, a Vietnam War veteran and triple amputee, lost. And that loss, coupled with others, allowed the Republicans to take control of the U.S. Senate. Illinois Democrat Dick Durbin noted that Cleland's defeat remains "something that gnaws at us."[76] Mary Landrieu, a Louisiana Democrat, is even more pointed: "For Democrats who were trying to work with the president on national security issues and support a more hawkish stand than might seem natural for a Democrat, this president discounts it, ignores it, and acts as if it's very important that the president make that the priority and make everything else come in second. . . . Unfortunately, the president has earned this polarization. It hasn't just happened. He pushed it to happen."[77]

History usually doesn't offer presidents too many second chances. Undoubtedly, George W. Bush would like to unite the country if he could. But he may not need to. The manner in which he has won reelection suggests that he has expanded his base—not by courting the "authentic center"—but by finding more like-minded followers. In a postcampaign mortem, Bush manager Ken Mehlman described how the Republicans used sophisticated market research to expand their voter base. According to Mehlman: "If you drive a Volvo and you do yoga, you're pretty much a Democrat. And if you drive a Lincoln or a BMW and you own a gun, you're voting for George W. Bush."[78] By using these marketing techniques, Republicans found 3.4 million new voters. Moreover, the Bush team identified 7.4 million infrequent GOP voters and 10 million unaffiliated voters whom they believed might support the president. These voters were bombarded with messages from the Republicans and the Bush campaign. As Mehlman later observed, "You felt like you were in the old Chicago organization that Richard Daley used to run because we ran for president in those places and among those people as if we were running for mayor."[79]

That strategy worked. On the final weekend, the Bush campaign focused not on a last appeal to the center, but on expanding its voter base. Republican cadres knocked on some 5 million doors, urging a vote for Bush.[80] The Republican base expanded, the center ignored, and the electorate itself underwent a makeover. According to the exit polls, 22 percent cited "moral values" as the most important issue. And of these voters, 80 percent supported George W. Bush, while only 18 percent backed John Kerry.[81] In fact, Bush actually *lost* Independents by one point and self-described moderates by an astounding 9 points.[82] As William Butler Yeats once wrote, "Things fall apart; the center cannot hold."[83]

The winner of the 2004 election has been determined. But what has yet to be divined is will George W. Bush now act in the spirit of John Adams—whose presidency roiled the partisan waters—or Thomas Jefferson—whose presidency calmed them? Time and chance will tell.

Notes

1. James Callender, quoted in Ron Chernow, *Alexander Hamilton* (New York: Penguin Books, 2004), 612.
2. See Stefan Lorant, *The Presidency* (New York: Macmillan, 1951), 40.
3. Bush received 271 electoral votes to Gore's 266. One Washington, DC, elector refrained from voting for Gore in order to protest the District of Columbia's lack of statehood.
4. Quoted in David McCullough, *John Adams* (New York: Simon and Schuster, 2001), 537.
5. For more on the development of the permanent campaign, see Sidney Blumenthal, *The Permanent Campaign* (New York: Simon and Schuster, 1982).
6. In 1796, under the peculiar rules of the Electoral College, the runner-up in the presidential contest became vice president. Jefferson, who had served as Adams's vice president, did not want a rival in the office, and he arranged for an Electoral College tie with the understanding that Burr would become vice president. That happened when both Jefferson and Burr received 73 electoral votes apiece. Burr eventually reneged on the bargain, and the election was decided in the House of Representatives.
7. See Chernow, *Alexander Hamilton,* 612.
8. Quoted in A. James Reichley, *The Life of the Parties: A History of American Political Parties* (New York: Free Press, 1992), 54.
9. Chernow, *Alexander Hamilton,* 609.
10. Reichley, *The Life of the Parties,* 56.
11. Adams won all the electors from Massachusetts and New Hampshire and an 8–7 plurality in Pennsylvania.
12. Joseph J. Ellis, *Founding Brothers: The Revolutionary Generation* (New York: Vintage Books, 2000) 203.
13. See McCullough, *John Adams,* 556.
14. Chernow, *Alexander Hamilton,* 635.

15. See McCullough, *John Adams,* 564.
16. Ibid., 557.
17. Quoted in Ellis, *Founding Brothers,* 231.
18. Zell Miller, Speech to the Republican National Convention, New York City, September 1, 2004.
19. Chris Matthews, "Hardball," MSNBC, September 1, 2004, telecast. Matthews once worked for Democratic House Speaker Thomas P. O'Neill, Jr.
20. Warren St. John and Rachel L. Swarns, "Politics Makes Estranged Bedfellows," *New York Times,* October 31, 2004, ST-1.
21. Zogby International, Iowa survey, September 8–9, 2003, New Hampshire survey, September 24–25, 2003.
22. St. John and Swarns, "Politics Makes Estranged Bedfellows."
23. Quoted in Damien Cave, "The Election's Over. Are You Still Losing It?" *New York Times,* November 7, 2004, ST-1.
24. See Zogby/Williams Identity poll, August 11–16, 2004.
25. See CBS News/*New York Times* poll, October 28–30, 2004.
26. CNN/*USA Today*/Gallup poll, November 3, 2004.
27. The total popular vote in the red states was 60,267,267. Bush won 34,412,879 votes (57%). Kerry won 25,700,985 (43%). The total popular vote in the blue states was 54,780,809. Bush won 24,693,351 (45%). Kerry won 29,845,081 (54%).
28. One elector defected from the Democratic ticket to back Dukakis's vice presidential candidate, Lloyd Bentsen.
29. ABC News exit poll, 1988. Eighteen percent of self-described Democrats backed George H.W. Bush.
30. CBS News exit polls, 1972.
31. ABC News exit polls, 1980 and 1984.
32. See Center for Responsive Politics. The information comes from the website www.opensecrets.org. The party totals include sums raised for the national committees and the House and Senate campaign committees.
33. Alexander Hamilton, "Federalist 68," in Alexander Hamilton, James Madison, and John Jay, *The Federalist Papers* (New York: Mentor Books, 1961), 414.
34. James Madison, "Federalist 10," in Edward Meade Earle, ed., *The Federalist* (New York: Modern Library, 1937), 77.
35. In 1820, one elector did not support James Madison, so as to preserve the distinction of having George Washington be the only president to achieve unanimity in the Electoral College.
36. Quoted in James Thomas Flexner, *Washington: The Indispensable Man* (New York: New American Library, 1974), 263.
37. George Washington, Farewell Address, September 17, 1796. Reprinted as Senate Document Number 3, 102nd Congress, 1st session, 1991. Ironically, each year the partisan members of Congress assemble to hear once more Washington's warning about the dangers of excessive partisanship.
38. See among others H. Ross Perot, *United We Stand: How We Can Take Back Our Country* (New York: Hyperion, 1992); Jesse Ventura, *I Ain't Got Time to Bleed: Reworking the Body Politic from the Bottom Up* (New York: Villard Books, 1999); and Ralph Nader, *Crashing the Party: Taking on the Corporate Government in an Age of Surrender* (New York: Thomas Dunne Books/St. Martin's Press, 2002).

39. The closest reincarnation was when Republican Abraham Lincoln placed Democrat Andrew Johnson on his newly formed Union Party ticket in 1864. After Lincoln's assassination, Johnson found it impossible to govern, as the Republicans in Congress distrusted Johnson and impeached him. Talk of unity resurfaced in 2004, when John Kerry toyed with the idea of offering Arizona Republican John McCain the vice presidency and the Defense Department's top job. See "How Bush Did It," *Newsweek,* www.msnbc.msn.com/id/6407226/site/newsweek.

40. In 1824, five candidates sought the presidency. While Jackson won a majority of the popular vote and a plurality in the Electoral College, the House of Representatives selected John Quincy Adams after one of Jackson's rivals, Henry Clay, announced his support of Adams who, in turn, named Clay to be his secretary of state. Jackson's supporters were angry and denounced the appointment as a "corrupt bargain."

41. Martin Van Buren, *The Autobiography of Martin Van Buren,* ed. John C. Fitzpatrick (New York: Augustus M. Kelley, 1920), 135.

42. Quoted in David Herbert Donald, *Lincoln* (New York: Touchstone Books, 1995), 138.

43. Woodrow Wilson, inaugural address, Washington, DC, March 4, 1913.

44. Quoted in David E. Price, *Bringing Back the Parties* (Washington, DC: CQ Press, 1984), 103.

45. William Howard Taft, *Popular Government* (New Haven, CT: Yale University Press, 1913), 29.

46. Knox served from 1940 to 1944; Stimson from 1940 to 1945.

47. See especially James MacGregor Burns, *Roosevelt: The Lion and the Fox* (New York: Harcourt, Brace, and World, 1956), 274.

48. For more on this, see John Kenneth White, *Still Seeing Red: How the Cold War Shapes the New American Politics* (Boulder, CO: Westview Press, 1998).

49. Arthur Larson, *A Republican Looks at His Party* (New York: Harper and Brothers, 1956), 14.

50. Dwight D. Eisenhower, Acceptance Speech, Republican National Convention, August 23, 1956.

51. Theodore H. White, *The Making of the President,* 1960 (New York: Atheneum House, 1961), 409, 415.

52. Samuel Lubell, *The Future While It Happened* (New York: Norton, 1973), 39.

53. Theodore J. Lowi, *The Personal President: Power Invested, Promise Unfulfilled* (Ithaca, New York: Cornell University Press, 1985), 113.

54. This was accentuated by Clinton's choice of a fellow baby boomer, Al Gore, to join him on the Democratic ticket.

55. Quoted in E.J. Dionne, Jr., "Buchanan Heaps Scorn on Democrats," *Washington Post,* August 18, 1992, A18.

56. Irving Kristol, *Neoconservatism: The Autobiography of an Idea* (New York: Free Press, 1995), 486.

57. Jim Jeffords, Vermont's junior senator, left the Republican Party in 2001, complaining that it no longer stood for "moderation; tolerance; fiscal responsibility." See Jim Jeffords, "Statement Announcing He Is Leaving the Republican Party," Burlington, Vermont, May 24, 2001. See also James M. Jeffords, *My Declaration of Independence* (New York: Simon and Schuster, 2001).

58. See David W. Moore, "Top Ten Gallup Presidential Approval Ratings," Gallup press release, September 24, 2001.

59. *Los Angeles Times* poll, January 30–February 2, 2003.

60. See Richard A. Clarke, *Against All Enemies* (New York: Free Press, 2004), 186.

61. This was only the second time since 1934 that a president's party had padded its congressional ranks in a midterm contest. The other was 1998, when Republicans overreached following the Monica Lewinsky scandal and sought Bill Clinton's impeachment—something most Americans did not support, though they favored a congressional censure.

62. See John Kenneth White and John J. Zogby, "The Likable Partisan: George W. Bush and the Transformation of the American Presidency," in *High Risk and Big Ambition: The Presidency of George W. Bush,* ed. Steven E. Schier (Pittsburgh: University of Pittsburgh Press, 2004).

63. Zogby International polls, December 4–6, 2003 and December 15–16, 2003.

64. Al Gore, MoveOn.org speech, August 7, 2003.

65. Edison Media Research and Mitofsky International exit poll, November 2, 2004. Of those who were angry at the Bush administration (23% of the electorate), 96 percent supported Kerry and 3 percent Bush. Dissatisfied voters (26% of the electorate) broke 82 percent for Kerry and 16 percent for Bush. Satisfied Bush supporters (26% of the electorate) voted 89 percent for Bush and 11 percent for Kerry. Enthusiastic Bush supporters (22% of the electorate) voted 98 percent for Bush and 2 percent for Kerry.

66. Edison Media Research and Mitofsky International exit poll, November 2, 2004. Five percent said they made their decision on Election Day; 4 percent said they decided within the previous three days; 2 percent said one week prior to the election; 10 percent said they made up their minds in October; and 78 percent answered "before that."

67. Zogby International poll, November 3–5, 2004.

68. Quoted in Reichley, *The Life of the Parties,* 64.

69. Ibid., 63.

70. Quoted in Lorant, *The Presidency,* 62.

71. George W. Bush, Victory Speech, Washington, DC, November 3, 2004.

72. John Kerry, Concession Speech, Boston, November 3, 2004.

73. ABC News/*Washington Post* poll, September 23–26, 2004.

74. George W. Bush, Inaugural Address, Washington, DC, January 20, 2001.

75. Quoted in Dan Balz, "Gore Pledges to Back Bush, Calls for Unity," *Washington Post,* September 30, 2001, A3.

76. Quoted in E. J. Dionne, Jr., *Stand Up and Fight Back: Republican Toughs, Democratic Wimps, and the Politics of Revenge* (New York: Simon and Schuster, 2004), 63.

77. Ibid., 64.

78. Quoted in Dan Balz, "GOP Governors Celebrate Party Wins," *Washington Post,* November 19, 2004, A9.

79. Ibid.

80. Ibid.

81. Edison Media Research and Mitofsky International exit poll, November 2, 2004.

82. Ibid. Independents backed Kerry over Bush, 49 percent to 48 percent. Moderates gave Kerry 54 percent of their votes to Bush's 45 percent. Zogby/Williams Identity survey, August 11–16, 2004.

83. From "The Second Coming," in *The Variorum Edition of the Poems of W.B. Yeats,* ed. Peter Allt and Russell K. Alspach (New York: Macmillan, 1957), 40–41.

11

Armageddon, Just Another Campaign, or Something In-Between?

The Meaning and Consequences of the 2004 Election

William Crotty

The George W. Bush administration was quick to call the 2004 election a "mandate" for its policies and its stewardship of the presidency. The election redistributed political power, restructured the parties' coalitions, and, in this case, established the Republican Party as the dominant political force in America.[1]

Then again Karl Rove, President Bush's political strategist, said the same thing after the 2000 election, one in which Bush lost the popular vote nationwide to Al Gore, his Democratic opponent, by 500,000 votes, and in which a conservative U.S. Supreme Court stepped in, stopped the recount under way in Florida, a state whose Electoral College votes were pivotal to the outcome, and in a split 5-to-4 decision declared Bush the winner. Given this and Rove's long-run association with Bush, he might be accused of wishful thinking and partisan bias. He may also be correct. The administration's objective was nothing less than to use the 2004 election as the basic structure for a generation of Republican control of national politics.

After the election, Bush moved quickly and decisively in restructuring his team of advisors. He made major changes in his cabinet, including dropping moderate Colin Powell as secretary of state in favor of loyalist and White House national security advisor Condoleezza Rice. The controversial attorney general, John Ashcroft, a lightning rod for critics of the administration with his harsh treatment of civil rights issues, resigned. He was replaced by a Hispanic, Alberto Gonzales, a man who, while less confrontational, shared the same views as Ashcroft. Gonzales had written the legal brief justifying detention without trial or access to legal procedures of "detainees" at Guantanamo Bay and elsewhere. Tom Ridge, director of the Department of Homeland Security resigned; John Danforth, the U.S. ambassador to the United Nations, also resigned. Commerce Secretary Don Evans, Secretary of Education Rod Paige, Department of Health and Human Services Secretary Tommy Thompson, Secretary of Agriculture Ann Veneman, and Secretary of Energy Spencer Abraham all resigned.

The new appointments were people with less public recognition and no national constituencies of their own. The intent was to provide Bush with a loyalist group of cabinet members to facilitate rather than to make or question White House policies. The cabinet was effectively reduced in influence to that of a bureaucratic department in the federal branch.

A new director took over at the CIA, former conservative Congressman Porter Goss. His appointment was controversial, although endorsed by the Senate. The fear was he would reposition the intelligence agency as a political arm of the administration. Once he was in office, a number of resignations followed and Goss announced his intention to make the CIA more responsive to the president's wishes.

The likelihood of opportunities to appoint Supreme Court members appeared to be a future possibility. The justices were aging and Chief Justice William Rehnquist had been hospitalized and was reported to be seriously ill with thyroid cancer. (In July 2005, Justice Sandra Day O'Connor announced her retirement. Bush nominated federal judge John G. Roberts as her replacement.) The balance of the Court was already conservative; new presidential appointees could move it further in this direction. A conservative to extremely conservative Court majority could be the norm for decades to come.

Immediately after the election in a rare (for the president) news conference, Bush announced that his policy priorities were to privatize parts of Social Security; introduce a new tax code favorable to industry and the wealthy; and to continue the war in Iraq and the fight against terrorism. All had been issues in the campaign and ones the candidate had been clear in promoting. More surprisingly, and seldom discussed during the general election period, Bush, with British Prime Minister Tony Blair at his side and endorsing his approach, declared his (and their) intention to push the development of Palestine as an independent, peaceful state, one that would not be a threat to Israel. The fact that Palestinian leader Yasir Arafat was ill and dying gave the timing of the announcement special significance; a new leadership would take over in Palestine. Bush sidestepped questions as to Israel's role in the process, what he would request its leaders to do, or if it could be urged to reinitiate the "Roadmap to Peace" plan that had received major attention in previous years as a potential solution to the continuing Israeli-Palestinian conflict.

There was also talk of nuclear weapons being developed in Iran, part of an administration campaign through the media in which many believed they saw similarities to the buildup of a climate of public opinion receptive to the earlier invasion of Iraq (and helpful in establishing the administration as the guardian of American security and the front against international terrorism in the campaign). The European Union and other international groups initiated a more conciliatory approach, negotiating with the Iranian leadership, who in turn both denied the allegations and invited outside specialists to inspect its facilities. The administration did not welcome the more compromising negotiations or the intrusion of others into the process (it had long been critical of Iran and, along with Iraq and North Korea, had labeled Iran as part of the "axis of evil" it saw itself as confronting).

The Economist Intelligence Unit (November 2004) summarized what it saw as the consequences on the international front of Bush's reelection in these words: "This victory confers a certain legitimacy on Mr. Bush. He is no longer the accidental president—or, less charitably, a fraudulent one, as many Democrats have charged. Like it or not, Democrats in America, and anti-Bush prime ministers and presidents in other countries, will find themselves dealing with a newly empowered and emboldened Mr. Bush."[2]

Then again the same electorate that voted Bush another four years had begun to show cracks in its support for administration policies in the postelection period: "At a time when the White House has portrayed Mr. Bush's 3.5-million-vote victory as a mandate, the poll found that Americans are at best ambivalent about Mr. Bush's plans to reshape Social Security, rewrite the tax code, cut taxes and appoint conservative judges to the bench. There is continuing disapproval of Mr. Bush's handling of the war in Iraq, with a plurality now saying it was a mistake to invade in the first place."[3]

The Democratic Reaction

The Democrats essentially licked their wounds. Kerry returned to the Senate after calling for a "national reconciliation" and announcing his intention to have a voice in national and party politics. He could take some satisfaction that the 55 million votes he received were more than that of any Democrat in history and the $222 million raised in his campaign exceeded the total of both of Bill Clinton's races and, as later turned out, he had raised more money than his Republican counterpart (an anomaly in presidential politics). The Democrats as a whole were left to assess the wreckage of the election and the party's uncertain future.

Still, the Democrats in the immediate postelection period were at best dispirited, at worst depressed and resigned to their fate. They had lost two close elections in a row. The first came after a highly successful, in domestic terms, Democratic administration that had managed to provide eight years of peace internationally. The deficit had been eliminated and the country was in good shape economically and otherwise. The heir to this Clinton legacy (1992–2000), Gore, nonetheless ran a confused campaign in 2000 and in a low-interest election lost to a candidate (Bush) with no particular qualifications or extended experience (unlike his father), or message. His one elective position had been as governor of Texas.

Four years later in a highly charged campaign, a well-financed candidate, John Kerry, leading an unusually unified Democratic Party and financed at a level no other Democratic candidate had ever enjoyed, nonetheless lost to an incumbent at a time when the economy gave signs of being weak, the deficit had reached historic proportions, an administration tax code redistributed wealth upward, and the nation was at war in Iraq, a war whose intent and execution had been severely criticized. Yet in an unusually polarized national setting, Bush was elected.

The Democratic assessments of the election's outcome were expectedly gloomy. Donald Fowler, former chair of the Democratic National Committee: "I think we have come to an ending point in a long transition that began in 1968. . . . The old Roosevelt Democratic majority coalition has creaked and cracked away under various kinds of racial, religious, social and international forces, and this election was the end point in that transition. . . . [W]e live in a country that is majority Republican now." And James Carville, a political consultant and strategist in both of Bill Clinton's elections (1992, 1996) and an advisor to Kerry: "I think we have to come to grips with the fact that we are an opposition party right now and not a particularly effective one. I'm out of denial. Reality has set in."[4]

The Democrats as a permanent minority party? It has lost two close elections: The first the closest ever and by decision of the Supreme Court and the second in a period most Americans felt the nation's security threatened. Drastic predictions of its demise may be prophetic; they also could be premature.

The Democrats' talk of being a permanent minority party should be viewed with a degree of caution. If true, this projection would provide support to a realigning assessment. The next election is only four years away and a close win by a Democratic candidate would serve to scuttle such talk. Realignment would have to await further election results.

Conclusion

Where all this leads is problematic. An unrestrained presidency, of limited accountability for its actions to the Congress or to international laws or covenants (or, for that matter, to the previous half-century of multilateral actions in response to international emergencies) was disturbing. A president and an administration starkly determined, whatever the costs, to pursue their own vision of a new (American-dominated) world order, disdainful of the conventional diplomatic and multinational approaches that have been the dominant form of crisis management in the post–World War II years was not a pleasant prospect. To some, it was alarming, an invitation for strife, uprisings, and continued terrorist threats in a go-it-alone world environment. To supporters of the president, however, the course embarked on by his administration would lead to the spread of democracy throughout the world and greater overall security.

In general terms, from the administration's perspective it would be business as usual. The previous four years would set the tenor and priorities for the upcoming four years. There were no surprises here; the White House ran unapologetically on its record and it now believed the American people had endorsed it in the election. It would proceed much as it had before, although with fewer dissenting voices inside the administration and a greater majority in both houses of Congress.

Two parties, two significantly different policy commitments, an intense, even brutal, campaign, and one winner: Americans had chosen, for whatever reason, the path they wanted to follow. The Bush administration was determined to continue as it had. Supporters and critics agreed that it had reshaped the American landscape significantly as well as the country's international relations with its Hard Right policy agenda, its restructuring of government, its deemphasis on social welfare programs, its continuing wholesale deficits, and its fight against terrorism, the latter providing the motivation for a good deal of what it did, including a scaling back of civil liberties. More of the same would be the order of the day. The broader, long-run consequences for the nation were unclear—yet to be established in the years and decades to come.

As seen in the previous chapter, John Kenneth White has referred to the Bush election as "Armageddon." Maybe so. Many critics saw Bush's first four years as a period marked by an insensitivity to social concerns and civil liberties, a lack of appreciation for dissent or views questioning its policies, and a heavy reliance on military force in foreign affairs. Bush supporters repeatedly invoked September 11 and its impact and the threat of international terrorism[5] to justify a new national security state.

Some had begun to refer to the advent of an "American Empire." If a new American Empire is in the making, there are basic questions that must be addressed as to the limits of empire in the contemporary period and the nature of the fit between democratic values and imperialist objectives. Such questions have yet to be seriously asked, but may well provide a context for critics of the administration's policies and the run-up to the next presidential campaign.

One campaign is over. Its consequences are enormous. Nonetheless, a new campaign has begun for both sides and the next election is a few short years away.

Notes

1. Walter Dean Burnham, *Critical Elections and the Mainsprings of American Politics* (New York: Norton, 1970); Arthur Paulson, *Realignment and Party Revival: Understanding American Electoral Politics at the Turn of the Twenty-first Century* (Westport, CT: Praeger, 2000); David Mayhew, *Electoral Realignments: A Critique of an American Genre* (New Haven, CT: Yale University Press, 2002); V.O. Key, Jr., "A Theory of Critical Elections," *Journal of Politics* 17, no. 1, 1955: 3–18; V.O. Key, Jr., "Secular Realignment and the Party System," *Journal of Politics* 21, no. 2, 1959: 198–210.

2. The Economist Intelligence Unit, "*Economist* Special Report: After the Election: Bush and the World," November 2004.

3. Adam Nagourney and Janet Elder, "Americans Show Clear Concerns on Bush Agenda," *New York Times*, November 23, 2004, A1.

4. Adam Nagourney, "Kerry Advisers Point Fingers at Iraq and Social Issues," *New York Times*, November 9, 2004, A20.

5. William Crotty, ed., *The Politics of Terror* (Boston: Northeastern University Press, 2004); William Crotty, ed., *Democratic Development and Political Terrorism* (Boston: Northeastern University Press, 2005).

Appendix

Presidential Elections and Party and Candidate Success

Year	# of States	Democrat (D)-Republican (R)	Federalist (F)	3rd party candidate	Electoral votes # and %	Popular vote % / (#)
1789	10		*Washington	No political party affiliation	F - 69 / 100%	Uncontested
1792	15		*Washington	No political party affiliation	F - 132 / 98%	Uncontested
1796	16	Jefferson	*Adams		D - 68 / 49% F - 71 / 51%	N/A
1800	16	*Jefferson	Adams		D - 73 / 53% F - 65 / 47%	N/A
1804	17	*Jefferson (P) Clinton (VP)	Pinckney (P) King (VP)		D - 162 / 92% F - 14 / 8%	N/A
1808	17	*Madison (P) Clinton (VP)	Pinckney (P) King (VP)		D - 122 / 69% F - 4 / 27%	N/A
1812	18	*Madison (P) Clinton (VP)	Clinton (Fusionist) Ingersoll		D - 128 / 59% F - 89 / 41%	N/A
1816	19	*Monroe (P) Tompkins (VP)	King (P) Howard (VP)		D - 183 / 83% F - 34 / 15%	N/A

Year	# of States	Democrat - Republican	Independent (I) Democrat-Republican	3rd party candidate	Electoral votes # and %	Popular vote % / (#)
1820	24	*Monroe (P) Tompkins (VP)	Adams (P) Stockton (VP)		D - 231 / 98% I - 1 / 0%	N/A
1824	24	*Jackson (P) Calhoun (VP)	Adams (P) Sanford (VP)		D - 99 / 38% I - 84 / 32%	N/A
		Democrat - Republican	**National Republican**	**3rd party candidate**	**Electoral Votes # and %**	**Popular Vote % / (#)**
1828	24	*Jackson (P) Calhoun (VP)	Adams (P) Rush (VP)		D - 178 / 68% R - 83 / 32%	D - 56.1% (642,533) R - 43.6% (500,897)
1832	24	*Jackson (P) Van Buren (VP)	Clay (P) Sergeant (VP)	(Anti-Masonic party)	D - 219 / 76% R - 49 / 17% 3rd - 7 / 3%	D - 54.2% (701,780) R - 37.4% (484.205) 3rd - 7.8%
		Democrat	**Whig (W)**	**3rd party candidate**	**Electoral votes # and %**	**Popular vote % / (#)**
1836	26	*Van Buren (P) Johnson (VP)	Harrison (P) Granger (VP)		D - 170 / 58% W - 73 / 25%	D - 50.8% (764,176) W - 36.6% (550,816)
1840	26	Van Buren (P) Johnson (VP)	*Harrison (P Tyler (VP)		D - 60 / 20% W - 234 / 80%	D - 46.8% (1,128,854) W - 52.9% (1,275,390)
1844	26	*Polk (P) Dallas (VP)	Clay (P) Frelinghuysen(VP)		D - 170 / 62% W - 105 / 38%	D - 49.5% (1,339,494) W - 48.1% (1,300,004)
1848	30	Cass (P) Butler (VP)	*Taylor (P) Fillmore (VP)	Free Soil Party	D - 127 / 44% W - 163 / 56% 3rd - 0	D - 42.5% (1,223,460) W - 47.3% (1,361,393) 3rd - 10.1%
1852	31	*Pierce (P) King (VP)	Scott (P) Graham (VP)		D - 254 / 86% W - 42 / 14%	D - 50.8% (1,607,510) W - 43.9% (1,386,942)

* Indicates election winner.

		Democrat	Republican	3rd party candidate	Electoral votes # and %	Popular vote % / (#)
1856	31	*Buchanan (P) Breckinridge (VP)	Freemont (P) Dayton (VP)	Whig - American Party	D - 174 / 59% R - 114 / 39% 3rd - 8 / —	D - 45.3% (1,836,072) R - 33.1% (1,342,345) 3rd - 21.5%
1860	33	Douglas (P) Johnson (VP)	*Lincoln (P) Hamlin (VP)	A. Southern Democrat B. Constitutional Union	D - 12 / 4% R - 180 / 59% 3a - 72 / — 3b - 39 / —	D - 29.5% (1,380,202) R - 39.8% (1,865,908) 3a - 18.1% 3b - 12.6%
1864	36	McClellan (P) Pendleton (VP)	*Lincoln (P) Johnson (VP)		D - 21 / 9% R - 212 / 91%	D - 45% (1,812,807) R - 55% (2,218,388)
1868	37	Seymour (P) Blair (VP)	*Grant (P) Colfax (VP)		D - 80 / 27% R - 214 / 73%	D - 47.3% (2,708,744) R - 52.7% (3,013,650)
1872	37	Greenley (P) Brown (VP)	*Grant (P) Wilson (VP)		D – Died R - 286 / 78%	D - 43.8% (2,834,761) R - 55.6% (3,598,235)
1876	38	Tilden (P) Hendricks (VP)	*Hayes (P) Wheeler (VP)		D - 184 / 50% R - 185 / 50%	D - 51.0% (4,288,546) R - 47.9% (4,034,311)
1880	38	Hancock (P) English (VP)	*Garfield (P) Arthur (VP)		D - 155 / 42% R - 214 / 58%	D - 48.2% (4,444,260) R - 48.3% (4,446,158)
1884	38	*Cleveland (P) Hendricks (VP)	Blaine (P) Logan (VP)		D - 219 / 55% R - 182 / 45%	D - 48.5% (4,874,621) R - 48.2% (4,848,936)
1888	38	Cleveland (P) Thurman (VP)	*Harrison (P) Morton (VP)		D - 168 / 42% R - 233 / 58%	D - 48.6% (5,534,488) R - 47.8% (5,443,892)
1892	44	*Cleveland (P) Stevenson (VP)	Harrison (P) Reid (VP)	Populist Party	D - 277 / 62% R - 145 / 33% 3rd - 22 / —	D - 46.1% (5,551,883) R - 43.0% (5,169,244) 3rd - 8.5%
1896	45	Bryan (P) Sewall (VP)	*McKinley (P) Hobart (VP)		D - 176 / 39% R - 271 / 61%	D - 46.7% (6,511,495) R - 51.0% (7,108,480)

1900	45	Bryan (P) Sewall (VP)	*McKinley (P) Roosevelt (VP)		D - 155 / 35% R - 292 / 65%	D - 45.5% (6,358,345) R - 51.7% (7,218,039)
1904	45	Parker (P) Davis (VP)	*Roosevelt (P) Fairbanks (VP)		D - 140 / 29% R - 336 / 71%	D - 37.6% (5,028,898) R - 56.4% (7,626,593)
1908	46	Bryan (P) Kern (VP)	*Taft (P) Sherman (VP)		D - 162 / 34% R - 321 / 66%	D - 43.0% (6,406,801) R - 51.6% (7,676,258)
1912	48	*Wilson (P) Marshall (VP)	Taft (P) Sherman (VP)	T. Roosevelt (Progressive Party)	D - 435 / 82% R - 8 / 2% 3rd - 88 / 10%	D - 41.8% (6,293,152) R - 23.2% (3,486,333) 3rd - 27.5%
1916	48	*Wilson (P) Marshall (VP)	Huges (P) Fairbanks (VP)		D - 277 / 52% R - 254 / 48%	D - 49.2% (9,126,300) R - 46.1% (8,546,789)
1920	48	Cox (P) Roosevelt (VP)	*Harcing (P) Coolidge (VP)		D - 127 / 24% R - 404 / 76%	D - 34.2% (9,140,884) R - 60.3% (16,133,314)
1924	48	Davis (P) Bryant (VP)	*Coolidge (P) Dawes (VP)	LaFollette (Progressive Party)	D - 136 / 26% R - 382 / 72% 3rd - 13 / 2%	D - 28.8% (8,386,169) R - 54.1% (15,717,553) 3rd - 16.6%
1928	48	Smith (P) Robinson (VP)	*Hoover (P) Curtis (VP)		D - 87 / 16% R - 444 / 84%	D - 40.8% (15,000,185) R - 58.2% (21,411,991)
1932	48	*Roosevelt (P) Garner (VP)	Hoover (P) Curtis (VP)		D - 472 / 89% R - 59 / 11%	D - 57.4% (22.825,016) R - 39.6% (15,758,397)
1936	48	*Roosevelt (P) Garner (VP)	Landon (P) Knox (VP)		D - 523 / 90% R - 8 / 2%	D - 60.8% (27,747,636) R - 36.5% (16,679,543)

* Indicates election winner.

1940	48	*Roosevelt (P) Wallace (VP)	Willkie (P) McNary (VP)		D - 449 / 85% R - 82 / 15%	D - 54.7% (27,263,448) R - 44.8% (22,336,260)
1944	48	*Roosevelt (P) Truman (VP)	Dewey (P) Bricker (VP)		D - 432 / 81% R - 99 / 19%	D - 53.4% (25,611,936) R - 45.9% (22,013,372)
1948	48	*Truman (P) Barkley (VP)	Dewey (P) Warren (VP)	Thurmond (States' Rights Democrat)	D - 303 / 57% R - 189 / 36% 3rd - 39 / 7%	D - 49.5% (24,105,587) R - 45.1% (21,970,017) 3rd - 2.4%
1952	48	Stevenson (P) Sparkman (VP)	*Eisenhower (P) Nixon (VP)		D - 89 / 17% R - 442 / 83%	D - 44.4% (27,314,649) R - 55.1% (33,936,137)
1956	48	Stevenson (P) Kefauver (VP)	*Eisenhower (P) Nixon (VP)		D - 73 / 14% R - 457 / 86%	D - 42.0% (26,030,172) R - 57.4% (35,585,245)
1960	50	*Kennedy (P) Johnson (VP)	Nixon (P) Lodge (VP)		D - 303 / 56% R - 219 / 41%	D - 49.7% (34,221,344) R - 49.5% (34,106,671)
1964	50	*Johnson (P) Humphrey (VP)	Goldwater (P) Miller (VP)		D - 486 / 90% R - 52 / 10%	D - 61.1% (43,126,584) R - 38.5% (27,177,838)
1968	50	Humphrey (P) Muskie (VP)	*Nixon (P) Agnew (VP)	Wallace (American Independent)	D - 191 / 36% R - 301 / 56% 3rd - 46 / 8%	D - 42.7% (31,274,503) R - 43.4% (31,785,148) 3rd - 13.5%
1972	50	McGovern (P) Shriver (VP)	*Nixon (P) Agnew (VP)		D - 17 / 3% R - 520 / 97%	D - 37.5% (29,171,791) R - 60.7% (47,170,179)

1976	50	*Carter (P) Mondale (VP)	Ford (F) Dole (VP)		D - 297 / 55% R - 240 / 45%	D - 50.1% (40,830,763) R - 48.0% (39,147,793)
1980	50	Carter (P) Mondale (VP)	*Reagan (P) Bush (VP)	John B. Anderson (Independent)	D - 49 / 9% R - 489 / 91% 3rd - 0	D - 41.0% (35,483,883) R - 50.7% (43,904,153) 3rd - 7.1%
1984	50	Mondale (P) Ferraro (VP)	*Reagan (P) Bush (VP)		D - 13 / 2% R - 525 / 98%	D - 40.6% (37,577,185) R - 58.8% 54,455,075)
1988	50	Dukakis (P) Bentsen (VP)	*Bush (P) Quayle (VP)		D - 111 / 21% R - 426 / 79%	D - 45.6% (41,809,074) R - 53.4% (48,886,097)
1992	50	*Clinton (P) Gore (VP)	Bush (P) Quayle (VP)	H. Ross Perot (United We Stand America)	D - 370 / 69% R - 168 / 31% 3rd - 0	D - 43.0% (44,909,326) R - 37.4% (39,103,882) 3rd - 18.9%
1996	50	*Clinton (P) Gore (VP)	Dole (F) Kemp (VP)	H. Ross Perot (Reform Party)	D - 379 / 70% R - 159 / 30% 3rd - 0	D - 49.2% (47,401,054) R - 40.7% (39,197,350) 3rd - 8.4%
2000	50	Gore (P) Lieberman (VP)	*Bush (P) Cheney (VP)	Ralph Nader (Green Party)	D - 266 / 49.5% R - 271 / 50.5%	D - 48.4% (50,999,897) R - 47.9% (50,456,002) 3rd – 2.7% (2,882,955)
2004	50	Kerry (P) Edwards (VP)	*Bush (P) Cheney (VP)	Ralph Nader (Independent)	D - 252 / 46% R - 286 / 54% 3rd - 1.0% (400,706)	D - 48.0% (57,288,947) R - 51.0% (60,608,582)

* Indicates election winner.

The Contributors

Mark D. Brewer is an Assistant Professor of Political Science at the University of Maine. He received his Ph.D. in political science from Syracuse University, where his fields of specialization were American politics and public policy administration. His research interests focus generally on political behavior, with specific research areas including partisanship and electoral behavior at both the mass and elite levels, and the linkages between public opinion and public policy. His books include *Relevant No More: The Catholic/Protestant Divide in American Politics* (2003) and *Diverging Parties: Realignment, Social Change and Political Polarization* (2002) (the latter with Jeff Stonecash).

Patricia Conley is a Visiting Assistant Professor at the University of Chicago. She received the American Political Science Association's E.E. Schattschneider award for best dissertation in American politics. Her book *Presidential Mandates: How Elections Shape the National Agenda* (2001) examines the relationship between election outcomes and presidential policymaking. She has published extensively on the American presidency, distributive justice, and the role of self-interest in public opinion formation.

M. Margaret Conway is a Distinguished Professor Emeritus of Political Science at the University of Florida. Her research interests include political participation, political socialization, and women and politics. Her publications include *Political Participation in the United States* (1985, 1991, 2000) and *Women and Political Participation* (1997, 2005) and a number of other books and seminal articles on political parties, political participation, and American politics.

William Crotty is the Thomas P. O'Neill Chair in Public Life and Director of the Center on the Study of Democracy at Northeastern University. He is the author of a number of books and articles and a recipient of the American Political Science Parties and Organizations Section Lifetime Achievement Award.

Christine L. Day is Professor of Political Science at the University of New Orleans. Her research examines the strategies and influence of interest groups on public opinion and policy. Her publications include *What Older Americans Think: Interest Groups and Aging Policy* (1990) and, with Charles D. Hadley, *Women's PACs: Abortion and Elections* (2005).

Thomas Ferguson is a Professor of Political Science and Senior Assistant Provost of the University of Massachusetts, Boston. He received his Ph.D. from Princeton and taught formerly at MIT and the University of Texas, Austin. A contributing editor to the *Nation* and contributing writer to *Mother Jones,* Ferguson is the author of many books and articles, including *Golden Rule: The Investment Theory of Party Competition and the Logic of Money-Driven Political Systems* (1995).

Charles D. Hadley is University Research Professor of Political Science at the University of New Orleans. His published research includes *Political Parties and Political Issues* (1973) and *Transformations of the American Party System* (1975, 1978), both co-authored with Everett C. Ladd, Jr., and *Women's PACs: Abortion and Elections* (2005) co-authored with Christine L. Day. He also has co-edited *Political Parties in the Southern States: Party Activists in Partisan Coalitions* (1990) and three volumes based on data collected for his National Science Foundation–funded Southern Grassroots Party Activists Project (with Lewis Bowman) as well as numerous articles and book chapters on presidential nominations, partisan change, southern politics, and women and politics.

John S. Jackson III is Professor of Political Science (Emeritus) at Southern Illinois University, Carbondale, where he has taught since 1969. Jackson is also currently Visiting Professor at the Paul Simon Public Policy Institute at Southern Illinois University, Carbondale. He is co-author of three books, with Bill Crotty, on presidential primaries and elections. He is also co-author, with David Everson, of a monograph on Illinois primaries and the author or co-author of numerous articles in academic journals and chapters in books. He formerly held major administrative appointments at SIU, including Associate Dean and Acting Dean of the Graduate School, Dean of the College of Liberal Arts, Vice Chancellor for Academic Affairs and Provost, and Acting Chancellor of the university.

Jerome M. Mileur is Professor Political Science at the University of Massachusetts, Amherst. He is editor of *The Liberal Tradition in Crisis: American Politics in the Sixties* (1974), co-editor *of Challenges to Party Government* (1992), *Progressivism and the New Democracy* (1999), *The New Deal and the Triumph of Liberalism* (2002), and serves as co-editor of the University of Massachusetts Press series Political Development of the American Nation. He has published extensively and has presented papers on political terrorism, among other subjects, at professional meetings.

Richard J. Powell, Assistant Professor of Political Science, University of Maine, received his Ph.D. from Northwestern University. He is the author of journal articles and book chapters on the presidency, Congress, elections, and state politics, and is co-author of *Changing Members: The Maine Legislature in the Era of Term Limits* (2004).

Harold W. Stanley holds the Geurin-Pettus Distinguished Chair in American Politics and Political Economy at Southern Methodist University. He is an editor of *Vital Statistics on American Politics 2003–2004* (2003) and has also published numerous articles and book chapters on presidential nominations, partisan change, and voting rights. He has served as President of the Southern Political Science Association (2000–2001). His current research focuses on southern politics.

John Kenneth White is a Professor of Politics at the Catholic University of America. He is the author of several books on American politics, including *Still Seeing Red: How the Cold War Shapes the New American Politics* (1997 and 1998); *New Party Politics: From Hamilton and Jefferson to the Information Age* (co-authored with Daniel Shea, 2002); and *The Values Divide* (2002).

Index

Page numbers in *italic* indicate tables and figures

SANTA FE COMMUNITY COLLEGE

WITHDRAWN

DATE DUE